Please return/renew by date shown.
You can renew at:
norlink.norfolk.gov.uk
or by telephone: 0344 800 8006
Please have your library card & PIN ready

G33

The Letters of JOHN CALMANN

The Letters of
JOHN CALMANN

1951–1980

With two forewords
by William Anderson
and François Duchêne

London · John Murray

CAL

Nof: PA

GIFT

© Gerta Calmann 1986

First published 1986
by John Murray (Publishers) Ltd
50 Albemarle Street, London W1X 4BD

Typeset by Fakenham Photosetting Ltd
Fakenham, Norfolk
Printed and bound in Great Britain
by The Bath Press, Avon

British Library CIP data
Calmann, John
    The letters of John Calmann.
    1. Calmann, John   2. Publishers and publishing
    —Great Britain—Biography
    I. Title
    338.7′610705′0924   Z325.C/
    ISBN 0–7195–4291–X

Illustrations

ACKNOWLEDGEMENTS

I would like to thank the editors of these letters, Mrs Diana Davies for her help in selecting them and Mr Roger Hudson of John Murray for his sympathetic and untiring support. To John's friends who so willingly supplied photographs and information—in particular to the two who wrote the Forewords to this book—I am deeply indebted and immensely grateful.

I would also like to take this opportunity to express my gratitude to the members of John's staff, including his eldest sister, who together contributed through their inspired devotion to the survival of John's newly-founded firm after his death.

Gerta Calmann

FOREWORD
by William Anderson

The first time I met John Calmann was at Oxford, in the rooms of our mutual friend Robert Symmons. In a matter of seconds we were arguing about the relative merits of the Florentine and Venetian schools of painting. I was not only trounced in argument by his infinitely greater knowledge of painting; I was ground down. I returned to my college smarting in defeat, convinced that he was the rudest man I had ever come across, and that I would never meet him again. Why was it that I found myself a week later hurrying off to John's rooms in the Canterbury Quad of Christ Church? Knowing none of the other people there, dazed by the speed of conversation, informed by my host when I did try to intervene that my remarks were banal, there, in his white panelled rooms looking out onto the crown of a copper beech, I entered a new world of friendship.

It was a new world, not in the sense of discovering a new set of acquaintances, but because of the quality of emotional response he brought to people, art, ideas and nature. It was in John Calmann's nature to say what he felt: that alone made him an original. Unlike most of his contemporaries he had survived an English education with his native responses inviolate and, as he was voluble, eloquent and epigrammatic in his conversation, of a combative tendency and harbouring many cherished prejudices, he could be formidable and explosive. What made him specially original in Oxford was the range of cultural references he drew on: he had travelled in Europe far more widely than most of us, he had grown up bilingual in German and English, he spoke excellent French and he had spent a long period in Italy before coming up to Oxford. Though Oxford taught him much in an academic way, it moulded few of his tastes and interests. He was too formed before he came up and too impatient of what he considered the provincialism and narrow-mindedness of his tutors. He was also eager to explore the opportunities for making friends and exercising his gifts for generosity and for drawing out the talents of others.

What he gave to Oxford was the greatest talent for making friends I am ever likely to meet. If he wanted you for a friend, there was little you could do about it. If he wanted you to like and appreciate someone else, again there was almost nothing you could do to resist. Sometimes in relation to him, I think of myself and his other friends as different colours he wanted for his palette. If he wanted to mix you with another colour or to contrast you with a range of lines or brushstrokes, you had no more choice in the matter than the paint in the tube squeezed between the thumb and forefinger of an artist. That makes him too manipulative, too scheming or arranging. It avoids the fact that sometime after finding him a dazzling and amusing acquaintance, you discovered in him a warm and observant nature, easily touched by the return of kindness, seeing things about you that no one else had noticed, telling truths that from anyone else could have led to a permanent end of friendship, and constantly ready with practical help. This is one example: some twelve months after our first explosive meeting I had decided to take the option on the Age of Dante in the Oxford history school for which I had to travel in Italy. I had no connections in Italy and no knowledge of Italian. He arranged the whole journey: we travelled together to stay with his aunt Carmen at Ascona and then he sent me down to Siena to stay with that remarkable family, the Vivantes, having written to them with a letter of introduction. There—and all because of him—I learned something of the inner spirit of Italian literature and verse.

What his friends at Oxford were lucky enough to receive from him was a share of what the many families of his background had been giving to England since their flight from the Nazi persecutions before the Second World War. These families brought with them the outlook that characterized the best of German culture. One day many of these letters will be quoted in the history that should be written as an acknowledgement of the debt owed by Britain to that cultural diaspora.

To become a friend of John Calmann meant that very soon one was drawn into becoming a friend of his family. The story of his family background is of great intrinsic interest and it is essential to know something of it to understand many references in the letters.

Gerta and Hans Calmann, his mother and father, had been allowed to leave Nazi Germany in 1937, bringing with them four children, their furniture and belongings and £900 which was all that was left after paying the tax imposed by the Nazi Government on emigrants. In England they had to learn to fit into a very different society. The Calmanns were a Hamburg Jewish family which had owned a bank for three generations. After army service in the First World War and a brilliant university career Hans Calmann joined the family firm. His job enabled him to travel and to study and collect classical art. As a schoolboy he also formed a collection of African tribal sculpture, buying pieces from sailors in the port of Hamburg. Though the Calmanns were not practising Jews, the older generation was imbued with the Jewish tradition and they lived in a circle of Jewish families in Hamburg. Hans's elder brother had renounced his right to a partnership in the bank in order to practise as an artist. Their mother—John's paternal grandmother—came from Pinsk in Russia but was educated in Germany. Her younger brother, Godja Halpern, was to play a leading part in the new state of Israel. John was very proud of his Jewish background though this applied in the main to his father's family.

On his mother's side only her grandfather, Gustav Hertz, was Jewish and he had been baptized at an early age in 1834. He was a lawyer and became a Senator of the Free City of Hamburg. His eldest son was the physicist Heinrich Hertz who produced the experimental proof for Clerk Maxwell's equations and laid the scientific foundations for all the future development of radio communications. He died too young to receive the Nobel Prize which would surely have come to him though another member of the Hertz family, Gustav Hertz, also a physicist, received his Nobel Prize in 1925. Gerta Hertz was the youngest child in a well-to-do laughter-loving family. Her father, a respected lawyer, insisted on providing his children with the best possible education; he sent Gerta to the London School of Economics where she studied for her doctoral thesis on the history of British education in India, later published in Germany. She travelled in India, returning to Germany in 1933 where she met and married Hans Calmann in April 1934. Their son John was born in December 1935.

Hans Calmann had been married before. His first wife, by whom he had three daughters, Marianne, Susan and Iris, had died in 1930. Gerta therefore had the task of bringing up three step-daughters. It was this family with the infant John that they brought to England in 1937. Though the Hertz family in general was not molested by the Nazis, several of Gerta's immediate family, some of whom appear in these letters, also took refuge abroad. Her brother Richard Hertz went to live in America and her elder sister, the witty and intelligent Gräfin Carmen von Finckenstein, to Switzerland where she was joined by her mother. All were to experience great difficulties and hardships but nothing compared to many members of Hans Calmann's family, including his elder brother, who died in the concentration camps. One of the most extraordinary passages in these letters is that where John describes himself sitting down in New York to read about the Holocaust for the first time, a subject that for obvious reasons had never been mentioned in his family, and forcing himself to absorb the monstrous story despite his terror that he might come across the names of his relations. (See p. 63)

True intelligence has been defined as the ability to adapt to different surroundings and circumstances. If that is a good definition then the Calmanns showed themselves to be supremely intelligent. From being a banker Hans Calmann set up as an art dealer, equipped by all the preceding years of private study and travel. In some fifteen years he was to establish himself as one of the most important dealers in old master drawings in the world. Gerta, despite the heavy burden of running a household and entertaining clients, also continued her studies: among her publications is the notable study of the eighteenth-century flower painter George Dionysius Ehret.

As these letters bear witness John was deeply aware of how much he owed to his parents and his family background. This background became part of the special gifts he could transmit to others through his friendships. From it he derived his love of art, his passion for justice, his deep interest in societies other than his own, notably India.

It is to the period immediately following Oxford when he spent over a year in the United States that we owe the fullest sequence of letters. His correspondence here has much of his quality as a raconteur in conversation: it is vibrant with the exceptional speed of his reactions to new impressions, and the skills polished at Oxford in making friends are wielded on a wider scale, if more diffusely, exploring and annexing various ranges of American society. His arrival in New York marks the beginning of one of his most important friendships, that with the remarkable Ben Sonnenberg who opened door after door for him. It is interesting that he compares Ben Sonnenberg with Leuwen *père* because he himself was not above assaulting his opponents or enemies, like Lucien Leuwen, 'avec des coups de bonne compagnie'.

Just as he kept the friends he made at school and at university, so he went on acquiring and keeping friends from all his sojourns abroad and his various jobs. As his friends of both sexes got married, he rarely failed to make a new friend of the partner if he or she had not been known to him before and that, I think, is a remarkable sign of his tactful tenacity in friendship. He also made friends with their children and in many families he was the grown-up visitor to be greeted by

5

children with joy because he preserved and exhibited the sense of fun and spontaneity and the air of complicity in innocent wickedness they most admire.

After his ventures into journalism and being an international civil servant, he decided to become a publisher. The range of his contacts made him an invaluable acquisition because he knew so many authors and even more he knew so many talented people whom he persuaded to write for him. Many people divide their lives between their work and their social life: not so with him because many of his colleagues became his friends and his older friends were drawn in to meet them. He admired talent, he admired hard work, and he could draw out both from his authors and subordinates: for a time he could show outstanding toleration of his stupider superiors and masters. It was inevitable that he should eventually start his own firm. This suited his temperament: his speed of decision, his impatience of unnecessary consultations, his ability to realize conceptions and put them into action. It also enabled him to develop even more widely his gift for drawing out the talents of others. This gift, which in him seemed instinctive and effortless, was a compound of imagination and memory joined by a sensitivity to the needs and natures of others.

It is now five years since he died. At many gatherings I hear his friends say 'John Calmann should have been here', a remark that will continue to be uttered until the last member of his generation has to say it to him or herself. What they miss is an incomparable zest, a sense that the social chemistry of the atmosphere in the room or garden changed once he entered it. What they also miss is a warmhearted and kind companion to go on long walks with, to enjoy music, painting, sculpture and architecture in his company, the more intensely because of his knowledge and taste. They miss the chatter over a meal he had cooked himself, and a voice on the telephone which immediately by its tone told you he knew you were in need of help whether the matter was serious or simply that you ought to be jollied and teased out of yourself. They also miss in him their younger selves.

I was recently in the Ashmolean Museum and was startled to see a sculpture that I had once known well in his drawing room. It is a marble fountain head in the form of a brightly intelligent satyr's head wreathed with vine leaves, carved by Balthasar Permoser—probably from the Zwinger at Dresden in about 1720. With characteristic generosity his family had presented it to the Museum in his memory. This head which once my fingers had fondled and explored while John had held it up and talked about it, now had the ban of the museum upon it: I could not touch it.

So to his friends will these letters seem like objects in the museum of time and there is a greater ban upon them than can be imposed by wise curators. Just as the fountain head, though, will give delight and pleasure to generations of Oxford visitors and undergraduates as a permanent emblem of the European culture he exemplified, so too these letters will preserve something of the spirit of a remarkable man.

I was once cooking him some steak when he had come to supper. A superb cook himself, he restrained himself nobly while watching my amateur efforts. Nevertheless he leaned over my shoulder and said, 'Let me tell you the secret of life. It is unsalted butter.'

WILLIAM ANDERSON is a poet and author. John Calmann was his publisher for many years.

FOREWORD
by François Duchêne

Letters and photographs can tell a lot about a person. What they cannot convey quite so well is the total impact of the living presence. In the case of John Calmann, with his immense vitality, the difficulty is to recreate something of the exhilarated anticipation so many people felt when about to meet him.

Talk was John's supreme medium and it was here his vitality was most infectious. Joining argument with him involved flaring eyebrows and the rattling of antlers, a noisy and often very candid trial of intellectual strength from which one disengaged hours later, drained, with only the faintest idea of what started it all. One also knew, though, when one met him, that he would soon be laughing not only *at* but *with* one's most pathetic jokes and ill-judged puns. He was ready to seize on the thinnest idea and run off with it by means of some quite unforeseeable mental association, nearly always entertaining, sometimes casually profound. He gave one the feeling the company was inspired, oneself astonishingly included, and that something or someone might shine at any moment. His friends duly loved him.

There was no more exuberant gossip than John Calmann and he could be wickedly amusing and gleeful. But his sharp eye was as accurate as a novelist's (he wrote two novels and several plays). He would be almost Proustian in conjuring up a social scene and pinpointing in the greatest detail the incidents which reveal hidden group assumptions or relations between individuals. He was as percipient and vivid talking about French and American circles as English ones. Insight at this level has to be basically serious—and also generous. I never heard John speak of someone facing a crisis without feeling he

9

knew, in his own flesh and blood, the confusions, sufferings and courage needed to live with ourselves and with others. More than one friend sought his help in trouble, and the help always came, unsentimental but compassionate, realistic and reinvigorating.

Very rarely, there came to the surface another quality which, once one had experienced it, could only be called assimilated passion. Three of his friends trailing behind him in mid-summer across a totally unshaded Greek island were taken aback by his reaction when one of them wondered aloud whether the shrine they were heading for was worth the sweat of the devastating walk. John rounded on them and lashed their faint-heartedness. This was the unfamiliar subterranean John, the initiate, the devotee, for whom art was no pastime, no cultural pretension, but a trek to the sources of life which brooked no compromise.

Anyone interesting is a fusion of diverse forces. A bewildering array were certainly present in John Calmann, but one of them at least was crucial. This was the remarkable background given him by his family. The Nazis added another. As a grown man, he suffered from nightmares about the Holocaust which had destroyed most of his relations. Privileged himself, he had every reason to know how fragile privilege can be and that the greatest qualities may attract disaster in a dangerous world. One sometimes had the impression that much as he adored life, to some extent he defied it as well. If John's style was at times pitched high, that was because it contained a great deal of embattled courage and suppressed tension.

All this was expressed in his admiration for Disraeli. Here was a loner with the courage to take risks in order to impose himself with triumphant panache on an ambivalent society: to be an aristocrat of one kind forcing an alien aristocracy to recognize his worth on his own terms. Here also was a renaissance man whose inner variousness encompassed the man of action and the novelist, the dandy and the philosopher, the romantic and the sceptic.

10

John Calmann had the same inner variousness and it fed his excellence as an enterprising publisher. He had an insight into several cultures and an incomparable network of friends in each of them. He had a deep knowledge of art and a broad one of several literatures. He was practical, he loved to be his own master and took creative risks, he revelled in exercising his judgement, he inspired his staff. As one of them said, 'life was often explosive, but *never* boring'.

That strikes the authentic note about John Calmann as all his friends remember him. It also recalls another epitaph, left not by or about him but by his ancestor, Heinrich Hertz, who also died young and spanned the cultures. Before he died, Hertz wrote his parents a brief letter. 'If anything should really befall me, you are not to mourn. Rather you should feel a touch of pride and consider that I am among the elect, destined to live only for a short while, and yet to live enough.'

FRANÇOIS DUCHÊNE was Editorial writer for *The Economist* between 1963 and 1967. From 1969 to 1974 he was Director of the International Institute for Strategic Studies, and from 1974 to 1982 Director of the European Research Centre, Sussex University.

John was a prolific letter writer and a complete edition of his letters would run to five times the length of this volume. Omissions, therefore, are inevitable, but the intention has been to show the wide range of his interests, the deep attachment he felt for his family and friends, and above all his energy and enthusiasm, which alternately stimulated and goaded all those with whom he came into contact.

Diana Davies

Hans Rudolf Calmann, later known as John Calmann, was born in Hamburg on 6 December 1935. He emigrated with his parents to England in March 1937. During the war from 1941 to 1945 the Calmanns lived in a cottage in Horspath, near Oxford, and John went to the village school under Mrs Black. His second school was the famous Dragon School in Oxford.

In April 1945 the family returned to London to St John's Wood and John entered Arnold House School under the Headmaster Mr Smart, who later helped him to find a place at Westminster School. His years there were very happy. Holidays were generally spent abroad. In 1950 at Cala Ratiada on the north-east tip of Mallorca he met a French family called Monconduit. The father was a renowned journalist on Le Monde. *With a view to an exchange with their son François and for the improvement of John's French, he was invited to stay with them during the Easter holidays in 1951 and 1952.*

TO HIS MOTHER   *chez Mme Monconduit*
17th April 1951   *11, rue de Bourgogne, Paris 7e*

Life continues here as ever and I find that it is now quite natural for me to be in Paris. It is no longer a kind of a dream through which I am wandering haphazardly, as it seemed at first. Now Paris seems almost as normal as London. I do much more though. I saw the Berlin [Staatliche Museen] pictures on Thursday with Madame. They are wonderful, especially the Van Dycks. His portraits are much more alive than Rembrandt's, although perhaps these have more interesting subjects. Watteau's *L'Enseigne de Gersaint*, which is obviously, together with Rembrandt's *L'Homme au Casque D'Or*, Petrus Christus' *Portrait of a Young Lady* and Velasquéz' *Duchesse Olivares*, meant to be the highlight of the show, is very well placed indeed, with a room to itself and no frame, except the beige velvet. I am not sure yet whether I like it best. Madame does, because she considers that both its colours and the cleverness of its composition set it above the others. But I can't get away from the idea that there are two pictures. The two

13

groups are separate and their connection is difficult to find. But it is difficult to explain to someone who has not got the picture in front of him.

To turn to something else, that evening I invited Madame to a Bach-Mozart concert dans la salle Pleyel. Goodness it was rotten. The acoustics were terrible. The whole was a concert of concertos for one-two-three-four pianos. The chief player was a Monsieur Lévêque. He played as if he was carefully hammering on each note. He seems to be a well-known master, but although he knows how to play, he does it like a machine, without any thought or originality. He had as his partners his pupils, who in the difficult bits of the Bach concertos made a long series of mistakes. In the background you heard a buzz-zz, that was the orchestra. They did not dare to play. However, during the Mozart, just when it should not have been, for some trick of the acoustics of that terrible concert hall you heard a nasty squeaking going on. Next to me Madame showed her anger and disgust by smacking her tongue against the roof of her mouth in time with the music, utterly spoiling it for everyone around. *Voilà la vie!*

Quite often I go out onto the Esplanade des Invalides and play a kind of tennis with François. It is rather fun, especially in the evening, when the Dôme des Invalides sparkles in the sunlight and the Eiffel Tower stands out most impressively against the blue-red glow of the setting sun.

TO HIS MOTHER   *c/o Mme Wolfram*
10 April 1952   *54 Cours Gambetta*
                                                   Aix en Provence

Aix is absolutely lovely as a town, and to a certain extent it is like a Southern Bath. Most of the houses are 16th, 17th or 18th century, especially those near the cathedral. The most elegant and amusing street is the Cours Mirabeau, a long avenue of maples, with old fountains with warm water pouring out of them. So far the sun has shone all the time.

Tomorrow, 'nous faisons la carême. Seulement du pain sec, et du poisson.' I shall go to hear a requiem in the evening; on Saturday I will go to a midnight mass, and on Sunday morning to another mass. It is just faintly disappointing watching the Catholic Church at work at the most important point of the Christian year, after I have given her so much support in my essays. But the Monconduits agree that the service we all went to last Sunday was abominable, since the priest mumbled, and refused to read the lesson, one of the finest parts of St Matthew. They only talked clearly when they asked us to give liberally to Church funds.

On the whole there is very little to complain of, except the extraordinary noise made by the frogs in the irrigation ditches during the night, the lorries and cars on the main road outside, and the hideously uncomfortable house.

TO HIS MOTHER   c/o Mme Wolfram
15 April 1952   Aix en Provence

It is very strange because nobody ever talks to me about anything interesting. Monsieur and Madame [Monconduit] never talk about the arts or history or anything with me because they consider I am too young. When I saw a La Tour reproduction in a bookshop window (one of the Berlin pictures)—a picture of the dying St Sebastian with a lot of women, a candle, handkerchiefs and so on—I said I thought Caravaggio was a better painter than La Tour. I was immediately quashed with 'you are too young to understand La Tour, when you are older you will realize his place is as high as the greatest painters and far above Caravaggio, who is small fry compared with L.T. etc . . .' Bosh! It does not depend on how old you are, but on how many pictures you have seen, and how much you have taken in. It is also difficult to know how far you are allowed to criticise the church. If you say certain priests at a certain mass were awful they agree if it is true. But if you say that the Pope Pio Nono was a reactionary and not infallible, there are shocked glances, and long arguments about Peter's successor, etc.

However, that does not prevent me from having a very good time. Yesterday I had one of the best meals I have ever had in France.*

. . . After a long and pleasant conversation on the banks of the ruisseau, out of which came the lunch truites, we all went high up into the hills above St Zacharie. It was really charming up there, with a view stretching for miles across plains and hills, all red, grey, green and blue, towards the setting sun. Wonderful country! First we walked up to a little chapel on the top of the hill, where we sat and watched, and then we prayed inside the chapel, which I thought was a sweet idea. The chapel was very pretty, with some charming 18th-century Ex Voto pictures. One was really excellent, much better than anything by Greuze—I would like to have pinched it.

Wednesday
After we had been to the chapel we went again near the villa [of a friend of the Monconduits], where there are the remains of a small Roman village. Here we sat under a circle of pines which stopped at the edge of a precipice. Thus we could see across an enormous stretch of country and the Mont Ste. Victoire, behind which the sun was setting. We ate something called croquants (hard with almonds inside), drank a Burgundian Rum date 1895, which was really overpowering, and also white wine. It was very amusing, and we looked just like a Fête Champêtre out of a Watteau picture. It was extraordinary but the figures were arranged just like that, especially Madame M., who does her hair in a 1700 style, and who had her back turned to me, with the result that she looked just like a Watteau drawing.

After this we all got into the cars and drove home. I was in

* At St Zacharie, a small hill town beneath Le Mont Ste Baume.

the roofless one and spent the time looking at the wonderfully clear sky and at the cars in the distance on the Route Nationale. All one can see are the two huge yellow eyes which seem to sprawl around like cats. It was altogether a wonderful day.

In 1953 John's mother took him on a car-trip during the Easter holidays to West Germany to look at baroque architecture. They were accompanied by John's prep-school friend Timothy Wilson-Smith (born 1927, Director, Christie's Auctioneers 1964–70, founder Carritt. The latter—older than John—was a friend of the family (born 1927, Director, Christie's Auctioneers 1964—70, founder Artemis Fine Arts 1970, the outstanding connoisseur of his generation. Died 1982). In autumn 1953 John won a scholarship to Christ Church, Oxford. To fill in the time until he could begin his studies he stayed another term at Westminster School and afterwards spent a few months in Italy to learn the language. However, in between there was another journey by car along the Danube as far as Vienna and from there to North Italy. This time they were joined by James Madge, a friend from Westminster School who later studied architecture. After a short time in Florence John was fortunate to get an introduction to the Vivantes in Solaia near Siena. Elena Vivante's friendship was of special significance to him and the style of life at Solaia inspired him with an enduring love for Italy, particularly for Tuscany. Of the three sons of the Vivantes two went to America: Paolo, the eldest, teaches in Canada and Arturo made a name as a writer.

TO HIS SISTER IRIS   *c/o Conte San Miniatello*
9 May 1954   *Perignano Pisa*

As you can see by the address, I am at the moment staying with Donato [San Miniatello]—only for a week though. You cannot imagine how beautiful it is here. No sound but the birds and the peasants shouting to their oxen. I have just been having breakfast in bed, served by a most amusing waiter—I think with my socialist ideas—who clicks his heels when he leaves the room. As I write I can look out onto a garden full of different kinds of trees, and if I walk a few yards through it, I can see blue mountains, which rise near the sea. Yesterday evening the blue was quite luminous—extraordinarily lovely, and far away the real Appenines, with a little snow on their peaks, as the spring has been very cool, and *wet*!

In fact this year's Grand Tour did not succeed nearly as well as last year's in that respect—in Vienna, which is rather sad anyway, it rained every day. The music we heard there was wonderful though, and on the last day the Italian pictures which had been hidden from our view, because of rebuilding, were shown to us in the restoration room, and in the as yet unopened Italian Gallery. Thus we saw Giorgione's *Three Philosophers*, just cleaned, which was really more beautiful than one can imagine, all the Titians, and a Correggio, an Antonello, and a lovely Tura and so on, that is to say we saw everything at least that I particularly wanted to see. In the Albertina we were lucky in seeing just a small box with delightful provincial German drawings, otherwise as usual the museum was shut in our face because of rebuilding.

The car was a nuisance. We had to abandon the luggage rack in Mantua because it started to slide off in the rain, with all our luggage slipping with it. It was an extraordinary scene, in a terrible storm on a dyke in the middle of a lake on which Mantua lies, and the beginning of a long journey from M. to Ascona. You cannot imagine the horror of it. All the luggage had to be taken into the car on top of the knees and bodies of those in the back. The discomfort was something terrifying, the driving very difficult, on slippery roads, through a misty and, no doubt because of the rain, depressing landscape. We left the rack at the next village leaning against a house, looking like an old bedstead.

I wrote to David [Carritt] about my visit to 'I Tatti', which was pleasant, but less so than I had hoped, owing to the insistence of the Rusconis to speak to Vertova★ all the time. She is very nice and I would like to meet her again. The R's and I get on very well now, their faults have softened a little, as they make some efforts to friendliness. B.B. has of course one or two marvellous things—a Domenico Veneziano which is quite perfect, the (very important) Signorelli portraits don't interest me very much, the Cima is heavenly (*S. Sebastian*) and the Sassetta good, but I don't like Sienese painting all that much, and his collection is made up largely of works by masters whom he has more or less had to invent.

The reason why I am so dawdly in this letter is because I am still rather sleepy. We went yesterday to a concert given by Bruno Walter—Brahms, Mozart and Mahler—and sat in the 'loggione' or Gods where the heat is considerably worse than the Black Hole since there are more than 120 people sitting there. Bruno Walter is not my favourite conductor. The Mahler was the best, what I heard of it, in between bouts of day-dreaming. My new suit is a sight. It will be ready on Saturday evening; it has slightly (only slightly I am glad to say) narrow trousers, but the tailor has spared me the worst of Italian fashion, by cutting the suit in what he calls 'a l'Inglese'.

On Monday I went to see a Miss Harrison who lives in a lovely villa in Maiano (near Settignano) with a view over 'I Tatti' to the hills and beyond. She is 85 and very lively indeed, very amusing, and much travelled. She went from Rome to Perugia (I think) in a carriage (dog-cart) in 1913 and has been all over Europe in dog-carts. She believes it is the best way to travel. The other evening I took a carrozza with Zara [Eve], her brother and a friend, along the banks of the Arno. For once there was a clear sky, with the moon shining brightly, very

★ Luisa Vertova, Bernard Berenson's secretary.

romantic. Certainly it would be fun to go in such a thing all over Europe.

I took a tram yesterday afternoon to Via Boccaccio and walked two-thirds of the way up to Fiesole, and sat for three-quarters of an hour looking out over Florence as the sun set, from 'Il Banco della Regina Victoria', a famous viewpoint where Vicky is meant to have sat. While there I read a few more letters in *Werther*, which is too delightful for words. Daddy thought it would bore me—rubbish! Could not be better.

TO HIS MOTHER   *c/o Contessa Rusconi*
29 May 1954   *Firenze*

The rush of events since I left school—the race round Germany, the novelty of Florence, being here, going there and seeing new things all the time, and the change from customary routine of school life—have left me pretty knocked about and I am looking forward very much to settling down in the country and relaxing for a little while—in fact it will be for three months! Altogether I have not had any kind of rest since that awful scholarship term which was a little like slave-driving on Keely's★ part (nothing wrong with it but it was so)—and so I feel more nervous at present than for a very long time. However, I should be very disappointed if you took that as an extra reason for my not going to Rome.

★ John's history master at Westminster School.

20

Miss Harrison, whom I mentioned in my other letter, is very fond of a church in Groppino. I shall go with her [to visit it]—a
, car shared is not very expensive. Perhaps Mr. MacMaster, who is British Consul here, will come too. Everyone says how nice he is. He is the first consul in years to take any interest in the English inhabitants, who now number about 400 or so, I am told. But before 1914 there were 6000—quite incredible. They all lived in flats in the Via Tornabuoni (if they hadn't got villas); that is why all the shops and cafés in that street are English by name!

On Tuesday I saw the wonderful Raphael and Leonardo drawings here. Particularly wonderful was the first sketch for the *Madonna del Granduca*. I also saw all the Baroccis—I have seen better, but what a good artist. I am coming to like him more and more. I think he is just as good as El Greco really, although that is heresy. Today I shall see Dürer, Correggio, etc. Very lucky that I get on so well with Maria Fossi,★ otherwise I would not have seen anything. Tonight dinner with Mario Witt.†

Assisi is very beautiful indeed. Today was Corpus Christi, and there were processions and services. I did not see all the frescoes therefore but will look again tomorrow. The Giottos are marvellous (so by the way was Piero's *Dream of Constantine* at Arezzo, what I did see of it). The view from my bedroom

---

★ Assistant keeper at the print-room of the Uffizi in Florence, later married Mr Todorov.

† Son of Professor Wittkower, married Miss Olschki, sharing with her in the management of the famous firm of booksellers.

window is quite spectacular, right across to Perugia but I pay through the nose for it. I hope Rome will be less expensive.

Yesterday evening I dined with Lady Berkeley, who turned out quite different from what I expected. She is explosive, talkative and very lively for 65 (or whatever she is), very nice, and you can't think how rich. She behaves like a Queen, and treated me pleasantly, but I left feeling like Addison, when he went at my age from one influential person to another trying to get their support and their interest. She is very straight from the shoulder, and completely terrifies Mr L.P. Hartley (author of *The Go-Between* and other books) who sits like a delightful old pussy listening and purring contentedly. A pleasant man, but so obsequious that I could not believe he really wrote that good book. You may have gathered that he was my fellow-guest as we sat on the terrace, wrapped in coats, eating chicken aspic and other delicious things by the light of two candles and the full moon, waited on by liveried servants, etc. Underneath us was the Duomo, a black outline against the clear blue sky and over it all hung the smell of honeysuckle. It was romantic and wonderful to say the least. I think of you often, particularly when I see all these wonderful things.

TO HIS MOTHER
21 June 1954

Pensione Gasser
Via Niccolo da Tolentino 50
Rome

Yesterday morning I walked round the Vatican—St Peter's is not very beautiful inside, nor is the façade, and the colonnade, fine as it is, is quite out of place. I went to see the crypt with Pollaiuolo's tomb for Sixtus IV, which is quite as wonderful as I remembered it, as are the early Christian things there. I spent so long down there in the cool (the whole of St Peter's is wonderfully cold after walking in the hot summer sun) that by the time I had walked the several miles to the entrance of the museum and trundled down the gallery of the Vatican, I had only three-quarters of an hour before having to return home, which I spent looking at the Sistina. In spite of the magnificence of Michelangelo, I find the Botticelli *Moses* pictures just as fascinating. No one could say that he is an easier painter, but he is less monumental, which may be an advantage.

TO HIS MOTHER *c/o Vivante*
3 *July 1954* *Villa Solaia*
Malafrasca per Siena

Everyone is very free and easy here, and frightfully nice—you would like [the Vivante] so much. If you come to Siena you should visit them. Anyway the place is worth seeing as it is a typical cinquecento-Piccolomini villa, slightly *north* of Siena. Ten minutes by car from the centre, and rather longer on foot, although the walk through the fields is fun. From the top rooms one can just see the towers of Siena, but from my room, which is one of the nicest and is all by itself in a little backwater next to the dining-room, I can only see the terrace with the lemons hanging like little yellow suns on the trees. They are much bigger lemons than ours at home and some have degenerated into funny shapes, looking more like Diana of the Ephesians than anything else!

The Vivante are terribly anti-fascist, anti snob, anti the aristocracy, and of course the priests! Signora Elena Vivante's brother★ was killed in an air-crash (or maybe was shot down by the fascists, that's what the Vivante say) after dropping anti-fascist leaflets on Rome. Signor Vivante is Jewish by origin, from Venice, very modest, serious, a very pleasant old man (70 or so).

★ Lauro de Bosis.

c/o Vivante
                                                    Malafrasca per Siena

Life passes very slowly, but pleasantly. I am reading
Pirandello, very hard going, as the Italian is difficult. I shall try
to find something a bit easier. Also Gibbon, who in spite of his
wonderful language, is a bit on the heavy side. Goethe's
Iphigenie pleased me no end—I read it aloud to myself, and
enjoyed every line. I should like to see it performed.

A little while ago I read *David Copperfield*, as I may have told
you, which is certainly among the best novels I have ever read.
Do try it again. Dickens is much more original and lively than
Pirandello, who is a kind of Italian S. Maugham. Of course it
is better than that, but the short story never can contain as
much as is necessary for a colossus like *David Copperfield*.

The race,★ when it finally took place, was very exciting, but
I had seen one of the *prova* so it was not new to me. The terror
of a man behind us, who was of the district of the sign of
Onda, that his rider would be bribed at the last minute, or get a
bad position at the start, was much aggravated when he saw
the jockeys discuss things among themselves, and making
signs at the bribers. However Onda won, and the man, who in
his terror that he would not do so had been screaming away,
his eyes full of tears, was so delighted that he just dumped his
baby son, who could not have cared less, on the bench, and got
up and shouted wholly unnecessary encouragement to the
rider who was in the lead from the start. If he hadn't won we
were frightened that he would bash us all up.

Christ Church
                                                    Oxford

It is very cold, but I am now firmly installed. I am not in Peck
as Iris [his sister] would have had me believe, but in Meadow

★ The *Palio* in Siena.

Buildings, right at the top, in a newly decorated room which is very pleasant, and I am alone which is a definite advantage. Downstairs is a boy called Jeremy Lemmon,* very nice, whom Tim [Wilson-Smith] once introduced me to, and who has a clavichord, on which he plays very well, among many other instruments. I have received of course invitations to many societies, but have decided nothing as yet. I arrived quite safely with the Stefano [della Bella drawing], and a Bali picture, but my prints did not fit into the cases and you will be so kind as to bring them please.

On Wednesday Armide [Oppé] took me to a concert given by her friend Szigeti [Joseph Szigeti, violinist], who did not play as well as he should have done, I thought, although Armide was delighted. *The Times* of yesterday agreed with me. I only praised it to Armide of course.

We met some extraordinary people backstairs at the Festival Hall, all women worshippers of the great man. Lady Forsdyke† was very charming, and so was a woman who runs an arty night-club in St James's Place, and looks after artists in distress. But altogether the aura of hangers-on to the great man was more than I could bear at some moments. Never mind, it was certainly interesting to see. Szigeti is a charming man.

How nice it is to be here. My window is rather small, but what I see are tree-tops, which are very pleasant. From my bedroom a lovely view greets me, onto towers and gables— because as I am so very high up, about sixty steps or so, I see over the opposite roof-tops. It is quite exciting walking across the quads to think that I really am here now, in spite of the continual drizzle. On Sunday I shall go to Bath with Iris to hear a concert in the Bach Festival which is taking place there. I put all the books into my shelf, which then proceeded to come crashing down. Food in Hall (my thoughts always come back to that at the moment) is moderately bad. A glass of cider

---

* Born 1935. Master at Harrow School.

† Widow of a former Director of the British Museum, sister of Sir Ernst Gombrich, and a musician in her own right.

cheers things up a bit however. I bought very decent cheap glasses at Woolworths this morning. The sheets are here, and wonderful. Everything has worked well. I am looking forward to receiving you here. I look most amusing in a scholar's gown.

TO HIS MOTHER   *Christ Church*
2 May 1955   *Oxford*

Anthony★ assures me the Conservatives are going to bring in a House of Lords reform if they come back to power, but I don't see how they can. The Constitution is one of those things which well-mannered people leave alone . . .

I am not seeing too many people, nor working too hard. This evening I was sitting in Nicky's room, playing chess with him, when in came Lords Lumley and Weymouth both pretty tight and after much reeling about and exclaiming they explained that he [Nicky Gage] had just been elected a member of the Bullingdon. He was rather worried by this—as he does not want to be a member—'How am I to explain?' he asked me. It was like an Evelyn Waugh scene (and not the best kind I'm afraid)—and they shut the *oak* we found out later when we went out. As you may know it is not considered quite decent for two people to be sitting in an *oaked* room.

TO HIS MOTHER   *Christ Church*
7 May 1955   *Oxford*

I went last night to see Joyce Grenfell at the New Theatre which was quite fun—but she has a ballet with her composed of three dancers who are among the most revolting and

★ Anthony Grigg, born 1936. Son of Lord Altrincham, younger brother of John Grigg.

tedious I have seen for a long time. Afterwards we had dinner at a nice little Indian place—a funny group of myself, a Russian (of whom I have spoken before), a very nice person called Simon Young who is the son of a well-known physicist or something now at London, and Harry Graham, another Etonian of some charm and intelligence—altogether a very Oxford evening with a great deal of laughter etc. and so English at the same time! I am all the time astonished how English the English really are. The conversation was a bit like out of Wilde—but much more personal of course. I am told that that is peculiar to Oxford, and that at Cambridge everyone is much more restrained and interested in being moral and so on. I don't believe it. Tomorrow perhaps I shall go into the country. I shall try to persuade Anthony Grigg to take me—he is a charming person and rather intelligent. It is very odd how most of the people here at Christ Church and outside whom I know are Etonians—they are like a coterie which knows no limits. A pity that none of my Westminster friends is here yet. However, I have no right to complain as everyone is very nice to me—and one ought to be grateful for that!

TO HIS MOTHER   *Christ Church*
22 May 1955   *Oxford*

There is very little to tell you of any great novelty—I have had the writer [Henry] Green's son here all evening—he is so much talked about (Sebastian Yorke is the name) but I do not find him very much more than charming. But he knows enormous quantities of people and that of course makes a great difference. What an advantage great charm is to people who realize they have it—the world sits at their feet. Arcadi* and I have decided to have a little party next Sunday—you will be astonished at who has been asked but I shan't give you a list

* Count Arcadi Nebolsine, born 1932, now teaching in New York.

until they have all actually come. I may say that I telephoned to Mrs Betjeman and she was very civil and charming, and said she hoped she and her husband would turn up! She will let me know. Arcadi on the other hand is trying for Berlin, Cecil and Sparrow and so on—we shall see! Arcadi is being particularly nice to me—for which I feel very grateful. He takes me here and there and introduces people to me the whole time in the pleasantest way.

TO HIS MOTHER   *Christ Church*
no date but before   *Oxford*
20 January 1956

Here everything seems to be going quite well—I wrote an essay again yesterday, but did not have to read it out. None of us is very pleased with this system—no tutorials, etc. I go to lectures and all that and work sometimes in the Bodleian which is very useful because as David [Carritt] said there is absolutely nothing else one can do there. Of course I shall go to [Edgar] Wind's lectures. There are several of them making a whole course, all on Julius II's tomb. Tell him if you see him in London that I am here. I doubt if he will be staying here all the time but I shall definitely try to see him. James Joll★ hopes to see him, and I may meet him there. James was extremely nice and I met a number of amusing people there—including Father Dominic, a Jesuit of delightfully worldly habits and a sharp tongue.

★ Born 1918, Fellow of St Antony's College Oxford, Stevenson Professor of International History at the University of London, 1967–81.

Christ Church
23 *January 1956* *Oxford*

I went to the Union for the first time last week, and heard a debate on the Establishment (of the Church of England). The only really amusing thing was the presence of the Bishop Chavasse of Rochester who was dressed in purple 18th-century clothes and was rather fun to listen to as a kind of ranting old-style Tory bishop. The other people in the Union were generally tedious, one could see from their faces. I shall try to speak there on Thursday evening—I don't suppose I shall be much of a success as I cannot make the kind of feeble joke that the audience laughed at and applauded—none of any kind in fact in speeches.

TO HIS MOTHER *Christ Church*
5 *February 1956* *Oxford*

I do hope you enjoyed your visit as much as I did—it was such fun having you both* here and going to Blenheim, and the lunch. It was so funny the way Carmen kept looking for Feldmarschall von Finckenstein in the tapestries of Marlboro'—I am sure he was on them. What a fascinating place it is. I wonder whether there will be any villas as grand round Asolo—I hope so. I went book-buying yesterday and I found an old copy of *Der Stille Garten* in 'den Blauen Büchern' series—first half 19th-century German painting. The photos are bad but some of the pictures obviously quite lovely—Kobell, Friedrich, Kersting, Begas d. ä., Schick, Runge u.s.w., and of course Spitzweg—but they are not much known here, just as I suppose English water-colourists are not known much abroad. The Ashmolean got a lovely Rubens drawing out of the Cooke Collection—which Woodward showed me—but he also showed with pride the Filipino which Buttery has

* His mother and her elder sister, Carmen Gräfin von Finckenstein.

cleaned; the result is not too good in my view, but they no doubt know best.

TO HIS PARENTS   *Christ Church*
no date (1954 or 1956)   *Oxford*

Thank you very much for the sherry, it will come in very useful, and I am sure it will be quite delicious—I have not tried it yet as I still have some other. I have just come back from Wind's first lecture at the Ashmolean—it was absolutely brilliant. The audience was smaller than it would have been at the Warburg, but that does not matter as the thing is inevitably printed and of course reported everywhere. The Vice-Chancellor and Bowra were there and of course Parker, and all the Oxford art nabobs, but really it was a tiny audience, which, considering the incredibly high quality of the lecture and the vast panorama of learning which he very modestly presented, was a pity—the loss of those who did not bother to go. It was all about the tomb of Julius II, at least it was meant to be, but today was in fact all about the significance of the Raphael fresco of the *School of Athens* and the other ones in that room in the Vatican. In fact it showed the philosophical background to that picture and also he tried to give one some idea of Julius's influence on the works of the artists whom he commissioned—that is what it is going to lead to. The whole was accompanied by very well-chosen slides and altogether clear and very interesting.

He was, funnily enough, able to back up his theory by looking at Joshua Reynolds's 'cartoon' of the *School of Athens* which puts caricatures of the Savants of Rome in the place of the various philosophers. That they, the Savants, were doing all the things which he says the philosophers are doing (as shown by their gestures) in the original, was not merely the result of some idle tradition which Reynolds had picked up in Rome but was derived from the 17th-century authority

Bellori. Wind could prove this because he had found, purely by accident, in the Harvard Library Joshua Reynolds's copy of Bellori, complete with notes by R. None of this is very clear, I am afraid, but it goes to show something of his range. I spoke to him afterwards and he sends you all his best wishes, and he hopes to see me sometimes before he leaves and gave me his address. His accent as Mutti says is atrocious. However, one was able to forget that at least some of the time. It all rushed on, rather unfortunately, as he has so much material that he can hardly get it all in!

TO HIS MOTHER   *Christ Church*
16 February 1956   *Oxford*

I am very sorry not to have written for such a long time. It was very naughty of me, but I have been very busy—doing thousands of things at once and really doing nothing properly. I will tell you all—first, last Wednesday I had Trevor-Roper to lunch which was very amusing I thought, although not everyone else thought so. It was really a monologue, or rather a series of them—one of them lasted twenty-five minutes! It was the story of the election to the professorship of Poetry in 1939, which he told as if it were a piece of history—the whole story neatly unfolded itself; he made his points as if we were taking notes so that it was a little unamusing—although the material itself, as it were, *was* so—interesting, but not very witty. I had Anthony Grigg and Mark Tennant and Fionn★ and Miranda [McKenna] as well—they thought him a little boring but quite nice. He is very clever—but also very shy I suppose and anxious to please I think. He noticed my heater, but made no comment fortunately—of course it is against college rules.

On Friday and Saturday I went to Cambridge. I borrowed

★ Fionn and Miranda O'Neill, daughters of the late Lord O'Neill and the late Mrs Ian Fleming. Fionn married John Morgan of the Foreign Office, now divorced.

Robin Hope's car to do so and enjoyed both the drive and the visit. I got back on Sunday morning in two hours—which is an average of 40 mph, all in a Morris Minor. I thought that was pretty good going. It was, however, neither dangerous nor frightening—the roads were quite empty. In Cambridge I saw the Fitzwilliam which I admired enormously. Such good pictures and very well arranged. They have such a lovely Courbet as I have never seen—and Hogarths and Titians and a Rembrandt—but you know all that. The pictures in Cambridge are very much better than here, as is the furniture —but not the drawings and not the sculpture, or bronzes rather. Then the architecture is not so good. As a town it is more intact but less impressive. There is no street like the High. The Tudor architecture is poor on the whole, except for King's marvellous Chapel. The 18th-century is by great artists like Gibbs, but not so much of it and generally less dominating than here. Still it has enormous charm—and all the pinnacles of King's in the snow were beautiful. In King's I tried to see Jaffé but he was out. Burgo Partridge, with whom I went there, took me to see E. M. Forster—who was also out. After that we stuck to undergraduates.

The next day among other things and amusing people I went to see Mathilde* for a couple of hours, who was very glad to see me and we had tea together. I brought her lots of food and things, having warned her in the morning. Except for our dinner on Saturday evening, which was spoilt by the sudden cliqueness and rudeness of the people we were with, I enjoyed the visit [to Cambridge] very much. It was very interesting to see how different they were from us—much more earnest, much more easily shocked, far fuller of enthusiasms, far more like young people than Oxford undergraduates. The tone here is so very much 'being as much like smart grown-ups as possible'. There they are much more natural, and therefore much less at ease, and very serious—too much so. They could do well with a little breath of fresh air—a

* His first cousin once removed, daughter of Heinrich Hertz, 1857–94. Physicist, discoverer of electro-magnetic waves.

little too stuffy at times, and very self-consciously serious too, with the result that he who is the most pompously intelligent is the most respected. And they have tin-Gods who are applauded at every word. I didn't like that. I suppose to an ordinary visitor the differences would not seem so obvious— but still, both I and other people have noticed them.

TO HIS MOTHER   *Christ Church*
20 June 1956   *Oxford*

After an enormous lunch and the party this morning [Jeremy Lemmon, Andrew Dawnay, John Buchanan-Riddell, Antony Grant, John Calmann at Home, Thursday, 20th June, Canon Simpson's House: 11.30], I still feel rather full and sleepy now (6 p.m.)! The party went very well—about 100 people were there—and took place under a brilliantly blue sky in a Canon's garden. The champagne was very cold and so it all seemed very pleasant. Afterwards we had lunch here (the five hosts) and ate so much that a heavy torpor seemed to drown us all at about 4 but a certain amount of rational clarity has returned now.

On Tuesday I spent two hours at a vast party at Cliveden House (owned by the Astors) given by Douglas Fairbanks for his daughter. Jacob Rothschild took me at about midnight— myself in the character of Adrian Berry who did not want to make use of his invitation. The house was built in the style of an Italian palazzo by Barry in about 1840, inside it is hideous but sumptuous, and its Italian gardens are absolutely splendid. They were lit up with a sort of yellow light—the house itself on a huge terrace in darkness. The Queen and the whole royal family were there, looking perfectly boring, but naturally their presence gave the whole a certain glamour. Tiaras, ribbons, medals, stars, jewels, etc. glittered on every head and coat, so you can imagine that there was plenty to look at. I didn't dance with anyone, nor talk very much, just observed the whole as one might a real-life version of a very Ruritanian film. I had a short exchange with the heavily decorated and excessively smooth Fairbanks. In the dining-room the sea of tiaras was quite dazzling—Alan Pryce-Jones sitting where it seemed thickest. The whole was a strange contrast to an exceedingly boring party given in St Anne's earlier in the evening, where the bourgeois had not managed to disguise themselves so well.

I have seen Alan Bullock, who is in charge of the B.Phil. He will let me know during the holidays if it is impossible for me to do it and will tell me next term what to do if it is all right for me to stay on. So . . . it all depends on a 2nd.

In autumn 1957 John took his degree in history (gaining a 2 plus) and was encouraged to stay on for a further two years to study for a B.Litt. at St Antony's College. His thesis was to be on an 18th-century subject and he chose the secularization of monasteries by the Emperor Joseph II of Austria. For his research he had to go to Vienna where he found lodgings in the decaying grandeur of the palace of Princess Schönburg. In Vienna John was joined for a short time by the parents of his American friend Robert Cumming. Professor William Cumming and his wife Betty taught English at Davidson College, North Carolina. Robert Cumming (born December 1935) took his degree at Harvard, and got a scholarship to Oxford (Christ Church) 1957–60, where he took a B.Phil. in history. He served in the US army reserve and trained as a Peace Corps volunteer in Thai language, history, etc. He spent two years teaching English at the Bangkok universities of Chulalongkorn and Silpakorn, 1962–63. He travelled in India and lived in a Hindu ashram in Bihar, 1964–65. On his return to the States he did anti-poverty work in North Carolina, then taught writing to underprepared students from low-income families at the City College, New York, 1968–73. There he married Deborah Smith and both now have professorships at Lauder College, Greenwood, South Carolina. In 1981–82 they returned to Thailand, Robert as Fulbright Visiting Professor. Both began translating contemporary Thai poets and Robert has also published his own poems.

TO HIS MOTHER   *Christ Church*
22 May 1958   *Oxford*

I have made a close acquaintance with my American friend Cumming. His manners *sont à merveille*, but he is too polite and shy I think. He is very intelligent, and simpler than would at first appear. Americans are of course serious—much more so than me—but he covers it with extreme modesty. Perhaps after two years here he will loosen up a bit.

The Americans are strange in that they have a much younger attitude to life than any of my friends, while being quite grown-up in manners and knowledge, etc. They also decry America the whole time. Cumming clearly likes where he lives though, the South, and he is enormously attached to his land—just like landowners everywhere. This makes him a bit more like a European than his friends.

TO HIS MOTHER   *c/o Fürstin Schönburg*
8 January 1959   *Palais Schönburg*
                                                        Vienna

Vienna is as we remembered it, a depressing place in which so far I keep finding that museums are closed, for holidays or for other reasons, which has been a great bore for Mrs Cumming, who has as a result seen much less than she wanted to. The Kunsthistorisches is wonderful in some respects: the bric-à-brac downstairs, like the salt-cellar [by Benvenuto Cellini], is excellent, but you will be pleased to hear that our bronze head is much better. The curls on the one here are more lively, and more separate than on ours, and they are perhaps a little more

35

delicate. On the other hand, one sees the whole thing very much from below, and so it is difficult to judge the quality of the details. The ears are very small, the patina dull compared with ours, and the preservation very much less good. There are nasty marks on the cheeks, and the expression of the mouth is softer and less pronounced. The face is decidedly fatter than ours and less elegant and sensual.

The pictures are all shown without glass and are in a remarkable state of preservation. The *Three Philosophers* [by Giorgione] is quite magnificent, so are the Titians, especially the one of the *Nymph and the Shepherd*, which Mutti likes so much. The Dürer altarpiece of the *Trinity in Glory* I had never seen in reproduction and was amazed. Its colours are so brilliant, and the concept so grand, I had hardly thought Dürer could *paint* anything so well, and on such a scale. The great room with the Breughels is in some ways the most astonishing. There is so much to look at in each picture that after I had seen them I had no energy left for anything else. I also can't make up my mind which I like the most, each one has so many virtues, and is so different from the others. Some have very little integration in their composition, but there is so much put into them that the details leave one no choice but to examine them. The *Vogeldieb* would hang best in the drawing-room, or the *Winter-Scene*. There are many other good pictures, Flemish and Italian, and one can go many times. I haven't yet been to the Albertina, nor to the Akademie and other museums but will do so in time.

The *Zauberflöte* was very well done. Unimaginative sets and wooden acting on the whole, but it is such a silly opera from every point of view, except the music, that you can't expect anything else. Sarastro was bad. The music is the best in the world, and very nicely played by the orchestra. The theatre has been very boringly restored inside with the exception of a sort of promenade gallery, which is pretty, and the remnants of Wiener chic wandering up and down. I thought the use of three *Sängerknaben*★ as the three boys was charming, and their

★ Members of the boy-choir of the chapel of the Hofburg in Vienna.

voices blended wonderfully with that of the prima donna (Seefried). I heard them sing Mass by Mozart in the Hofkapelle last Sunday: visually and musically a most delicious performance and a really wonderfully unprotestant *douche* for the Cummings with whom I went, and who loved it! They enjoy everything hugely, and I keep a firm control of myself when Mrs C. praises some masterpiece of 1880s baroque! They have been very nice to me, however, and we spent a merry day on Sunday when the weather was good, had lunch on the Leopoldsberg, and saw Schönbrunn in the afternoon, which has been restored again since we saw it, with too much new gold in some rooms. But wonderful outside in the blue-pink winter light.

Yesterday evening the youngest princess [of the Schönburgs] took me to see parts of old Vienna in the lamplight. She had borrowed a car for the purpose, and we saw really *very* pretty *Stadtpalais*. The house here, a *garten palais*, is 1720s—very heavy in style, but with a fine drawing-room. The people who call have without any exception names like Thun, Razumovsky, Czernin, Esterhazy, Nostitz, etc.

We also met Thornton Wilder here, who came round one day and is a friend of the elder princess. He is a very nervous man of about 55, looks well over 65, and thrilled the Cummings by asking them to dinner. I hope to see him again when he comes to tea on Saturday. He seemed very friendly and amusing.

There were originally eight sons [in the Schönburg family], but six were killed in the war. The two others live away from Vienna, which they don't like. The eldest princess is about 45, the younger one 25. There is another married one who lives in the basement, whom I met for a moment. The eldest *lives* for the palais, which she is vainly trying to save, not having the first clue really of how to run it. The youngest plays the piano well, and the first evening I wandered through the dark rooms of the ground-floor in which one could just see a little of the gold glitter reflecting the street-lamp outside, and pushed my way like in a Cocteau film into the enormous and very grand drawing-room where she sat wrapped in coats and rugs playing a Chopin valse with a great deal of temperament.

Vienna is really quite dead, and an evening spent with a Hungarian boy, who lives here, in the Augustiner Keller did not convince me that it is anything but a large and generally boring provincial town with a few last vestiges of cosmopolitan grandeur. The Keller was so respectable, and full of such sweet old Hungarian music, and the people so quiet, and the wine so very second-rate, it was a little as one might have expected Graz to be, but not the capital. I am told by the Hungarian that the nobility lead a very smart life, but judging by the youngest princess's conversation they all go to Paris or London. A dead world.

TO HIS MOTHER   c/o Fürstin Schönburg
2 February 1959   Vienna

I came home last night at ten, after eleven hours with Hylton,* and had a further five hours with the eldest princess, who suddenly began to tell me about her life in Berlin during the war. It began really when she told me that she had worked for the husband of a cousin of hers in the *Auswärtiges Amt*,† as a sort of secretary and general assistant. He was very anti-Nazi etc. etc. and she lived in their house, and then it became too hot for him, and he got a posting to Roumania. I thought for a moment of our visit to the Rantzaus in '53 (it had already cropped up in my mind much earlier in the day for different reasons) and asked her if it had been a Rantzau‡ she had worked for—'Yes, of course'. What a Zhivago-like

* Hylton Thomas. See Letter of 27/11/59.
† The German Foreign Office.
‡ Josias von Rantzau was taken prisoner by the advancing Russian army and against all the rules protecting members of diplomatic services, was imprisoned in the Peter-Paul Fortress in Leningrad where he died in solitary confinement.

coincidence (this Rantzau was the brother of your friend of course). Then we talked about other things—his friends, the bomb-plot—and I remembered that story about a blind friend of yours who was visited by Stauffenberg and later killed himself—'Ahlmann', she said, 'mein Busenfreund'. And then she really got going: she was in the *thick* of the bomb-plot— was to have gone to a quiet celebration lunch with Hassel on the 20th July '44—saw him and a friend called Trott and many others in prison etc. etc. Unfortunately I can't remember all their names. I just listened, fascinated, while she told story after story about that group of Hitler's enemies—how slowly (they started already before the war) they worked, how disorganized they were. She said that she had been in the midst of it all without really knowing what it was all about. You can imagine I found it all most disagreeable, but fascinating. She also told me about some Prussians who ran a secret hide-out system for the Jews right on into the war, and many other strange things.

John failed the B.Litt. examination. There were probably several reasons for this: he had become disenchanted with Oxford and was convinced that he would be unsuited to the academic life. He had also spent much time writing a play about Prince Frederick of Prussia, encouraged by his literary agent Margaret Ramsey who later refused it. In the summer of 1959 he travelled with his mother and Robert Cumming in the Haute Savoie. Later John's father joined them and they drove to Genoa where John boarded a Greek cargo boat bound for New York. From there he flew to Los Angeles to stay with his relations, the Hertz family.

Richard Hertz, John's uncle on his mother's side, had served in the German Foreign Office but resigned in 1937 and emigrated with his wife and family to the USA where they acquired citizenship. Richard was, however, re-instated by the German Foreign Office in Bonn after the German defeat and he was German Ambassador in Korea when John arrived in California. The rest of the Hertz family

remained at home in Los Angeles, where John visited them. Richard
Hertz died as German Ambassador in Mexico in 1963.

TO HIS MOTHER   *c/o Hertz*
18 September 1959   *2264, Mandeville Canyon Road*
                                                    Los Angeles

I am now installed here since Sunday, almost five days, and am
just beginning to get used to the family and the city. I will try
to describe both. The air trip was very comfortable really and
passed off very quickly. Five hours was too quick I suppose—
but they still speak English here, and I have no feeling of being
in a foreign country, only in a slightly strange one. It is of
course much stranger than New York.

Peter and Richie [Hertz, his cousins] were sent to private
schools at one stage or another, which saved them from public
education for a while at least, which by itself is simply
dreadful. All the Americans are worried about it, the
newspapers talk about nothing else, particularly now that
Russia has hit the moon, and that Khrushchev in his speeches
has made clear to them that Russia is really doing very well.
He has been very frank—and the newspapers have completely
misunderstood him. As far as I can see the Americans are in a
panic that any discussion with the Russians would be the same
as appeasement—they always cite Munich, as if that had
anything to do with it. Even Richie, for all the Zen-
Buddhism which his father taught him in Seoul just now,
thought nothing of the statement 'Korea would have been
settled much better with 3 or 4 (!) atom bombs,' which he
made the other day. [Walter] Lippmann, the journalist, wrote
an article saying he thought America should realize that
Khrushchev meant it when he said that Russia and the US
were equally powerful now, and that the only hope was to see
how one could survive and live side by side. The Americans,
however, are very frightened of this and have done their best

in the newspapers and in the questions they put to annoy him and attack him. Mme Veuve Macarthy even held a meeting in New York as a protest against Khrushchev—and thousands are wearing black arm-bands to show their disapproval! Many religious leaders, particularly Catholics, have protested publicly and from the pulpits. Trust the Churches! Eisenhower in the meanwhile has left K. to go around by himself, and has gone off for the weekend to play golf. (The papers printed it today.) One has no idea in Europe of the extreme conservatism of the Americans—their complete misunderstanding of socialism for instance. The American public has a capacity for believing anything it wants to, to a degree far surpassing the English. The intelligent Americans I met on the ship were all very violent in their criticism of the country, though they had very different attitudes and backgrounds. In this utterly unhomogeneous society I can understand why they have such a passion for conventions, for rigorously sticking to codes—even the Beatniks, now covered by *Life*—and conservative hatred for anything outside them. Hence the attitude to Khrushchev.

In a way it is funny they [the Hertzes] take such an interest in me, since they have no idea about our family at all—much less than I had of them. But it is very far away here from Europe— and I know how distant it must seem to them, more so, funnily, than the other way round.

TO FIONN O'NEILL   *c/o Hertz*
2 *October 1959*   *Los Angeles*

Outside the brown leaves of a plane-tree screen off the brown hills of scrub that rise suddenly in the middle of this part of the town. The garden is filled with pale gladioli, oranges and lemons, endless shrubs of a vaguely green-brown nature, and a plant with a mauve flower called 'Impatience'. The sky has

41

no cloud, the air is dry and warm and for miles round there are similar houses with similar gardens.

The people are not at all beautiful—the girls have a tendency to being cute, the boys are not even that!—and at first the atmosphere is vaguely provincial. But that is quite wrong. It is an embryo city. I drove down Wilshire (correct spelling) Boulevard yesterday, with its immensely expensive shops, and I caught a whiff of Harrods or even 5th Avenue. More Harrods really. You must imagine that the Americans are really awfully like the English—in spite of all the obvious differences—like the English a hundred years ago perhaps. They are wonderfully confident that they're right, and that they are good-hearted. But you've heard all that before.

My uncle has just arrived from Korea, where he is German ambassador (my aunt and the children remained American while he went back to being a German, which caused rather a split in the family) and is as extraordinary as I remember him. He is a huge man, with great vitality, and most opinionated about everything under the sun: he combines great social ambitions with a voluptuous enthusiasm for Zen Buddhism, the last resort of many scoundrels. The social ambitions were encouraged in youth by a central European grande-dame of the finest water (my metaphor is drawn from mineralogy), a Helene von Nostitz, than which no better name exists, who popped him into the German FO. Then the Nazis came and he left to teach philosophy to the Americans—a mission that failed, in so far as he became a worse and worse philosopher, less and less in touch with the world of his dreams, and very poor. Then the return to Germany and the FO in '51, and now the tail-end of a diplomatic career—and very much a tail-end it is, though by all accounts he had a brilliantly successful life in Seoul, that joint outpost of America and Asia. You'd enjoy all the nonsense he talks; he would have made a good playboy though he's a bit selfish, I think, which isn't too good in a playboy. On the one hand, he wishes to be thought of only as an intellectual, on the other as the intimate of princesses. That's a game one can only play with an iron character and real

42

gifts—whether social or intellectual. In the end he is always disappointing or disappointed—the latter more often. Dame Edith [Sitwell] took him up a few years ago; you can imagine the awful deception when he met the three sedentary witches and discovered that they owed their success more to snobbery than to charm!

I don't feel depressed by California—yet—nor overcome by a desire to get back to the European hearth, though unless I go back to New York soon and see some slightly more familiar faces I may get restless. I'm not really sure why I'm here, or what I want from America though of course the best would be to sell a play here. I've just sent a new one to London, and am waiting for the agent's opinion.

TO WILLIAM ANDERSON   *c/o Hertz*
5 October 1959   *Los Angeles*

I began Proust on the ship—*Swann*. I am very confused about it. He is very derivative I feel, from Dickens and Saint-Simon. But there is a wonderful sense of prose there. Sometimes tears are brought to my eyes by the extreme sensibility. *Au fond* it is because I distrust princely nostalgia—I feel it too easily myself to regard it as the basis of great experience or great art, and this distrust makes me impatient with Proust at times, or unable to enjoy more than the flavour of what he conveys, without receiving really anything *new*. But you will regard this as very heretical. The Oxford term must have begun by the time this reaches you: I can't imagine it without *me*—as soon as my back is turned I feel it must disappear.

It just takes time to find one's way into this miasma of conflicting styles and incoherent suburbs. My cousins are fun, though trying at times. Their vitality is just terrific, their *joie de vivre* a full blast after the sophisticated jingle of champagne parties in the Woodstock Road [in Oxford]. In order to make myself heard I have to shout and scream with the best of them—occasionally they pause to listen to what they call my persuasive reason and common sense. To call *me* by those names must indicate the violence of the proceedings. Also I am official interpreter of England and Europe: of course my opinions on these subjects are strictly European, I have not yet got a world-based *Weltanschauung*, that's been made very clear—just as they are absolutely America-minded in face of me. I am often told by them that American culture and literature is 'getting somewhere'—unlike our own dry European stuff, subtle and witty though we may be. In face of this I have given up most pretensions to subtlety and have stuck to hard-hitting arguments, which are the only ones that carry weight. It is difficult to say whether we are 'getting anywhere'. When I read some press-cuttings on a new book on the Establishment, which my mama sent me, I was frightened by the introspective sterility of England—but I also know that I personally don't want to 'get anywhere', or my 'culture' to, in their sense of the words. At Oxford and among our friends I always cherished the romantic illusion that we would of course bring some new life and spark to England at least, and in spite of the regular habits which you all seem to be adopting I still think that way as a matter of course. How can I explain all that and not sound a fool? My plays have been well received by them and I can at least point to the fact that I am *trying* to see what I can do. To part of my family at any rate such an attempt seems awfully small fry compared to, say, the

* Born 1936. Specialist in race relations and social policy, Professor of Social Policy, University of Birmingham, since 1980.

mighty actuality of Hemingway. I hate Hemingway, and Faulkner is totally unreadable as far as I'm concerned—that puts me in a difficult position.

I was able to substantiate my claim, I think, that there are no American painters and never have been (except for Sargent whom I like of course). But this sort of fight is pretty dull in the long run. I am trying to understand what they really like about American culture without putting across my own. But sometimes it is astonishing just how little there is to offer here: after all, the minutiae of a French cathedral, of a 17th-century poem etc., are distinct and, in their possibly unimportant ways, delightful. Here things are 'great' or nothing. How much we depend on the minor masters in everything, even in furniture and architecture and in all the sights of our everyday life in Europe. Minor masters are simply bad here. Imagine then the surprise when I said I thought many Americans were inarticulate: 'we go out to people', was the reply, unlike the stiff Europeans. They go out to people, but either it is the smallest of small-talk, or deepest of deep-talk, but never intellectual gaiety.

TO SIR JOHN BUCHANAN RIDDELL*   *c/o Hertz*
17 October 1959   *Los Angeles*

Of course, we—I mean you and I and our friends—are a very specialized group of people, with limited interests, untrained in talking about our jobs (I have none), our cars, our women and our sports (we play none): these topics are the neutral territory of the Americans and if one goes beyond that here there is danger of either finding nothing, or too much—great deeply felt convictions which are impossible to discuss. Harvard or other 'good' college graduates are different, I hope, but here in the West it is obviously pioneering country.

* Born 1934. City banker, Private Secretary to the Prince and Princess of Wales, 1985.

At first I was ready to accept it, now I am ready to rebel against it. The conformity is so overpowering! Everything is so predictable, so déjà vu: one super-market costs a little more than another, one 'home' has a slightly larger garden than another, one car is a little smaller (none is small), and so in spite of the fact that everything is quite new, or at least post-1953 or so, once one has the hang of things one has got the lot (the whole bit, as they say here). There are no secrets to discover, some districts are richer, others less so, but variations are in the lushness, in the conveniences (I use the term in the widest sense) with which each house is endowed; the atmosphere is without charm and without romance. Romance is after all part of the past: nothing here is part of the past, it is all transitional to the future.

I have been to a club or two in the evenings . . . The first, called misleadingly Club Renaissance, had a black queen singing a camp song or two, and some folksingers, who surprisingly enough had some charm and talent. The second was much more ambitious, and there I saw a vast coloured woman and her troupe singing spirituals and quasi-religious negro music excellently, with enormous gusto and vitality. The woman first appeared in a purple gown covered in sequins; you and I and Jeremy Lemmon could have all climbed in it together and left some room, if we had had the extraordinary desire to do so. She alone filled it amply and out of it bellowed a deep and very beautiful voice. There were some pretty boys and girls in the troupe, and they stamped up and down enjoying their religious ecstasy as if they were genuinely moved by it and not putting it on for us. It was the first time I had been really stirred by anything in L.A. The blacks offer all the exoticism here, if you discount the beatniks, whose hideout I haven't yet visited.

I went to the beatnik place here† the other night. It is
dreadfully commercialized, though vaguely sinister, but the
surroundings, an imitation of Venice and northern France
combined into a rather touchingly grotesque mixture, have
some interest. The beatniks themselves, looking just as they
did in *Life*, selling artefacts 'by Ginsberg' in the 'shoppes',
wear a uniform, and in the midst of their revolt reflect the
American urge to belong somewhere. I think small-town life
in this country must be the best—not because the people will
be nicer, surely they won't—but because it must make the
Americans a little less lost in a world of anonymous beings
with whom they are directly associated by a political bond,
but with whom they have so little personal contact. Arthur
Miller does bring that out well, I mean the feeling of being
lost. The beatnik world is a small community—an in-group
with special codes, morals and sexual practices, and even
language—but it has of course produced absolutely nothing of
real merit, and I include all that drivel by Ginsberg we got so
excited about because of Robert P. Cumming's bringing it to
Oxford. Am I unfair? I hope so. I think the old thing would
agree with me if it was not part of his personal 'mission
civilizatrice' to support them. I agree they have talent perhaps,
but so had Robert Bridges.

As for K. Tynan—yes, he is a good critic, I suppose, but
such a dictatorial one, and of course he produced Osborne
which is a strong point against him, in my 'umble opinion.

★ Born 1935. Vice President of Magdalen College, Oxford, Editor of the
English Historical Review. Married 1958, Joanna, daughter of Sir Richard
Musgrove Harvey Bt.
† In 'Venice', a part of Los Angeles.

Thank you for your 'blow', which hit me last night just as I arrived very tired after three days' sight-seeing in the desert. Naturally I am very disappointed. But I can see, I think, why you don't like the play—obviously it isn't good enough as it stands. I am very well punished for sending you a thing straight off the machine, as it were. I would, however, be glad to hear more exactly what you think is wrong. If you do have a moment to spare, write what you think, I like being told that—even when unpleasant.

I read a great deal of Arthur Miller before writing the play, not the right stuff for me to be influenced by perhaps, and anyway I'm sure I haven't properly understood the technique. What I have against him and so many plays today, even good ones like his, is that none of the characters is ever allowed to say anything worth listening to—their actions are interesting, their conflicts may be exciting (this is where I break down), but never can they express an idea intelligently without it becoming so trite that it makes one sick. All Arthur Miller's characters in his modern plays are either inarticulate or platitudinous. Nevertheless, his plays are good and very intense. I would like to learn how to present that intensity together with a few ideas—and in my play [*The Free Country*] there are one or two of them, though the ones in the last scene are plain dull.

How am I really, you ask. It is awfully difficult to describe. I feel slightly banged on the head by the fact that my agent hated

* An Oxford friend, married (1960) William Plowden, Director-General, Royal Institute of Public Administration.

my last play—and I can see why, though it has its moments!—and that I am getting slightly claustrophobic in L. A. Hence I shall leave here, and no doubt some things will get better. My car will whisk me away to San Francisco on Wednesday, and then after a few more excursions I'll go back to New York via Chicago. In my letters to everybody I keep describing America—because it is so very difficult to describe myself just now. Everyone writes—'don't be so impersonal'! But America is so much larger than anything I can get hold of, all ideas and feelings are squashed by this huge society around me, which, though I am protected from it by the presence of my cousins, who have a certain family likeness to me, I can feel creeping in all the time and obliterating my clear view of anything.

I often ask why I think I can become a writer—and whether it wouldn't in some ways have been better to become a soldier and then a businessman like everyone else.* But that is the safe way, and I have got out of the habit of playing it like that. I feel that if one is going to take risks at all, one must have great brains and great energy—if I have either they look damn well small in this hot-house of energy here. I am a sort of tourist through life—and have been since I got a degree at Oxford. While I always encouraged you to greater adventurousness, I have always had a secret longing to be able to sit quietly and lead a satisfactory humdrum life. But then there is always the question of money—and my vision of tranquillity is not one that holds a job in view. The idea of Morgan-Grenfell every day is not my bliss-view and so one is driven back to the risks. It may also be my cousins, who have overpowered me quite a lot by their vitality and nervousness, and that as soon as I get away from them I'll feel better. They are so full of their own energies that they destroy that which they touch. However it may be, I do feel cramped here. On the other hand it is very difficult to know whether one hasn't got some inherent restlessness and whether this won't come up at every turn and at every opportunity. I have a horrible suspicion that if I had a

* National Service came to an end while John was in the USA.

regular work-day week I would be twice as happy, that I would be able to survive with only half the 'nerves'. But where would one's ambition go then? And after a few weeks or months the same dissatisfaction would grow up that one had before.

TO ROBERT CUMMING   c/o Hertz
28 October 1959   actually at the San Marcos
                                  Motel, 101 Highway,
                                 Buellton, California

It was so nice to hear from you—because I think of you very often, at least as often as my absence from Oxford makes you think of me. I don't think of my friends as a group—but as a 'set': the difference is that the former implies some important almost aesthetic connection in which people work together for some common end. Sometimes Bill Anderson tried to get them to do this, or Nicholas [Deakin] and I. A set is a purely social term and means the group that meets very often (and contains many cousins), and knows few people outside it. You often think I am safely harboured in England in a group—or used to think so. I never was, though being quite an efficient host could have given you that impression. Groups are rare and impossible things; sometimes I want them very much, now I don't, or not often. Sets make life easier because they give one a social formula to belong to, but a group, like Bloomsbury, or the people round Dr Johnson, or the salon of Julie de l'Espinasse in the 18th century, which hopes to interact and have a common standard and philosophy, at least to some degree, and jointly to improve *the times*, is only possible, I think, among people of very great intelligence who have leisure and a little bit of disinterestedness. How could anyone of our age have that properly? Unless you perhaps, because the sensitivity of your heart is so much greater than your ambition —though admittedly not always than your convenience.

I have preached to you in this letter, and boasted, and blown myself up, when you asked me to *rally you*. How can I encourage you? I need it myself. For instance my play was no success with my agent at all—quite the contrary, but now I have another idea for one, so who cares? But still . . . one day I'll have to have some success otherwise my doubts will become serious. So far I have always conquered the ones about myself, so great is my own power of self-reassurance (with it I even managed to survive some other sharp blows this year), but I have a horrible feeling this innate stream of spiritual aspiring won't last for long now. I can't say I'm happy or unhappy, just confused.

I like your letters for the affection they speak of, but why is that affection so bound up with regret? I don't believe I was everything in your life, though I tried hard to be, at one time. I think it is being a student and Oxford more than my absence which may be saddening. I really can't express my delight at leaving all that behind. Without any question whatever, the last year was the most shattering of my life—and I had never been really scorched before. (Please don't take this as a shot at you.) Now I am having to build a fortress with the very fluidity of my ideas in a surrounding which is only unfamiliar —and that is difficult but worthwhile.

TO NICHOLAS DEAKIN   *c/o Hertz*
12 November 1959   *Los Angeles*

I wonder very much what the 'new left' discusses—is it the same as at 157?★ I like to think so, we had such enjoyably violent evenings there. I hope there aren't only discussions on the significance of radicalism—but also on what changes could actually be brought about. Paul† is of course very good

★ 157, Walton Street where Bill Anderson and Paul Thompson shared a flat in Oxford.
† Paul Johnson, born 1928. Author and journalist.

at telling one about that—and I often agree with him, and I think he'll make a very good Conservative in thirty years' time! (I know you'll pass that on.) If you knew how leftist I feel in this arch-conservative city! Wherever I go I find a tendency in myself to lean over backwards in the face of extremes to achieve some kind of balanced view. But in the end balanced views do not achieve very much, because all extreme measures of change will be compromised by those expected to carry them out. (Well, *maybe*.)

TO HIS MOTHER   *c/o Hertz*
13 November 1959   *Los Angeles*

Iris Murdoch by the way wrote she was glad I had given up the 'academic race-course'. 'It's important only to win one's own race', she said, which was nice of her. In the meanwhile Alasdair Clayre* has, I'm glad to say, got the best entry into All Souls since before the war, which he deserves, and now we can hope the standards of this institution rise. In spite of a few limitations he is a remarkable person.

TO FIONN O'NEILL   *c/o Hertz*
14 November 1959   *Los Angeles*

I am toying with the idea of turning *The Europeans* [by Henry James] into a play, and hope no one else has thought of doing it. Such a delightful book and it would go easily into a play, especially if one could give it a modern setting and rearrange the characters to suit a modern situation. I have an example in the shape of Bienchen Goldschmidt-Rothschild [née Henkel-Donnersmarck], who lives just down the road from here, and

* Born 1935. Fellow of All Souls, Oxford. Poet, novelist, writer for broadcasting, television presenter and producer. Committed suicide 1984.

whom you'd absolutely adore. She was the first hostess of Berlin in the twenties. The strange thing is in spite of having to live at present in L.A. (in an admittedly charming house with pool and a picture *by* Goethe, a relation of hers—as are also Talleyrand, Delacroix, Metternich, the Rothschilds, the Sassoons, the royal family, etc.), in spite of being 60 now, in spite of illness and worry, and in spite of being cut off as she feels herself to be from the brilliant life she enjoyed once, she is still *une parfaite grande dame.* And it is so unmistakable, not by the condescension (which she doesn't use), nor by the airs, but simply by the overwhelming charm and vitality. Still nearly six foot tall, with such a perfect nose! A tyrant I'm sure behind the scenes, but on the surface pure elegance, and kindness too.

After this slightly naïve portrayal of a retired grande dame, (why is it that all such portrayals always seem slightly naïve— even in Proust I think) what more can I tell you that won't make you smile only at me, but also at the subject. I am looking forward to leaving L.A.—not only because I dislike the city so much, but also because I am getting a little worn-out without real work, and without the quietude necessary for writing.

TO HIS PARENTS   *Chicago*
23 November 1959

Although winter is disagreeable I am greatly relieved to find it. Actually one needs the winter I think just as much as summer, and the eternal balmy California is softening to the brain. Chicago is rather exciting after L.A. in that it is a city, but, I'm afraid the nice part of it is very limited, and the rest is like London suburbs. It is grimy with dirt, has a lovely drive called Lake Shore Drive, with a view across skyscrapers and water, icy winds, and rather a tough population. Of course I was a little disappointed to find that Mr Maxton and Mr Silver were both away. However, I was received at the museum as if I was a crown-prince of a kingdom of which Daddy was the ruler. I had warned Maxton of my arrival and his secretary had prepared the apartments. On Saturday I had lunch with Harold Joachim* in the cafeteria, where we met by accident, and afterwards he took me on a little tour of the drawing exhibition, which was very nice. Good Watteaus and other things.

There we met Mr Vincent Price—the L. A. collector, whose collection I hadn't been able to see because of his not being there—who was very agreeable, sent you his regards, and was bothered intermittently by schoolgirls (Saturdays the museums are full of children here) who begged his autograph. He is a very well-known actor here. With him was a small 70-year-old *Gräuel* [Horror] who suddenly revealed that he had been one of the restorers of the Pasadena masterpieces—which were published in the *Los Angeles Times* (a disgusting newspaper) at 10 million dollars. He gave us as he said the 'inside dope'. 'You know', he said, 'if you have to clean a picture, strip it right down to the original paint to find out if it is genuine. We worked on these pictures for about a month, many of us together of course, using pure ether—now if a picture can withstand that it's old.' 'I see', I replied, 'but what about the attributions?' 'Well, you have to strip a picture right down, etc.' Such a charming expression, I thought, for cleaning, and very appropriate for what goes on in America. Anyway that settled that as far as the masterpieces were concerned. Clearly rubbish. The people who are involved with this business are 'professional finders' I'm told, and crooks. Unfortunately I didn't get this restorer's name, but you can tell David [Carritt] this whole thing.

---

* John Maxton, Keeper of Paintings of the Art Institute of Chicago. Louis Silver, a collector of drawings and rare books. Harold Joachim, Keeper of Prints and Drawings at the Art Institute of Chicago.

TO ROBERT CUMMING   *Woodstock*
27 November 1959   *Illinois*

I am staying with Hylton Thomas* and his family in
Woodstock and we spent the holiday [Thanksgiving] eating in
their cousins' house here in this little town. It is quite a small
place in the middle of farm country about sixty miles north of
Chicago. Snow is on the ground, and the presence of turkey,
icy winds and lots of good food like mince pies made me feel
that I was taking part in a rehearsal for Christmas. The
Thomases are very nice, with a pleasant middle-class house,
comfortable and old-fashioned. Their cousins are school-
teachers in the local school, and one of the preachers came
to the dinner, which was large and filling. We sat around
and talked until eleven at night—a little late, especially as I was
getting hungry again in spite of the large quantities of food
earlier! I nearly fainted at one point—though I don't think
anyone noticed but me. There was nothing madly exciting
about the whole occasion, but it was American homeliness at
its most relaxed and charming—I know people of equivalent
classes and types in Europe would often not be so 'liberal' and
easy-going, nor so welcoming to a stranger. I talked a great
deal to Hylton, who is always a combination of slightly
nervous American professor and highly intelligent, educated
person. In America he is more at ease than in Europe, which is
strange as he prefers Europe in many ways.

I have been reading today in Miller's *Colossus of Maroussi* and
am a little disappointed by it. He raves about Greece and its
people, but does not always say why. He has a picture in his
mind of his reader: an American with highly provincial prejudices who thinks materialism is everything. I don't happen
to be that reader, though I am pretty materialistic perhaps, and
I don't think anyone is as crude or naïve as he thinks his readers
will be. Anyway he needn't tell them so. He is very naïve
about Europe—telling one a few historical facts which are
blatantly rubbish and his interpretation of Greek history has a

* Art historian and Professor at the University of Minneapolis.

violently nationalistic bias. He forgets to mention that modern Greeks have to learn ancient Greek just as much as we do. He also made some unpleasant remarks about the English—why not?—but he didn't say more than that he didn't like them. So many Americans feed like parasites off the culture of Europe. Since he likes so much about Europe, why didn't Miller in his book at least say it was necessary, in order to protect Europe from some of the less agreeable elements, to fight the Nazis etc.? The culture does not exist separately from these unpleasant phenomena: Miller is after all an unread man who responds like a child—and that is also his strength—but he has nothing to say about Europe which is valid as a criticism, only occasionally some well-worded flight of fancy in describing his reactions to the beauties of Greece. Europe is not easy to write about any more than America is, and Miller is too much of a polemicist (against America)—he is always comparing places in a slightly naïve way, and insisting on some point he wants to get across to you, as a debater might do—to be able to tell you anything about Greece, only about himself. That is of course a very common phenomenon among the Americans—they often talk better and more vivaciously about themselves than about anything else, except money.

Is this unfair criticism of Miller? I'm afraid it is. But he deserves it—and in fact I loathe the cult of emotional 'world-feelings', of 'gosh how beautiful', even when written in his lively language, the cult of deliberate ignorance and the attacks on intellectual achievements, which he so absurdly overdoes. He is very thirties of course. The whole of that generation (for which I have practically no respect) was loud in its carping and criticism of the world, but abject in its failure to *withstand* the powers that abused the world at the time, and abject in its lack of imagination in thinking up at least short-term solutions to some of the problems of its time. In reaction to the cult of 'progress' Miller is even prepared to attack the tools he himself makes use of—and that is always paradoxical to the point where I lose interest.

American literature and thinking—I think also of you and

56

the people I have met through you—don't seem to have recovered from the pseudo-romantic outbursts of that time, from the feeling that unless you have a theory of progress you can only have a sort of intellectual nihilism. Old-fashioned humanism, that of some of the educated classes of the 19th century, and of some of the 20th century even, is commonly disregarded. Even beatnikery is a carrying-on of this phase of rebellion, without of course the ideological causes like socialism that sometimes were woven in with it. Beatnikery is frankly the cult of self-adulation, and it succeeds in that. It is one step from that to black and silver uniforms, the goose-step and the concentration camp. Hylton tells me I should read Orwell's essay on Miller—perhaps that would help me to like him more—but I suspect I'd still be fairly critical.

I see that I haven't written to you for a whole month, and haven't told you yet how much I liked San Francisco. I met some charming people there, including a very nice poetess—I know nothing of her poetry—Eve Triem and her husband. He was about 78, and she in her sixties. They were very intelligent, independent people, with great charm and many ideas about books, people and history. They had read a staggering amount, and if they had never been to Europe, they made up for physical travel with many journeys of the mind and many tales to tell. Also a delightful Negro writer with whom I sat up and talked about life and literature—and another Negro student I met in a bar with whom I talked differently about the same things. The Negroes when educated are such friendly and intelligent people and have so much to talk about and with so much character—not quite such sufferers from the universal American religion of uniformity.

In New York John was invited to stay with Mr and Mrs Ben Sonnenberg at 19, Gramercy Park. This was to prove of great importance to him. He never wavered in his gratitude and loyalty to his hosts, whose generosity in offering him a share in their life is an ever-recurring theme in his letters from America. After about three months John found a job with the Wall Street Journal *and moved to an apartment in a rather slummy street not far from the Sonnenbergs and Wall Street. Ben Sonnenberg (1901–78) was a leading figure in public relations in the United States.*

TO NICHOLAS DEAKIN
6 *December 1959*

c/o Ben Sonnenberg
19 Gramercy Park
New York City

Mr S. is a figure from romance. Do you remember Leuwen père in *Lucien Leuwen* [by Stendhal]? He resembles him closely. He is very intelligent, very warm-hearted, absolutely aware of what he is doing all the time, talks exotically, is shrewd to a really amazing degree, can tell a great deal of a man from a very short survey. He has not only got money but the *passepartout* for every door in the U.S.—and that's his job. Few people have heard of him, but it indicates the stature—success-wise—of people if they have. He said to me—'I'm a petrol-truck with more openings than you can use. I'm geared to be hitched to a diesel-engine, as yet you're a Ford two-seater.' And that's also a little how I feel.

What have I done since last Sunday when I arrived? I have seen one or two friends of mine, or Bob's [Cumming], and have gone out with Mr S. once. I saw Arcadi Nebolsine who was a friend in my first year at Oxford—did you ever meet him? He's much the same as before, and I like him in spite of the strangeness of his character—I should say because of it I suppose. I walk about the city, have gone to the Cloisters, to the Museum of Modern Art, etc. Most extraordinary of all have been my three chats with Mr S. who *doesn't* go out every evening, and who is fascinating to listen to as he describes his past, or the present situation. In the evening I'll go to Macha de Gunzburg—Jacob's [Rothschild] cousin—I suppose, and Michel Strauss', and later to a dinner, with Democrats to speak afterwards: Eleanor R., Kennedy, Humphrey, Johnson, etc. This in company probably of the Alistair Cookes. The bon-bons are dropping ready-made from the sky and right now I am stuffing myself! *Pourquoi pas?* I have no feeling that luck goes on for ever, or that when I'm forty some disaster won't overtake me, reducing me to teaching English to students in the Solomon Islands—*il faut cultiver notre jardin et en conserver tous les fruits.*

For years—at Oxford—I have been living in the future; the present was a sort of Forest of Arden in which life was serenely provided for by the berries of the bushes. But in the future— then we were all going to come into our own. That part of it is of course less easy than one thinks and it is a slow process, for me at any rate, to learn how to live in the present. I am making a career—all right—but in this society one has literally to grab hold of every advantage offered, because otherwise it won't be an advantage any more. The main chance and all that. Why do I say all this? Because I feel guilty at leaving behind the sweet-smelling honeysuckle existence of an intellectual with no real material ties, with at least the means of not being committed to any one industry or interested party. I would like to dream and reminisce—now I have offered my service in a competitive society and realize that one's independence is going to be affected. The great achievement is in the end to profit from that society and remain independent of it in some way—to snatch an hour to dream as it were from within the aggressive materialism.

TO HIS PARENTS AND SISTER IRIS   *c/o Sonnenberg*
9 December 1959   *New York*

It seems already as if I had been here since Doomsday. I have Ben [Sonnenberg] junior's suite in this unbelievable house and from the window of my study I look up Lexington Avenue on a panorama of the usual tall buildings and in the distance a skyscraper and the towers of the Waldorf. No. 19 must be the only remaining, or one of the few at least, of the private houses in New York entirely lived in by one family. It is composed of two buildings—19 and 20—has a lift, a number of drawing-rooms and bedrooms, a vast servants' quarter, a library, where we generally gather, and a 'Red Room' on the top floor of this part of the house with a built-in cinema, the walls covered in red damask, Victorian chairs and sofas in the same colours, and bad but amusing late 19th-century pictures (some by Rothenstein quite good), a portrait sketch of the young Victoria by Etty over the vast mantelpiece, and a large theatrical thing from the old Empire Theatre (here) of Otto Skinner, the actor.

My own sitting-room—I look into it across my desk—has brown felt walls, a thick red plush carpet—the carpets are all so thick that I get a shock every time I touch anything made of metal—some 19th-century pictures (one by Lucas, the follower of Goya, over the mantel), a wall-full of drawings (there is a very large collection of drawings, generally charming but not too good, spread over the whole house), mainly late 19th-century English and American, a number of sofas, chairs, books (very nice ones, all Ben junior's, stolen, according to Ben senior, from his own collection), telephones (one for inside the house, one for outside), brass bits and some good furniture. The furniture throughout the house is good and all of it English. Among them some remarkable pieces. The good drawings are two Baroccis in my bedroom, a Degas, a large Ingres portrait of a couple, some nice Berthe Morisots, Signacs and Daumiers and other things. Also a little Gentile Bellini Madonna. The nicest picture is really the self-portrait by Fantin Latour—though there are some other ones.

At a quarter to nine my breakfast is brought into my bedroom (the time is my own arrangement), after breakfast I usually write letters, find out what is doing in the house, maybe, as I did this morning, have a chat with papa S., telephone to Mrs S. (who is by the way a charming woman), telephone to friends and, more recently, 'jobbing', as I call my attempts to have interviews. Yesterday I had my first one (not bad going after only a week in N.Y.) with Henry Holt and Co., a publisher of which Mr S. is a director. I learnt from the very nice man that I met there that I did not want to go into publishing. What *do* I want to do? you will ask. I am now in the process of making a list of publications whose editors, etc. I shall try to see next week. Mr S. said to me this morning, 'There's plenty of cheese lying around for you to pick up—I'm just not going to ram it down your throat. Say whom you want to see, and I'll make sure you do.'

It all looks very easy. It is also rather exhausting. I said this to Arcadi the other day and he replied: 'Oh so you are exhausted already, even you? Yes, you see America is very exhausting and really for no reason at all. Everybody just talks, so there is no *good* reason, but everybody is exhausted.' This is not because of the pace—the pace in America is no faster, if anything slower, than in England. I think it is because so many people do nothing except think about doing things— and make others do them. The amount of organization people is incredible, though not more than a society of this size demands I suppose. But they have to live by bluffing one another, selling themselves to one another—and that's how Ben senior made his money, by acting as middle-man between people who were not good at this. I get into the habit now, very slowly, of talking 'big'—making a big show of what I can do, talking more than everybody else if possible and all that—of course it breaks down as soon as I meet someone like Mr Burnshaw at Holt's yesterday. 'What are your skills?' he asked me. 'Nothing,' I replied, 'I'm just out of Oxford.' All wrong of course.

My birthday was celebrated in great style. My hosts gave me a bottle of Eau de Lanvin, large enough to last me a life-time considering that I think it's a little dangerous for a man my age to wear. People might think I was trying to pass myself off for thirty! At dinner quite suddenly a large and very beautiful birthday cake appeared with twenty-four candles. I was really tremendously touched. Mr and Mrs Alistair Cooke, and the *New Yorker* columnist and publisher Jeffrey

Hellman, who were the other guests, screeched with delight, as you can imagine.

Outside all the skyscrapers are lit up and the pretentious bells from one of the thousands of clocks are booming out a quarter-to-six above the traffic in the square. I must be one of the most spectacularly well-looked-after of the millions in the streets. Next week when Mr S. comes back from Florida where he goes tomorrow early for the weekend, I'll make a round of the magazines and journals.

TO VERONICA GASCOIGNE   c/o Sonnenberg
12 December 1959   New York

At a party I went to given by a publishing house for the Duke of Bedford's book (he shook all the guests' hands, which was rather touching) I met a woman of great charm, and some good looks, called Mrs Rolo. We talked for about two hours, during which time I discussed the theatre with her, etc. She said, 'Wasn't there a young Englishman here earlier this year with a funny name also interested in plays? Maybe you know him, he has such a funny name.' 'Was he very charming, good-looking and amusing?' I asked. 'Yes', she replied with a smile. I leave you to guess the rest. Ask Bamber* about her, I'll probably see her again.

I am looking forward to work in some ways—and fear it in others. I fear the destruction of all time for reading, writing and just plain thinking. Last night—after Garry† left—I had the mad impulse to look at Ben junior's shelf of books about the Nazis. I have put off reading about them so long because I think I'd rather not know, etc. However, I read a book about the concentration camps until 3 a.m.—it was a bit of an

* Bamber Gascoigne, Veronica's brother, born 1935. Author, playwright, critic, television presenter.
† The Hon. Walter Garrison Runciman. Born 1934. Fellow of Trinity, Cambridge, Chairman of Walter Runciman & Co. Ltd. Sociologist.

ordeal, disgustingly fascinating. Some pages I simply had to turn over without reading. The author, a survivor of Buchenwald, sometimes says before quoting some eye-witness account or terrifying Nazi document: 'I will give only a few examples to protect the sensibility of the reader who only has to *read* these things.' One example was more than enough usually for me. Sometimes if he gave the name of someone on whom an outrage was committed I became terrified lest a relation of mine was going to be mentioned. I hope my parents who have so far avoided reading such books, never succumb to any whim to do so—on the other hand I'm glad I did. The extraordinary thinness of the partition which divides our nature from that of ghouls and monsters is revealed by it—because I don't have the naïve belief that only Germans are capable of these things. Maybe only the Germans would do this to millions and allow the rule of the non-commissioned SS officers. I think Jung is right when he says that brutality is the next step—the undercurrent—of sentimentality. But I prefer the latter in all its manifestations, and hope that in our lifetime we won't see the sugary superstructure collapse again. The SS were often alarmingly sentimental about their own misdeeds. *Mais je ne veux pas t'ennuyer avec tous ces détails.* In any case the thing made such a profound impression on me that I had to tell you about it.

(Later in the same day.) I'm sorry to have indulged in such murkiness, but I am going to send it to you all the same. Too often one forgets that these events happened in our lifetime and to people one might have known.

TO HIS MOTHER   *c/o Sonnenberg*
19 December 1959   *New York*

As to the places Mr S. takes me to—I go there as one of those fish that precede a whale-shark, munch some of the prey and then leave. Yesterday evening he took me to a dance given in honour of the Editor of the *N.Y. Herald Tribune* by a woman whose name I forget but who is evidently very rich. It took place in a penthouse opposite the Frick Collection—with a fantastic view from the terrace of the city lit-up and Central Park. It was a very pretentious party, with Stevenson and Harriman and filmstars and smart women (Mrs Lasker of the fortune and the collection), champagne and a few young girls, but only very few. These were very elegant but not terribly interested in insignificant young men. Rather more interested were the middle-aged women, of course. The party was not at all chic, and completely lacked charm in some way. The reason for this is because like all American parties they lump all sorts together and each person vies with the next—there is no solid core of people with some education which smart parties in England—or Europe—have. Finally, there were practically no Jews (not true I discovered afterwards), who are often much nicer and more amusing than ordinary American successful people. I'm sure most of the people there thought it was a very wonderful party simply because there were so many celebrities—but that is *le goût américain*, they overplay their joy in the glamour of public success because they have so little private glamour. The pictures on the walls were ghastly, the furniture tasteless and the expense of the whole thing out of this world—or almost, because I suspect they saved a penny or two on the champagne.

The evening before I went with Mr S. to a party given by Nathan Millstein for Rubinstein—that was much better and contained a group of intellectually or artistically pretentious people who knew at least how to look nice. After fifteen minutes of that we jumped back into the Rolls and went on to one given by the British information officer Mr Robin Cecil— a very nice man. There I talked to an editor of *Time* Magazine —a very cold fish with a snobbish Republican wife who was friendly, but I know the type by now. Apart from a select few, rich Americans have very little taste as to how to behave in private life. Those that have agreeable manners are then really delightful—*mais c'est bien rare!*

22 December

Yesterday I felt so ill that I waited until today to complete the letter. I sat in my room all day and read—I have read a great deal since I arrived in New York, and all the time I don't spend job-hunting and meeting people I spend reading, writing letters, and in the museums. Arcadi [Nebolsine] is taking me to lunch today with two ladies, a Princess Eristavi, and Princess Vera of Russia. I have met his parents, by the way, who are really charming people; she is still a very good-looking woman with the most enchanting smile, and his father a very sedate but handsome man with a pleasant manner. And oh! so European in that they are so relaxed and easy-going and familiar. I haven't found that anywhere except with the Rothschilds in L.A. No wonder one feels ill in this country so easily. The people really live at an unnecessarily excessive level of tension. At first I didn't realize this but now I can see. Mears, the butler, has been very sweet about warning me against too good a life. He said yesterday as I nursed my sore throat and tiredness in my sitting-room in front of the fire: 'Everyone when they arrive here goes rushing about thinking they can manage it all—but it just isn't possible.' So imagine, I skipped a party last night, given by my friend Garry Runciman for Richard Wollheim.

TO JACOB ROTHSCHILD   *c/o Sonnenberg*
27/28 December 1959   *New York*

Yesterday at tea-time I visited America's foremost critic of modern art, Mr Greenberg, in his bohemian flat in Greenwich Village. He was very nice—the walls hung with the works of Abstract Expressionists and Pollockesques given him by the great artists of this hemisphere. Occasionally he sells scraps of cardboard with doodles by Pollock for a little song of 12,000 dollars a piece. In fact, the Bottichelsea-like appearance of the place with little rooms and Bohemian clothes is a trompe-l'oeil, since Greenberg's collection is at present worth more than most of the millionaires' collections of Impressionists, etc. He does not, however, pretend that it is the greatest art of all time, and I found him delightfully approachable about it and friendly and relaxing. This last quality is so rare in America that I feel a thrill each time I find someone with whom it is not necessary to prove the validity of one's existence. He is of course un peu old-fashioned avant-garde. I don't think he would bathe in the nude like Burgo Partridge's parents, but he does have a little of the atmosphere of the thirties Trotskyites, one of whom of course he was. However, there was none of the squeamishness of Spender, nor the fashionable bounce of Cyril Connolly. You of course might have liked the modern pictures too.

Mrs Lasker, the most famous collector of modern art in New York perhaps, told me how much she admired Giacometti (we were looking at one at a party) and was horrified when I said I didn't. Apart from collecting him, she has given as a little annual present to the city a few hundred Christmas trees, which run all the way up the centre of Park Avenue. I think that's an idea for you: Stars of David at Chanouka all along Threadneedle Street! It may interest you to know that the Jews are accepted by rich Democrat society (since that party needs their money and support), but more rarely by Republicans. This is not the only reason why I find rich Republican society disagreeable whenever I have met it. Now that it is more or less certain that Nixon will be the next president—unless Governor Bowles of Connecticut or Stevenson manages a sudden last-minute coup, which is most unlikely judging by the defeatist attitude of all Democrats I've spoken to—I suppose we must all reconcile ourselves to an ever-increasing Republican society, rich or not. All the nasty people I met in California were pro-Nixon—and the nice ones there were very much in the minority. It is rather a ghastly prospect.

Il y a deux jours il [M. Sonnenberg] me dit: 'allons diner à neuf heures du soir dans un petit bistro òu je vais souvent. Après il y aura des parties.' Vers neuf heures et quart nous montâmes dans sa Rolls Royce et quelques minutes après nous nous trouvâmes dans le plus élégant restaurant de l'Amérique—Le Pavillion—qui appartient à un restaurateur assez désagréable, M. Soulé. Pour avoir une table dans le meilleur coin de son restaurant on doit payer je ne sais quelle somme, ou avoir une introduction du Président. M. Soulé s'avança vers nous: 'Mr Sonnenberg, where would you like to sit tonight?' Mon hôte me présenta (je dus serrer la main du restaurateur et être presque aussi respectueux envers lui qu'il était envers nous!) et Soulé dit encore: 'Would you mind sitting next to Mr Dali?' 'That will be all right', dit Sonnenberg. On nous montre son coin préféré. Dans la salle il y avait quelques producteurs de films, avec leurs stars, des milliardaires, des éditeurs, etc. Les Dali se mirent à côté de nous peu après—Mme D. parlait russe avec Mr S., et Mr D. en regardant le moustache de mon hôte (qui ressemble à un 'walrus') dit: 'You and I have the most important moustaches in the world,' et il riait à sa canne surmontée d'une décoration en émail dessinée sans doute par lui-même, et ce n'était pas très beau.

I went to see a man at the *Wall Street Journal* just before I started writing to you. I liked the way people were standing around in

   * Born 1919. French painter and writer; biographies of Delacroix and D'Annunzio. Other English titles: *Dreamers of Decadence* (1971), *The Symbolists* (1971). Committed suicide in 1977.

   † Born 1936. Lecturer in English, Queen Mary College, London University. Playwright and novelist. Plays include *Butley* 1971, *Otherwise Engaged*, 1975.

the vast office with 2000 typewriters going at once and talking to each other—the young ex-Harvard boys in their natty suitings (though with no coats on) being greatly deferential to the columnists and editors in dirty old clothes and bowler hats lying on their desks.

You are very troubled by Cambridge: when I was in England I was worried by the two Universities as well—but one is worried about the situation in which one has to swim, and I'm in a different pond now. I think you should enjoy the part you yourself describe in your letter as being romantic— the visual effects, the atmosphere of dedicated decay, the humus of centuries of people studying. *Mais tu le prends tant au serieux*. I agree that if you are interested in education and all that, the universities are a source of concern, to put it mildly, but you know very well that you are only there on lease as it were—it was a way of giving you an official status for a couple of years. I disliked that about Oxford—though I think when I was there we were less narrow than at Cambridge, less bound by the conventions of one group, or a few ideas. I hope anyway that you won't decide to remain in the academic world; it makes you angry as far as I can see, without giving you a feeling you are doing anything.

I agree with you about married couples; certainly the younger ones I know are ideal examples of emotional stability and sexual contentment. I certainly wish also for such a solution to my own vagaries—but not yet. I'm not frightened of marriage as you say you are, but I know it would mean that I had resolved on a pattern before I had discovered the varieties of life. I don't hope to know them all, but I'd like to have a glimpse of some of them. A voyage of discovery can only be made alone—half the wish for it goes if there is a heart of which one can be sure. Or rather not heart, because there are hearts of which I am sure, but a co-existence of which one can be sure.

I am having lunch today with Mr S. and some friends of his, including, I think, a cousin of Nelson's [Aldrich]. Every circle touches and retouches—it is extraordinary how small the world has become—or should I say how small the world is that I meet. In L.A. it was different. There apart from the Baroness [Goldschmidt-Rothschild] there was no one who had ever heard of any of the dramatis personae of the European life I have led, or heard of others leading. If they were interested in anything outside the 'yard' it was the World Series and the Country Club. For them a filmstar meant everything—a celebrity was a distant star under which it would be wonderful to sit. But often they did not care about that either. It was a village society without a green. Funny that a society should look dead at birth.

10 January

Interrupted again: this time by lunch with some publishers at a literary lunch club called the Coffee House: present the junior executives of Doubledays and their pretty wives. Before that a visit to the Parke-Bernet Galleries with Mr S. There we saw a shabbily dressed rather nice-looking woman in an old fur coat, whose face was very familiar. We shook hands, then Mr S. and I got into the lift. 'Who was that?' I asked. 'That my dear boy was someone you should have recognised yourself.' 'Who was it?' 'Greta Garbo'—a gasp from the other passengers—and a rather irritated one from me. Why hadn't I known *while* I shook her hand?

69

I have in the meanwhile a chance of a job—starting conveniently in the middle of February at the *Wall Street Journal*. I would have the lowliest of occupations and get 75 dollars a week, which works out gross at 3900 dollars a year. This seems a lot by English standards—but it is the basic living wage in New York. Under that one could not afford to go on the underground. There is a chance that when once in there they would discover my talents—or I would discover them to them—and get onto the editorial side. Mr S. thinks that just having a job there would do me good—and that once my foot is in the door I can't fail to have a brilliant career. Anyway I wouldn't be tied to them—and it is the second best paper in America. To have worked for them is a good sign. At least I have had an offer now and feel rather pleased by that.

On Saturday after lunch we went to Wildensteins. It was certainly appropriate that we drove there in the Rolls. The firm is housed in a vast palazzo in the most expensive part of town and has a number of showrooms of unbelievable chi-chi or too good taste. No doubt the millionaires are impressed by the flunkeys and the boiseries and the high stools on which the drawings are sold. Among other things we were offered a drawing by Bernini—a very attractive self-portrait, or portrait of a young man as I would say, *trois-crayons* and rather delicious. I was asked quietly by Mr S. what I thought it would cost—so I said between 800 and 1000 pounds. We then asked Riesik, who was showing it to us—25,000 dollars! It was quite absurd, and all the prices were like that. A very fine 15th-century landscape—attributed to Van der Goes—was priced at 18,000 only; a couple of figures by a 15th-century Florentine—charming but no more—20,000 etc. The portrait by Hyacinthe Rigaud of the Abbé Dubois—a very good picture by Rigaud standards and of great historical interest—was shown to us. However, I imagine it's about half the price of a large portrait of a general by David that I also saw there.

The David—if it were not for fashion—is not better than the Rigaud, but I don't expect there's a single American collector who has the eyes to see that.

It is the most absurdly fashion-ridden country in the world —and its attitude to works of art is at present like the Tulipomania of the Dutch 17th century. Much though I admire those pictures I would almost pay not to possess them, because they are so very vulgar. In fact the Americans often succeed in vulgarizing the things they have—much as a Sargent-Campoli performance of Beethoven's violin concerto at the Albert Hall destroys the music. The acquisitive urge is the first mover in the minds of the Americans generally—the love of art comes well below. Apart from that I think all this worship of French art is indicative of how sterile American enthusiasm has become—there comes a moment where one can't see the Impressionists anymore. I am beginning to suspect them of being slick and repetitive—and they don't gain by being hung all together. The nicest thing at Wildensteins was a lovely flower-piece by Delacroix, which Mr S. didn't understand at all.

TO HIS MOTHER   c/o Sonnenberg
13 January 1960   New York

You are quite wrong in thinking that Steven★ is too little serious in his approach: he has written the most readable history in the English language today—the nearest approach to good historical writing we have, and that is a very serious achievement. He also has a sense of humour—too many historians lack this, with disastrous results. History books are for pleasurable instruction not for miserable plodding. We have had to think of the Middle Ages as a superior moral age for far too long. I am very glad he has upset that absurd

★ The Hon Sir Steven Runciman, author of (among others) *A History of the Crusades*, 3 vols, 1951–54.

Victorian prejudice and given away the secret that it was a barbarian age in which there are a few golden moments.

TO NICHOLAS DEAKIN   c/o Sonnenberg
15 January 1960   New York

I long to see a really good modern comedy, of the quality of Sheridan or even Shaw; neither Broadway nor the West End has produced a fine one in years, and the reason is that *au fond* they are more difficult to write than tragedies. In comedy it is necessary to touch on the greatest issues of life and make them sparkle. We must leave feeling that they are bearable. In tragedy we need only be confirmed in a sneaking suspicion that they are not.

TO HIS PARENTS   c/o Sonnenberg
20 January 1960   New York

Mrs Alistair Cooke is painting my portrait. She is a charming woman. I won't be able to give you the picture when it's finished as it costs 600 dollars or thereabouts. We have very pleasant conversations while she paints. I agreed to sit because she complained of a lack of models. That's all the news. Don't believe the alarming picture my host will give you. He's been threatening me satanically with the things he's going to tell you. When he begins, warn him of all the things I can tell you about *him*! and don't blame him too much for being such a good host.

The newspaper [the *Wall Street Journal*] is quite good, covers mainly financial and economic events—like our *Financial Times* I suppose—and is the only national newspaper in America, as everyone keeps repeating all day long. It is written in bad English, but by American journalistic standards is lively and amusing—and makes all that stuff palatable. It gives me some interesting information I think. Yesterday, for instance, I was sitting next to a director of Loeb's (Bank) who, when asked what he thought the financial outlook was for the year ahead, simply quoted everything I had been proofreading for the past few days. Naturally he gave no sources, and I said nothing.

Very soon now the rather fancy life I have been leading will come to an end as I have found an apartment into which I hope to move next week or so. It took me ages to find the right one—and my host had to put up with me for more than two months as a result. I think he didn't really mind—as he was able both to enjoy himself amusing me and to use me as an additional amusement for his guests.

Just now I was interrupted by one of my superiors who was a Rhodes scholar at Keble in 1951. We discussed Oxford for a moment, then he said, 'Well I wonder what the good of all that education is in this age and country of specialization. I've never been able to make use of Keynes or Ricardo in my leaders.' Well, well. I have of course nothing to offer except education at present and what good is that, indeed?

TO WILLIAM ANDERSON   c/o Sonnenberg
15 February 1960   New York

Sometimes I would like to be at a point near to America, but not quite on it, if you see what I mean. There are moments when I have a *nostalgie de Londres*. But when the weather is brilliant like today, and the snow is glittering in the park outside, and the distant skyscrapers loom above the canyonesque avenues into unclouded blue, one has to confess that appearances for a moment are on New York's side. (The details are all hideous in this city, it is only the overall effect that is fine.)

Abstract art here is all the rage—one can escape from it nowhere—it has become a sort of religion, especially as everyone says that it is very important to react to it personally and that only one's own tastes matter. They say this because they know that they actually never say anything except what the critics have told them to say. If I violently disagree with current fashions, like that for Giacometti for instance, I am accused of 'taking a line', not of having an opinion which they don't like. Few people believe that one is capable of having a strong opinion of which one is also sure! As you know, I always seem too sure, so in matters of art I am unpopular among the people I meet, who are not of my age or don't share my interests. The people who discuss the horrors of action painting in enthusiastic terms range from bankers to dealers, from artists to businessmen. The Americans, in spite of all their virtues, are occasionally absurdly fetishistic.

TO FIONN O'NEILL   *215, East 25th Street*
24 February 1960   *New York*

My parents sent me a photograph today of a house which they may be buying in Somerset. It looks quite nice on the photograph, and apparently has a pretty garden—or one with distinct capabilities. The front has Palladian windows—that essential feature of English country life—but the sides have Victorian bay-windows, which my mother with her severe preference for the 18th century would have to remove.* I

* This was not Perridge House.

74

think it would be fun for her to have the house, and give her something amusing to play with—though I am sure a house in Italy would be much better. For one thing the climate is preferable, even to Somerset, and for another I think they are much more relaxed when they are on the continent. However both my parents have a strong desire to identify themselves with England and really to make a home out of it equivalent to the style they lived in in Hamburg. It would, as it were, be a final triumph over Germany. During the summer my mother told me a lot about how she and my father had lived in Hamburg, and when I met my cousins I realized even more what a close and integrated society they lived in, and how secure it all felt. They didn't really mind being jolted out of that security in the sense that they wanted to get out anyway— but leaving by force rather than pleasure makes a great difference. For me of course it would be terrific, though I yearn also for a house in Italy. In time maybe one can have everything!

I have been very surprised and pleased by one thing here in America: my father's clients, who range from museums and millionaires to young men with a little money and a lot of enthusiasm, by whom he is terrifically highly regarded. Every museum I have been to has laid out the red carpet for my visit. I know of course in London that he has had some success—but many people here regard him, quite apart from his success as a dealer in drawings, as one of the most remarkable dealers in the world. Very curious. Americans of course have a flattering tendency to exaggerate virtues, as well as vices, and have a habit, a pleasant enough one I admit, of telling one to one's face how nice or charming, or clever or whatever one is. After our English habit of being tough with each other this is rather delicious massage for the tired ego.

On Sunday my friend Polly Grant, who was at Oxford with me for years, and I had dinner. I collected her from the house of her aunt and aunt's sister, Mrs Bella Roosevelt. Their mother—a Mrs Willard of fame and great fortune—built the house on Sutton Place, which with its large gardens and beautiful view over the river is the most elegant street in New York (and is only a few hundred yards long). The house is filled with charming things dating from Mrs Willard's days. Among them in the vast and very high drawing-room are five pastel portraits of members of the Spanish Bourbons of 1780. I asked what they were and Mrs R. assured me that they were by Goya. She says that her mother got them in Spain when she was the wife of the first American Ambassador to Madrid (Mr Willard I mean) and that she has complete documentary proof of their authorship. 'Pastels', she added, 'by Goya are practically unknown.' I told her how right I thought she was. They are rather nice portraits and of course of enormous interest if they are by Goya. She had another quite good oil portrait of what I thought was Charles III (but her sister Mrs Herbert said he was Charles IV because she thought Goya didn't paint in the days of Charles III, which isn't true of course), but it has to be cleaned. Otherwise nothing of outstanding interest, except for the atmosphere of the whole which is what I call *très vieille Amérique*: good furniture, books and family (late 19th-century) portraits—inevitably a couple of Sargent drawings and a portrait of her father-in-law the President (Theodore not Franklin of course). She had just been to tea with Mrs Murray Crane (whose salon Philippe [Jullian] had mentioned to me in a letter) and who had a fine collection (or rather jumble) of things so I'm told. Mrs Crane, according to Mrs Roosevelt, is the only woman who still has a salon in New York. I suspect that should be transcribed—the only woman over seventy who still has one.

I admire your capacity for reading and am glad you do it with so much attention. I have never read enough with the result that I always have to rely on my experience of travel and things seen rather than things read (apart from history books). Things seen—I mean things which I have studied with my eyes principally—are valuable as experiences and give pleasure, especially if one gets practised at it, but to strengthen mental powers books are an absolutely essential discipline. And after books conversation. I think it is very difficult in this country to find highly trained conversationalists—even in New York. People here have a tendency to lecture each other, and sometimes to avoid committing themselves because they think the things are too serious. They are always mistaking my very definite viewpoints for statements of faith; they don't realize I often say something definite merely to stimulate the argument. Slightly dogmatic viewpoints ought to have a more stimulating effect than soft-spoken evasions. Why all this hesitation and evasion? This fear of committing themselves seems to me to express modesty, of course, but also lack of intellectual mettle. And it appears in all sorts of public expressions of the American mind, like newspapers and magazines, where stories are always being slanted under the guise of objectivity instead of openly expressed opinions. This 'slanting' is intensely disagreeable to me—we have it at home of course, but there is usually a bit more expression of opinion, especially in an excellent French newspaper like *Le Monde*. *Mais laissons tout cela*—I have quite enough of newspapers going on around me to give me food for depressing thought, and I see in letters a possibility of thinking of amusing things.

My parents have at last decided to buy a house in the country, which they are doing without my ever having seen it which is sad, since it will one day be my home too. One day I hope you'll come to England and stay. I think you would find my parents very different from your own in some ways—in

77

others quite familiar. My mother is a very much milder version of Carmen and Richard, but not less intelligent. (In fact she has some kind of wisdom which they, with all respect, don't have; while they are considerably less introspective and more dynamic on the surface.) My father is very much the opposite of yours in his strong adherence to rationality and empirical reasoning—and yet there are similarities which both of them would hotly deny, similarities which stem from the fact that they were brought up at the same time in the same country and received much the same sort of education. Your father reflects, however, the plush and intense tastes of the late 19th century much more than mine, whose romanticism leads him more to the High Renaissance.

I hope you go to Europe in the summer—and stay there for some time. Not because I think you should live there for ever, but because I think you'd enjoy getting closer to the monuments round which Western culture is built and because once one has seen the Mediterranean, life does take on a different dimension. Italy has more to offer the eye, the ear and the heart than any place on earth: man seems to have concentrated his capacities to embellish life in that small area, and though much has been spoilt, and much has disappeared from sixty years ago, there is still an enormous amount to see and everything is now within reach.

TO NICHOLAS DEAKIN   *215, East 25th Street*
18 March 1960   *New York*

You refer to London's 'slow round of life', which disappointed me: you of all people should be in the midst of the parry and thrust of social business, taking a leading role in Europe's most glittering city! Every day I have a few minutes in which I wish I was home, but fortunately enough distractions occur to make me forget. I have moved five blocks to my apartment—which is like moving from

Olympus to Boeotia, though I am glad to say that Olympus in the form of Mr S. occasionally opens its doors to me still. When I go there it is like the arrival of Hermes after a couple of adventures in the world—I am asked all about it and then go back. On Wednesday night for instance I went in a small party to the opening of an exhibition called 'Business Buys American Art'—a really grotesque evening but one which was a splendid display of what New York can do. There is nothing like it anywhere in Europe that I have seen—the strangely ugly multi-millionaires prancing before the even uglier objects their various firms have bought. The nicest thing was a drawing by a middle-aged American from Europe (judging by his accent) owned by the Ohio Oil Co. A vice-president of Philip Morris told me he really regards the Ohio Oil Co. in a much better light now—thinks they have bought well, shown initiative, and generally brought off a brilliant publicity coup. And he chose them only as an example—all the others could be seen in the same light.

Right now I am sitting in the office—once more it is Friday and there is practically nothing to do. I wrote an article the other day on the art market which may be printed if I manage to improve it—and they get round to re-writing it. This paper re-writes every reporter unless he is one of their prize men. And I am not even a reporter. If it is published my status will have changed in my own mind even if not in that of my employers, but it will be a beginning. The other people who work with me have begun to speak to me—occasionally—and a nice person just out of Princeton and I have discovered a common bond in our newness and isolation. Also in the fact that we are very severe in our criticism of the paper, which I can assure you is very far indeed from being a socialist one. Its primary concern is to boost American business and it always adopts a cheerful tone; its editorial page is stuck in 1905. They firmly believe (in the editorials) that there ought to be less federal government interference in local affairs, that government generally should curtail its powers, that individual freedom is best—and no taxation without representation. (This last is backed by an allusion to Cromwell of all people!) It's all very Whig but it won't do. Now that I get *The Times* every day from London I can really get a grip on the news, which in the smaller compact British paper gives more information than any of the eighty-page horrors here.

TO ROBERT CUMMING   *215, East 25th Street*
31 March 1960   *New York*

The English in New York all behave in a very curious way to each other—they seem to be out battling in this wild colony, and are quite ruthless in their treatment of each other. They certainly don't clan together. In fact I feel it myself—I haven't come here, I say when invited to see people I slightly knew at Oxford, to meet the English. But I don't put on battle harness when I do meet them as others do.

I often long for Europe from the visual point of view. I would like to walk down the street and see those details that make every European street a memory-evoking place. Those few cornices, those occasional pieces of carved stone, those sudden bits and pieces, that recall history or delight the eye.

The other evening at the Sonnenbergs I was introduced to Senator Javitts, a delightful man. Mrs S. said to him: 'You're too nice to be a Republican you know—you should be a Democrat. I had to vote against my own party to vote for you.' Sheila★ tells me this was everybody's attitude. He is unusually agreeable for a politician. Sheila said that when she was working for the Museum of Modern Art, Javitts rang up the director one day, and said wearily: 'Alfred, I've explained to the Senate what an artist is, now how would you explain the word professional?'

★ Sheila Lafarge, freelance editor and translator, also a painter.

There was an exhibition of Courbet at the museum [in Boston] which was really fascinating.

Courbet was a very strange painter, but he resolved what seems to me to be a very present difficulty in the visual (and maybe other) arts. He managed to create a realistic (representational of course) style of his own, which expressed his literary and emotional attitudes to contemporary life in terms which were none-the-less to do with painting as opposed to sentiment or bookishness—like that of the Pre-Raphaelites. His pictures, even his landscapes, do tell stories, or express opinions of nature if you like—so did Poussin and Claude—but they are painted with a technique very much his own, and they have a vision that is original and personal, and that has none of the déjà-vu of modern paintings.

South Africa has made the Americans sit up. It is after all only recently that they recognized that it exists as a continent —apart from the necessity of supporting Nasser or Liberia for business reasons every now and then. But of course it is very far away, as everything is outside the twelve-mile limit off their shores. What is wrong with Cuba and Venezuela in American eyes? In the first one it is not so much that Castro exterminates his enemies without trial (that can always be explained), but that he is 'red' and that business opportunities for the American businessman are bad and getting worse. And in the latter, Premier Betancourt is blamed for following a policy of economic structures bad for American business, which has invested so heavily there—but then of course it could get worse: i.e. more extreme leftists could get in which would make life worse for the businessman and hence for the Venezuelans also. (This is the attitude expressed in a hopelessly muddled leader in the *Wall Street Journal* on Venezuela.) While it's true that America has put bread into all our mouths, and that Americans work several hours a week for other people (as a result of taxation), it's also true that the

American businessman has profited hugely from *aid* to foreign countries, and that the complaints come when the profits aren't big.

US generosity is backed by a sharp eye for profits—and it is these that the US has thought about more consistently than anything else in the last few years, at home and abroad. Hence the total lack of planning, lack of beauty, lack of interest in, say, the rebuilding of New York since the war: the concentrated smooth ugly dullness of new architecture here (apart from about three buildings) is a supreme example of their creed that everything profitable is justifiable. However, I suppose it is not surprising that a country to which always the poorest, least educated and most proletarian of European oppressed have gone is still dominated by prejudice and attitudes reminiscent of the philosophy of small retailers in the following of Danton. What is surprising is that there is anyone not like that I suppose. More even than Russia this is the land of the triumphant proletariat—and as such is the complete confutation of everything Marx said. That all sounds almost bitter—it's not meant to be—just irritated. I am just as irritated with things in other countries, as I continually point out to Americans when I complain to them. However, I can't say that I enjoy working for this newspaper, which combines stuffiness with an editorial policy almost macabre in its absurdity. Apart from that my work is so mechanical and dull that it irritates me more to think about it even than actually to do it.

My mother sent me a cutting of David Carritt's article in the *Evening Standard* on Bacon (the painter, in case of any confusion). I am so glad he wrote it. It is high time that not only in America (where it has not happened yet), but also in Europe, the case against all the most recent trends in modern painting should be thoroughly exposed. Buffet, the tail end of Picasso, the abstract rubbish, Bacon, Freud and the whole crew of successful and unsuccessful should be chastised for their cynicism, or their stupidity. Both are unpardonable, and both dominate. When I say that here, people never have any reply to me but to say, 'You are too young, too stupid and too inexperienced.' It may be true, but it's no reply. 'We can't tell you why these things are good,' said Clem Greenberg to me, 'but you are just stupid not to recognize their qualities, when you haven't trained yourself to like them.' *Voilà tout.* (Greenberg, one of the founders with Dwight Macdonald of the *Partisan Review*, is a leading authority on the modern American 'masters'.

TO NICHOLAS DEAKIN   *215, East 25th Street*
13 April 1960   *New York*

What one wishes for in South Africa is a triumph for the moderates. I see no reason why one should hope for a wild black reign of terror any more than for a continuation of the present ghastly set-up. I think in particular Holland should be brought into the picture; the Dutch have a very considerable cultural influence in SA and they should be encouraged to give voice to the general disapproval. This might find some response down there. However, I suppose the Dutch may also sympathise with the Apartheid outlook—who knows?

You have a picture of me as being a country-house conservative with ivory-tower views. Quite the wrong picture. I have always had a strong regard to the place of government and its strength in any society, particularly a large one like ours, and believe that the government should initiate policies of reform which are not necessarily the ones most popularly canvassed. I don't happen to agree with many socialist points of view since I think that they have often been produced in a spirit of opposition and not of construction, or that they are half-hearted, as with education, or that they are absurd as they have sometimes been over foreign policy (in office I think they'd be quite different with regard to this). I think you're quite wrong in distrusting Macmillan with relations in Africa—he has recently done very well there and, compared to America with Cuba or Latin America Britain has shown up quite well in the past few months in her relations with 'trouble spots'. Where we are doing badly right now is in Europe—but that's so complicated I don't know any more what to think. It is far away and I have to rely on reported opinions. I still loathe Adenauer.

TO HIS SISTER IRIS   *215, East 25th Street*
18 April 1960   *New York*

I am still in the office where, it being Friday, there has been nothing for me to do all day except read *The Times*. This newspaper has now become a major office event. People crowd round and ask me what it is every day, and tear out pieces of news, take away pages, crow over the front-page advertisements—unheard of of course here as indeed in any other newspaper. *The Times* certainly has amusing details and it takes a lot of time and technique to know how to find them all. Each person that reads discovers, I find, quite different things in it—and the editor's secretary, who has been *thrilled* by it, loves the In Memoriam and Deaths registers, thinking that the comments—'passed away peacefully after a long illness' or 'came to rest at last after a painful illness borne with courage'—were editorial interpolations. She was a little disappointed when I told her that you could pay to have that put in! The stock-market news is garnered by others. Altogether my subscription has brought a lot of attention to my desk. My own article★ which I wrote in such a short time and which has a lot of new information—certainly new to the readers of the *Wall Street Journal* who have most of them never been inside an art gallery in their lives, although as they earn an average of $20,000 a year they might be interested in the vast sums involved in the art business today—has not been

★ On the Isabella Stewart Gardner Museum, Boston.

84

published and won't be until the end of next week or the beginning of the next. A pity.*

You would particularly like the Gardner Museum. The courtyard, which is surrounded by the four outside walls of a Venetian Palazzo, daubed in a very pretty uneven pink by the fair hand of the (not so fair) Isabella herself, is filled at all times with flowers, protected from the weather by the fact that a vast iron-glass station roof covers the whole building— encasing it though letting it appear to be in the open air, as sunlight can easily penetrate the glass. This time the trails of bright orange nasturtiums hung to the ground; up the steps to the french windows on the first floor there were pots of tulips, and under the arcade (because there is an arcade like a cloister round the courtyard at the bottom) there were endless pots with vast amaryllis in all colours.

As you can imagine this is the most charming way of designing a museum—and the inside follows the same delightful principles. Everything is placed where Mrs Gardner wanted it to be—the result is that each masterpiece (and there are many) is discovered by the unaccustomed visitor as if he was the very first to see it. The gloom (in the corners), the awkwardness of some of the positions, the reflecting glass on some of the pictures, the conglomeration of all sorts of things, some good, some amusing, some plain bad, make the discoveries more exciting still—and one feels sometimes like the young B. Berenson must have felt when he came upon a picture by a favourite master hidden in some tiny church in a poor village of the Abruzzi, knowing that it must be there. But such feelings of course are in rather a drawing-room frame— they haven't the sort of romantic exploration that BB was able to enjoy in the untidy, dirty Italy of the 1890s. Still it gives one a whiff of that if no more. The presence of music is charming too. There is a concert there on Sunday afternoons, and excellent players perform. A female voice rang out over the nasturtiums, high above the amaryllis, and wafted in to where I was looking at the big Titian through wide-open Italian

* It was never published.

85

windows. If it had been a little emptier one might have felt one was in a splendid Venetian house relaxing with the Jamesian circle one Sunday afternoon fifty years ago. Unfortunately hundreds of tourists feel just the same way as I do, and democratically one has to share all these experiences. One can't help grudging people that—unfair though it does sound.

TO SIMON GRAY   *215, East 25th Street*
20 April 1960   *New York*

I am now starting *The Wings of a Dove*, and have got quite far in it. James's style is very difficult at times—and I think he has a tendency to explain too much in analytical passages and too little in conversation and action. I enjoy reading it and am interested in the static world he recreates. But it is very static; he seemed to think that the year 1880 was never going to pass. However, you will have a cross reply—your devotion to James has always surprised me. His world and his characters are so opposed to yours—I mean in the sense that his characters are all in the frame of conformity: you are also within that frame, I suppose, but how differently you regard it! The Jamesian world is one in which I can in more nostalgic moments easily see myself—partly because I know the Italian end of it so well, and partly because through my parents and through English friends I have become attached to what remains of that world. But it has gone in most ways— irretrievably—and so-called social security has to be found in different and possibly less exclusive terms.

My attitude to this country is so different from yours, but then you came to this continent under pressure and you left it with relief, whereas I came under my own steam, and can go whenever I like. It will, I expect, be a relief to get back to Europe in a way. The familiar is always a relief. What an inestimable advantage one has in a way over the Americans in being a European: not in the sense that this makes one automatically superior to them in intelligence or other virtues, but that one can enjoy the culture that is still lying around left over from past centuries' glory, without self-consciousness and without strain. Here the culture, for all its efforts to be otherwise, is removed from its origins, from the things, ideas and visions from which it is derived and to which it is always straining to return. The Americans are terribly proud of abstract art as being their own peculiar achievement—even that, in all its unspeakable horror, is derivative. You have no idea how much they pay for these ghastly things: up to $80,000, money to burn. I think no single art fashion has ever been so grotesquely lacking in talent in all history as these abstract painters—but what's the use of exclaiming over it. Everybody loves them in their passion to be modern. They said the same about Lord Leighton in 1880. People are very surprised by my vehement attacks on them: in the first place it is strange to go against fashion, and in the second to be vehement about art. Those are luxuries which I can still afford.

TO FIONN O'NEILL   215, *East 25th Street*
21 April 1960   *New York*

I haven't heard from you for such a long time that I am writing again in the hope that I might stimulate you to action. I have seen Ben (Sonnenberg) junior who gave me news of you, and made me anxious for your company, which I do miss. I can't say I miss everybody all the time—I miss most of my friends some of the time—but I miss our frequent meetings, in which all the important details of the week can be thrashed out, and the development of each bit of business, whether social, literary, human, or romantic, can at least be hinted at—if not always analysed—as discretion permits. Now you see I have been reading Henry James—and look what happens to my style. What a determined effort he always makes to get everything into *one* sentence, and never quite manages.

Sometimes the effect is that I don't understand what he's talking about—and that is of course very dull.

People become very professional here: nothing can be done 'just as a pleasure'—as with my writing for instance. I would like to be able to live by my writing certainly, but here you have to take it so seriously that you talk of it in a semi-professional jargon, and with an intensity that is quite disgusting. I think people who talk 'seriously' about their 'writing' are as disagreeable as people who talk seriously about themselves. Both are necessary sometimes, when there's a crisis, but I loathe the way people treat their own work with veneration. There is nothing less venerable than anything produced by yourself. The only thing one should be concerned with is whether it gave one satisfaction to produce it, and whether it said something one would like other people to know. One can be silent about the rest. All that stuff about the 'agony of creation' . . .

There are some strange examples of this bigness complex—allied as it is here in NY to the necessity for building upwards—in the new 'glass boxes' that are springing up all over the main parts of the island. You can imagine nothing more boring and dull and occasionally grotesque than these high square glass and steel oblongs that are really machines for working in. One can feel almost the presence of some Druid lurking in these impersonal stones, metals and windows—but it would be a Druid of dedicated dullness, dressed in the suit and button-down shirt of the American businessman, sworn to abandon Art for ever. Not all America is like this, nor indeed all NY which in its crass way has a nostalgia of its own and an occasional beauty—the beauty of size and sweep and conflicting lights—but there is a tendency (regretted by New Yorkers) to make all the beauty accidental and dependent on the light, and none on the architecture.

Sometimes in the evening when I get home I wonder just why I am doing all this—not because I am not enjoying it, but because time seems to be going so enormously rapidly that I feel I ought to do more with it. I could live as I am for ever (if my father continued to give me money)—but it would be a little aimless as an existence, and I am aware of having aims. My natural laziness makes it so easy to do nothing when I get home, not write, nor read, just see friends—and then rise late and go straight to work. One has after all to discipline one's life in order to get anything done—and that's more difficult for me than for you even. I'd like to rewrite 'Frederick', and I have some other things in mind.

I read a very sad book of letters the other day*, written by a girl of 18 (she is now 80) to a friend describing a really miserable love-affair. A spectacularly good book (in German): tragic, young, romantic and charming, without any sickly sweetness. It might have had Richard Strauss music in the background, though perhaps not as sentimental. It's very easy to fall in love—the difficulty is to remain that way. Having known you—and your cousin—one has such high standards of what women should be! Write to me about what you are doing if anything, and about the wicked world in which you live. I wish I was there for a moment to drink in a little taste of England. It is April after all.

TO HIS PARENTS   *215, East 25th Street*
22 April 1960   *New York*

I wrote a letter criticising the EEC to Jaap†, who replied very crossly—but good-humouredly—having partly at least misunderstood what I said. I pointed out that though greater co-operation between England and Europe was obviously very important, the political connection that is desired ultimately by the members of the EEC is of dubious value. *How* can anyone say that political association between governments—with the hopeless corruption of the Italians, the ideological corruption of the French, the backward

* *Summer in Lesmona* by Magda Pauli.
† Jaap Van Der Lee, then working in Brussels as a director in the EEC.

89

colonial policies of the Belgians, the anomalies of the Luxembourgeois—would together make for progress and co-operation? As for the Germans, there is nothing to tell one they have made any great strides towards democracy since the war, beyond not actually being Nazis any more. Naturally he didn't quite see eye-to-eye with such a point of view! Although he denies it, I think most of the continental powers are delighted to cock a snook at England, and delighted to put the onus of her separation on English policy. I think there has been bad policy on both sides. It takes two to bring about separation of the present kind. But Jaap thought I regarded the continentals as 'vermin', which as you can imagine I did not. I said the governments were untrustworthy and unstable, which, with the exception of Holland, they are. Though I must say I was impressed with the way De Gaulle carried out his visit in London. Judging by *The Times* it was a success.

TO HIS MOTHER   *215, East 25th Street*
27 April 1960   *New York*

I have been reading Sylvia Sprigge's book on BB.★ It is as bad as the critics say, yet the information is of course of such interest that one's attention is held. As a piece of journalism it is fun: as an appreciation of so many-sided a character it is hopeless. She has, according to the *Times Literary Supplement*, taken the measurements, like the 19th-century sculptor, of every feature, but the final bust bears no resemblance to the original. When young he must have been fascinating, particularly in those early years before he became at all famous, and when with his wonderfully greedy appetite he was exploring in the mountains and villages of Italy. What a family the Pearsall Smiths were! Logan and the two sisters, who married BB and Bertrand Russell. Not bad as a start. It is strange too that BB should have been a friend of Santayana's at

★ *Berenson*, 1960.

Harvard, and so closely connected to Russell. Mrs Sprigge, however, spends a lot of time interpolating her own nonsense—and what undelectable nonsense it is—time which could be spent on giving more information to her readers. She has written the book in a terrific hurry to be the 'first'—and has included so much rapid discussion of the 'art world' that is quite absurd and rubbishy. BB was much more fascinating than she makes him appear; she hints at his fascination, but it is of course impossible for her quite to capture the secret.

The book has made me angry because it is interesting: if it were not, there would be no point in discussing it. It is interesting because no one with the slightest capacity for writing (and a journalist must have an inkling of that) could fail to have caught some of the excitement of the characters about which she writes; but every detail—like her description of the Gardner Museum—is badly done and misjudged. The whole charm of the Gardner is that it is as Mrs G. left it, but Mrs Sprigge attacks it for that. Of course the book will sell like mad, because it is 'first'. But there will have to be better ones.

TO NICHOLAS DEAKIN   215, East 25th Street
28 April 1960   New York

At this time last year I remember going with Veronica [Gascoigne] to that wonderful house north of Oxford: Aynho Park. We wandered very happily in the park and sat under the enormous trees looking across that typically English expanse of grass and hedges, with trees, and more trees and a feathery tree-lined horizon. In the evening, having been through the house, we walked over to the end of the terrace (built I'm afraid by the indefatigable Lutyens), and watched a very red sun sink behind the big undulating plain which the house dominates. It was warm, and there was little mist . . . *mais tout cela n'est qu'un souvenir. (Souvenir, souvenir que veux-tu?)*

I have been reading Sylvia Sprigge's life of BB . . . Someone is going to have to come along to write a book that will convey the excitement and enthusiasm of the early years, and study the way in which this passion for culture was consummated. It was in a sense like the wedding of the Doge and the sea: BB's life was a festival of culture, and the values which he encouraged have imperceptibly been impregnated into our modern view of the arts—or at least mine, both through my parents, and through contact with the many people who have taken part in BB's quasi-religious tryst. The golden eighties. Today the moss-covered, decaying, messy, damp, sluggish, dirty, empty, romantic Italy has been lost, and with it the sensation of discovery of lost arts, and the enjoyment of monuments in an atmosphere of a half-forgotten dream. What really do the hordes gain with their destructive, culture-conscious (but untutored) greed? I want to take travel away from no one, but why should some of its pleasures be taken away from those who really know how to use it?

Well, you will get justifiably cross about all that—never mind. The Europe we know has lost so much that if one was to start examining everything that had gone one would be driven to despair: and most of it of course comes from the destruction brought about by the Nazis and the communists.

When unhappy Americans become critical of their own society they often go to rather silly extremes. It is so easy apparently for people—who have as it were just begun to think of human and social problems in society today—to slip away from the indefinite practice of humanism into the armament of causes and ideologies. In the moment when they enjoy to the full the pleasures of individualism they advocate everything that tends to the individual's destruction. It has for some reason always been difficult (and I am glad in a way) to make a cause out of the individual. People without ideologies rarely fire the militant critics with any enthusiasm. They are possibly the only people I trust. *Voilà l'esprit juif!*

Yesterday evening I went for a walk with Mr Sonnenberg from his house to Greenwich village—the Soho-Chelsea of New York. We went into a good bookshop which remains open until midnight. He said that he wants to see advance proofs of the catalogue Daddy is producing so that he can choose all the best drawings for himself. However, in a long discussion yesterday I convinced him that unless he is prepared to spend a fat sum at a time he'll never have the great collection he craves, and that dribbling-spending, as he practises it, will bring him fun but no masterpieces. He saw that—and finally admitted: 'Well I can't resist nibbling—so I expect I'll never have a great collection.' He won't give up trying. I warned him though—tactfully—that the decision should be to conserve his buying power and enthusiasm for the really good things, and if he loves things like a fine Rembrandt and a Watteau sheet with hands he must be prepared to pay what they are worth. It was a frank but very affable discussion, and he understood me completely.

He doesn't mind being spoken to in a very direct fashion— he likes it in fact—and I must be one of the few young men who don't say 'Yes Sir' every minute but manage to be absolutely independent. He likes to be in control—and his extraordinary determination to give at all costs was demonstrated in the book-shop, for instance. I bought a couple of books—the famous paperbacks that are conquering America at present—and then he pointed out one—a novel: *The Memoirs of Hadrian* by Marguerite Yourcenar. Did I know it? No. Here I'll get it for you. It is a matter of pride to him that he gives something. He knows all the houses in which people have lived in 'the village' who subsequently became well-known and reminisces as we pass them. It was amusing to walk with him—he was unusually quiet and relaxed. Horrified of course by the girls in jeans, and the new buildings. Nearer home he recommended the hot chocolate in the 'Automat'—a sort of cafeteria—but when we went in, it was sold out. We sat down among the Lower East Side Jews and had milk instead. I expressed surprise that he should know about the 'Automat's' specialities—and he pointed to a corner: 'That was my table'. It was a typical gesture. He is a dotty man in many ways, but he could not do without it.

My friend for some years at Oxford—Marthe de Rohan-Chabot, now de la Rochefoucauld—wrote to me in reply to my letter of welcome. Philippe [Jullian] had told me she was coming here. She wrote: *Vous êtes un ange de m'avoir écrit. Je suis enchantée à l'idée de vous revoir à New York.* What unusual warmth from a French woman. She comes here shortly and will call me. I remember her as very charming and amusing.

I am looking forward to going to 'the Cape' [Cape Cod] on Saturday morning. It will be nice among the sand-dunes, if it is sunny. The following weekend Frances Fitzgerald★ (the step-daughter of Ronnie Tree) and Mautner† are giving a dinner for me in Cambridge. So you see I am not quite neglected—though nothing is happening *this* week.

TO ROBERT CUMMING   *215, East 25th Street*
6 May 1960   *New York*

I think the main point is that one should enjoy writing—I have ceased to wonder whether I'll be a good writer or not, though I would be grateful if I did become so, and naturally I *want* to be one. Like Alasdair [Clayre] I am trying my hand at a novel right now—but I wonder whether Alasdair has the imaginative range—any more than I for instance—to write one. For all his brilliance and wisdom he always struck me as slightly too impartial in his judgement of people. There is

★ Born 1940. Journalist, wrote *Fire In The Lake* (1972) on the war in Vietnam for which she was awarded the Pulitzer Prize.
† John Mautner born 1936. Taught German at Columbia University, now retired because of ill health.

94

plenty of wisdom there and not quite enough love. Am I wrong? This is not an attack on him, because you know how much I admire and respect him. Give him my love when you next see him—I may at last pull myself together and write to him at Cape Cod this weekend.

Yesterday evening I went to see *Ben Hur*, as it is generally known—a perfectly ghastly ordeal. It is in every way one of the most frightful emanations of the Hollywood culture I have ever come across: monstrous in its size, its dullness, its brazen lack of values, and mushy sentimental religious squalor. Even the spectacle is dull usually and has been better seen elsewhere: the chariot race is good but far too long to hold one's excitement. Also the sheer brutality and gruesome nastiness with which physical tortures and misery are exhibited make one feel quite sick, especially as the blood is so artificial and always gleams so brightly. No wonder it was awarded half a dozen 'Oscars' and more.

TO FIONN O'NEILL   *215, East 25th Street*
26 May 1960   *New York*

You write with the combined assurance of youth and of some grande dame of the '18ème siècle' explaining the passage of time to her confidante. You have both Sophie and the Marschallin—I wish I could have a little of Octavian, and only the vitality of Ochs.★

Do you ever see Bill Anderson? I stick to my prediction that he has a great deal of splendid things latent in him, and that one day they will come out. At least that is how I felt when I left Europe.

Last Friday I was given a dinner in Boston, to which I flew after work. My host was a friend of Bob Cumming's whom I first met in Vienna—a very intelligent and peculiar Jewish boy from outside New York, with plenty of money and an

★ Characters in *Der Rosenkavalier* by Richard Strauss.

95

addiction to being psycho-analysed. A girl-friend was hostess—a delightful person, with a kind of radiant distinction that was most captivating. We ate a vast amount at a good restaurant, and the company had that sort of glamour that our friends sometimes had at the University, with all the assurance and lack of responsibility, and certainty of being the most important people in the world that goes with it. The whole occasion was very flattering to me—everyone very respectful and charming, especially of course the girls! Frankie Fitzgerald sat next to me, and as usual was elegant and attractive. You'd like her—she reminds me, in a very distant way, of you.

The Americans themselves are fundamentally more interesting than the foreigners and I include the English. There are so many varieties and it amuses me to see how those who are more elegant, or more educated, make a great point of that—just because they feel that they are in such a minority—much as the 18th century (like Lord Chesterfield), looking back on the excesses and grotesques of previous centuries, and of the less distinguished contemporaries, was self-consciously poised in its brilliance, and aware of the novelty of its outlook. This makes some Americans appear much more snobbish than we are.

I—who depend for at least a third of all my delight on my eyes, which, Berensonlike, I have been training for years to see all the details and the touches which personalise and attract in the things which man has made for himself and in nature—am very thirsty for an English park, an Italian piazza, or some Gothic church in France rising high above a river bank, above blue roofs that terrace down to a sluggish Burgundian stream, spanned by a grand bridge built by one of Louis XIV's brilliant departments. That is really my last thought of Europe—Burgundy where I ate and drank so fantastically well last summer, looking at all the strange monuments of a society that was spectacularly rich in its enjoyment of the fat things of life: ruled by a family that expressed its decadence in monstrously over-decorated and delicious monuments like the church at Brou! Here nothing speaks of the distant past, so that things even of the middle of the last century one finds strangely nostalgic and comforting. We are at home the self-consciously emotional descendants of other ages: we are at all times aware, I mean educated people, that the things of the past speak of other lives, and give us a sort of touch of the continuity of things. That is such a comforting thing—one doesn't realise till one gets here just how important it is. When I see an 18th-century church here I feel I am breathing in antiquity—how astonishing it must be to Americans when they see Rome for the first time. But there are moments of nostalgia here—they are produced by the light. When one walks at sunset and sees the skyscrapers light up against the Western sky, the electric light against the dimming sunlight, it can be breathtakingly beautiful: at last the city takes on an almost tangible personality of its own.

TO NICHOLAS DEAKIN   *215, East 25th Street*
2 June 1960   *New York*

In Europe we aren't yet accustomed to regard aeroplanes as things of every day: somehow machines are very much more at home here. My mother for instance, who has just moved into her house in the country, failed to buy an ice-box: that would be the first thing anyone would buy here. In poorer homes like mine, so great is the danger of bugs, etc., that one has to put all one's food in a locked place like the ice-box to save it from decimation.

The girls I know in New York are infinitely more interesting than most of the men I have met. There seem to me to be many more bright, intelligent, educated girls here than bachelors—unlike my experience at Oxford and London, where the quantity of interesting men easily surpasses that of the girls. But then this is of course a woman's country—unlike England.

My week-end in S'bergia was very funny: he and his wife

tease each other incessantly, often for want of anything else to talk about. She is *au fond* bored, though she'd never admit it. She likes comfort more than anything in life and certainly knows how to create it and share it. She is a woman with an enormous heart, who ought to have had dozens of children to lavish her energies on. Her husband, however, would never stand for it. We rode to and forth from Boston in little planes —the kind the leading executives now have in order to conduct business in many different places on the same day, down in Texas and New Mexico. There they are used as ferries. In Provincetown, which has a certain amount of charm, we saw a few arty-crafty people in the street, and queers, and tourists: it is a sort of St Ives (as you undoubtedly know) with some rich and famous concentrated around. Mr S. told me that 'if you weren't so argumentative, I'd have called in Conrad Aitken and Edmund Wilson for a drink, but being as you are . . .' (a typical S'berg tease). When we got back to New York (the plane was full of returning business men) on Tuesday, Monday being Memorial Day, having digested the morning papers, a big Cadillac picked us up at La Guardia and swished Mr S. to Park Avenue, me to my slum on 25th street.

TO ARCADI NEBOLSINE   *215, East 25th Street*
16 June 1960   *New York*

I am very anxious to hear what you think about Oxford. The crumbling spires themselves will be smaller, less voluptuous and more concrete than you remember them: it is like a first visit to Venice after seeing a great deal of Canaletto—it all seems a little shabby and then you see it is more subtle than what the painter managed to convey to you after all. I do hope however that you enjoy yourself and don't seek to find fulfilment of some social commitment that you have been looking for all these years. Allow things to be as they are, and enjoy what is after all only a tourist's view, not that of a permanent committed resident.

Of course you feel out of it and find everyone less glamorous. After the initial glamour of being young has worn off it needs genuine and innate excitement to keep up the appearance of being extraordinary. We can all thrill at a person of nineteen, with nothing to lose, who by force of personality, or vigour, or beauty or other external virtue fascinates, simply because they are new to everything, and at the very start of the race. The question that is important after University life is over is: can one retain that freshness of purpose, that feeling of coming *new* to everything which, for instance, made Voltaire at 80 as exciting to the blind Mme du Deffand as he had been forty years before? Shaw claimed that he approached only the surface of things, because he wished to appear to have come to them fresh, and without the prejudices and convictions which we acquire from experience. I don't admire Shaw particularly, but I see what he meant. The great test is to be able to settle into one's own ways without losing a sense of the novelty of things: because glamour and novelty are inextricably intertwined.

On Tuesday I went to a party given by a sculptor, Lewis Iselin, from the NY family, whose daughter I met at Harvard. It was moderately nice, with middle-interesting intellectuals *de bon genre*. Real elegance you will find less and less of as you go round Europe and England: the reason is this—the very rich who surround themselves with elegance are usually not exciting in themselves, and those who could make something of the elegance depend on others richer than themselves. Here David Winn is an exception, and when he grows older he may create something bright around himself. Don't underrate him.

215, *East 25th Street*
New York

I have been reading *Miss Lonelyhearts*: Nathanael West is much
better than the beatniks, who have tried to get some of this
surrealistic flavour. Like most contemporary New York art-
products beatnickery is entirely derivative with about as much
real originality as say the *Boy Friend*. West's other book on Los
Angeles [*The Day of the Locust*] I liked a great deal—he writes
with punch, and what a relief that is after one ploughs through
all the blancmange-like prose of most people today.

What is happening to the Labour Party? I tend to dislike the
left wing of it in any case, and never admired Gaitskell too
much—but I feel sympathy with him now that he is under fire
from irresponsible (?) trade unions. Query, because you know
better than I at this distance. *The Times* says the events in the
party are 'tragic'—certainly it would be awful if they ceased to
offer a proper opposition, completely.

TO JAAP VAN DER LEE   215, *East 25th Street*
24 June 1960   *New York*

Although it has taken me some time to reply, I am still greatly
indebted to you for taking so much time and trouble to answer
my last letter, which clearly annoyed you a great deal. Thank
you for your answer, which I think shows you misinterpreted
some of what I said—though maybe, looking back on it, I did
write in rather an ambiguous way. What I meant about the
governments was this: the Six, whatever they say to deny it,
are a political association as well as an economic one, and I can
understand hesitating before wanting to join with them in a
political association that goes beyond the regulation of trade
and industry. I think everything should be done to make it
possible for Britain to join Euratom, and the Six, in economic
association, and in aid to Africa. The political implications of

such co-operation are obvious, but while the governments concerned can contain men of the leanings of some Christian Democrats in Italy, or pursue trials like the recent farcical affair in Algiers concerning Alleg, or in fact use torture as the French have for years, etc., etc., I see no great advantage in a *closely-knit* political organisation. There would be carping, and quarrels, and back-biting, and even violence in no time.

Much more important politically speaking would be an association between the US and the rest of the Nato countries to co-ordinate their foreign policy, and their aid to Africa, to which the US has so far contributed little or nothing, since she regards the Europeans as Imperialists there. But I ought not to go on, because I think this is directly in your line of country, and you know exactly what is needed and I do not. Have I made myself clear about the political aspects of the Community—and that I do want economic association? But —to take an example—until the Italians allow everyone to say what they like about the Mafia or the Church for instance, be they Italian or foreigners, I'll continue to regard their government—though not them—as a disgrace. Supporting that government politically means supporting the un-believable conditions in Southern Italy—conditions condoned by the actions of the late Pope, who considered all Socialists as sinners. You should hear what Italians have to say about their rulers.

Have you seen a film called *I'm All Right Jack*—a very good satire on modern England, with a couple of really delicious Macmillan-supporters in it? By that I mean they are exact portrayals of that kind of person who figures large among supporters of the present government. Have you seen what is happening to the Labour Party? It is dragging itself through crises and looks as if it will move more into the realms of absurdity than before. What a pity that they haven't a leader of real calibre. Bevin has gone and Attlee is like a decaying tortoise in the Lords—the real vitality seems to have gone with the departure of the best minds. The insularity of the

T.U. is terrifying in England, as is that of their counterparts here.

I am very interested by everything you say about Africa, and what my mother reports of your journey there. What chances are there of there ever being a co-ordinated Africa Bureau, as it were, of all the interested nations: England, France, Belgium and Portugal? Would the Portuguese, described in *The Times* as the first and last of the great imperial rulers, join with the others? Do you think the independent African peoples are going to continue to subscribe to the frontiers drawn up by the mutually suspicious and carefully balanced imperial powers of the last century? Is Ghana going to lose its Parliamentary aspects, and its guarantees of British Common Law? I would be very interested in going there—I wonder if there are jobs either in newspapers in Accra or in some European money-dispensing agency there I could get next year for a few months. I'd also like to go to Nairobi and to Rhodesia, and see on the spot how it is. I have learnt so much about America by being here, and working in a newspaper, even if I haven't learnt too much about how to be a journalist.

TO VERONICA GASCOIGNE   *215, East 25th Street*
27 June 1960   *New York*

I miss my annual visit to Italy badly—it has become a matter of essential habit to me. This will be the first year since 1953 that I haven't been there for at least a few days. My first proper visit was in 1950, when we went to Positano, Paestum, Naples and Rome. During those eighteen days in Rome I think we must have seen more than most people do in months. My father with his indefatigable Baedeker-based knowledge of what there was to see didn't fail to enter any church of any interest whatever, let alone ice-cream bars, restaurants, and visits to such places as Frascati, Tusculum, and the Villa Farnese at Caprarola. Have you ever been there? It is a five-sided villa north of Rome, with splendid gardens, and vast and beautiful rooms. It was built by the Farnese in about 1540. We had lunch afterwards on the Lago di Bracciano, eating in a little bistro on piles above the water's edge. When we went to Frascati to see the Villa Aldobrandini, we crossed the Campagna on a little local train, and then walked up from the station to the Villa gates. We were told we could only come in with an introduction or in a carrozza! Back in the piazza we were told by the driver that his carrozza cost 6000 lire for a visit to the Villa, and a drive in the park. Prince Aldobrandini clearly thinks 6000 lire means good character. Once inside the gardens, we couldn't see the inside of the house because *sua altezza* was at home, but we were persuaded to drive up to Tusculum at the top of a hill in the park—we pushing the carrozza from behind while the tired horse dragged it from in front. Tusculum was where Cicero had his villa and one has a magnificent view of Rome and the 'environs'. You can see what an impression it made on me—it is a sort of substitution for going to Italy to remember the whole occasion.

Also I have been made more nostalgic by reading Marguerite Yourcenar's reconstruction—*The Memoirs of Hadrian*—an excellent thing in its way: full of fine passages of observation and rumination, and some interesting bits of history that I didn't know. It suffers from the fault of all historical novels that very occasionally the author gets out of tune with the setting that she herself has created from her historical knowledge, and one is reminded that the whole thing is after all a reconstruction. But these moments are unusually rare. I didn't know that Antinous, whose face peers at one in so many museums, sometimes ridiculously languorous, sometimes turgidly romantic, sometimes sexy in a sort of Hollywood-esque way, was the discovery of Hadrian: they had a long and sad affair, the Emperor philosophically wistful over the melancholy 20-year-old's beauty. He had hundreds of portraits made—hence the ones in museums. I always thought he was an entirely legendary figure.

TO ROBERT CUMMING   *215, East 25th Street*
6 July 1960   *New York*

Thank you for your letter, which arrived today, full of
splendid descriptions of Perridge [John's parents' house in
Somerset]. I am so glad you went there and that you liked it: it
makes me feel that I will like it too.

July 7th
The news arrived yesterday from Fred Myers that you had got
your degree: many many congratulations. It's proof of how
hard you worked and of course you pretended not to. I feel
particularly pleased because it was I who suggested you do
that degree in the first place, and felt sure that you could get it,
in spite of your doubts. I am glad also that the University gave
you a better deal than they gave me. Fred's call came just as I
was lying on my bed trying to control the most agonizing
irritation on my back which I have had for the last twenty-four
hours—the result of sun-burn received over the weekend at
Cape Cod.

   While on the Cape I went with the S'bergs, with whom I
was staying, to a party given by Gilbert Seldes, one of the first
publishers of Eliot, Frost and Pound, etc., to which a number
of amusing people came. A group led by A. Tate contained
Spender and others, and Schlesinger was there, with whom I
had a longish chat, about the presidency—of course. What else
does one talk about now? Schlesinger's son was there, as was
Dwight Macdonald's and E. Wilson's—all the sons one might
say—however they did not make one father! If it hadn't been
for the after-effects of the sun which have left me in such a state
of nervous irritation, I would say the weekend was very
relaxing and pleasant. I was amused by the crowd at
Provincetown, made up of spanking lesbians, wild fairies,
artists, tourists, businessmen, hangers-on, natives and 2000
sailors from a ship which was visiting for the weekend. It
made an enjoyable insalata, to be observed in comfort from

the tidy white S-berg house. (It belonged to Dos Passos and O'Neill before them!)

I think I shall have to write an American book when I get back home—not only to annoy you, or make money, but also because I think there is such a lot to talk about here. Really I have learnt an enormous amount about how people can live and about the fact that intellectual standards do not apply in the judging of peoples. It is still too early (I hope not too late) to hope for a high standard of cultural civilization here: what one must look for is a high standard of social virtues—and that is where one could praise the US most and attack it most, because it provides a splendid environment for some, and a very bad one for others. For a foreigner the most terrifying thing is the fact that the world's 'top' nation is led by men largely ignorant of foreign countries and peoples, and by an isolationist view—still—of their cultures. The other evening Jack Paar—who runs a show on TV every evening and is one of the most famous men in the country—indulged in an attack on France and the French that was revolting in its tastelessness. He described the French as people that cheat with their change, speak an unpleasant language, and as mean and dirty. The S-bergs, hardly anti-American, naturally, and very irritated by my constant criticisms, were disgusted and switched the programme off in anger. It wouldn't happen anywhere else.

I was told by Arcadi that you were sad to leave Oxford: it did captivate you at last. I think you will have invested it with some nostalgia of your own by now—certainly among the many memories those yellow-coloured walls and absurd decorations revive in me, will be my walks with you. Oxford looks always as if it existed at least in part in the memory of other people—as if it were pieced together out of their reminiscences and imaginings. Are you sad to be leaving England too? I think even England, which irritated you so much, may have finally won your heart a little. I judge from your letter with its 'rave notice' of Somerset that you have discovered its beauty. And London? I don't think you ever gave the city a chance—but one day you must live there properly—and here too. New York has its strange similarities with London, in spite of having such a vigorous life of its own. But we are less violent at home—I mean fewer gangs and hoods—and we have ridiculous licensing laws. The all-night cinema—although very expensive—and the all-night bars are two of the great boons here.

TO JOHN MAUTNER   *215, East 25th Street*
20 July 1960   *New York*

I have been reading *Dodsworth* [by Sinclair Lewis]—the trouble with the book is that after page 100 it begins to become repetitive. While Lewis tries hard to be sophisticated he actually seems to remain *terriblement* bourgeois—much as E. M. Forster does in his novels. I also read yesterday *Giovanni's Room* by James Baldwin, a sensitive Negro living in Paris. It was highly praised when it came out, but it seems to me to be awfully turgid—and deadly serious. I wish Americans could write about the emotions as if it were sometimes possible to think they are invalid and idiotic and laughable—that is, to laugh at themselves—and have a little of the rough and ready cynicism towards their moral predicaments which one finds so concisely put in Rochefoucauld. The book is full of 'guilt'. Thank God I have a completely pagan absence of guilt, and when I feel sorry for someone it is out of sympathy for them and not because I feel I ought to. I have inherited either from my parents, or from my experience of Italy, or be it from an early discarding of religion, or from arguments with friends at Oxford, a pagan view of life: that we are responsible for the things we make ourselves responsible for, but that we are not inherently responsible for all the misery in the world, nor for all the weaknesses of the flesh. Turgidity and guilt are the twin muses of much American writing I have come across—it is hinted at in Nathanael West, but *he* had a sense of *irony*:

John with his Mother and his Sister Iris, Ischia, 1954

John at Solaia, the Vivante family's house, 1956

John and his Father in about 1959

Ben Sonnenberg at Gramercy Park, New York

Perridge House, Somerset

John in the 1960s

Fionn O'Neill (Morgan)

John and Bob Cumming at
Selinunte in Sicily

John and his Father
in about 1970

From left: Marianne Calmann, Iris Goodacre, Hans Calmann,
Gerta Calmann, John Calmann and Susan van der Hecht

Bob Cumming in New York, 1968

Hans and Gerta Calmann
at Perridge

John at the American Booksellers' annual Convention, 1979, with
Liz Ingles and Alexis Lichine

John's Mother in the garden at
Perridge

John in fancy dress, early in 1980

America awaits her Voltaire, and I think he sits on Cambridge Street.

As to T. S. Eliot, I will not argue with you about a sacred cow. *Nous avons tous nos vaches preferées.* But he too is dominated by guilt, and I loathe his prissy Anglicanism, with its fake Gods, fake mysticism, fake devotion, snobbery and preciosity. I admire his intelligence, and occasionally his taste. I think he has written some good stuff, but it does not touch the heart. He lacks the Byronic touch, and that is necessary in a poet. Even Matthew Arnold had it up to a point. He lacks heart, warmth, feelings for the passionate brilliance of the visual world, and a grand imagination. He is petty-fogging and brittle: but lacks the brilliance of Pope, or the intuitive vision and simplicity of Jane Austen. In his private life he is ridiculous—though that is true of many great artists I admit. Do you know that he once said Goethe was an insignificant poet? *Au fond* he lacks humanity and that is *le pire de tout.*

Have we the physical resistance required to overcome the huge pressures put on our judgement? Eliot for one had not—otherwise he would not have retired to the ivory tower of inane snobbery and Anglo-catholicism. If you had lived as close to all that quatsch as I you would be as stern in your judgement as I am. It is the culture of spiritual death. It is the culture of the *alte Fürstin.** (As for Marie Taxis, she never let Rilke have the run of Duino: she had him to stay—for her it was a pleasure to condescend, for him it was material flattery, and a chance to be cumfy.) Think of the humiliation of being patronized by the Schönburgs, or the Esterhazys, or the Rasumovskys, or the Rohans. The greatest French and English writers did their best to escape their patrons. Patrons are always demanding in the end, and few will bow to the will of their pet genius. Mozart hated every minute he had to depend on his patrons: and they neither appreciated his supreme qualities, nor gave him enough to avoid illness and tragic death, far from the assistance and care of good doctors. Enough on patrons.

* The old Princess (Schönburg—see p. 35ff).

Time has altered all the circumstances of our cultural surround, but not the essential duties of culture: it has always been isolated, but in the past it was the pet of those in power. Now it is the gloss of those who wish to be in power, or the dedication of those who will never have it. The best is full of quirks, and it is usually snobbish. In spite of all that it will probably survive, because some people will always be there to enjoy it for itself. You remember the Marschallin? *'Die Zeit, die ändert doch nichts an den Sachen'* . . . and . . . *'Allein man muss sich nur nicht vor ihr fürchten. Auch sie ist ein Geschöpf des Vaters, der uns alle erschaffen hat.'*★ I think the relationship between culture and the arts and society is fluid—and what seems a decline at one moment is always revived by a new flow of invention. In the midst of the 'dark' ages what brilliant inventors and artists were at work! What does it matter if we are entering a new 'dark' age? I think we have a few moments of pleasure left. Let them be moments of pleasures as great as those in the conversations in the *Phaedo*.

Mais je suis devenu sérieux, presque sentimentale—it must be the neon light and the banging of typewriters in this lovely office that has produced this reaction.

TO HIS MOTHER   *215, East 25th Street*
24 July 1960   *New York*

Mr S. confounds arguments about Kennedy's youth with the example of the emperors taken from Suetonius, the Penguin translation of which I gave him. He says the emperors weren't very old either when they succeeded each other, even the good ones, and he says they were all men who had already committed crimes, and fought for their positions. Kennedy he says has done the same, though he adds, 'He has shown what a

★ In Richard Strauss's *Der Rosenkavalier*: Time makes no difference in the long term . . . And yet one need not fear it, since it too is a creation of the Father who has made us all.

108

man can do with 50 million dollars.' Kennedy has at least as much. He is frightened that the K. family will be the principal beneficiaries of a Kennedy presidency—he says that J.F. has extraordinarily strong dynastic ties. Apparently at the Convention there were twenty-seven members of the family, and when the nomination was announced an inner caucus of supporters went to a party in his honour. There were only twenty-seven people at it. Perhaps he will prove himself yet.

Harvard is a sort of oasis in America of old-fashioned culture: it is also a Mecca of both education and *le bon ton*. But like Oxford or Cambridge it has a cult, and its devotees and products speak in the accents of its superiority. It also supports a ghastly institution known as the Business School that exists to make young men into members of the Republican party, and to ensure that they will be obedient to the adventurers and tyrants of Wall Street (who have not of course been to the school), whose will they will serve, and whose attitudes they ape. They firmly believe, to use the famous words of the president of General Motors, 'that what is good for G.M. is good for America'—and indeed the world. One thing I have learnt from the *Wall Street Journal* is that the world of business is one of the chief forces to the bad in the United States. Coupled with Mr S.'s and his wife's insistence that all self-respecting intelligent young men should join the Labour Party in Britain, who knows what will happen to me?

Back here I finished *Dodsworth*. Some of it is interesting and well-written, but (much as E. M. Forster) the attitude of the author is terribly bourgeois, his knowledge of Europe limited, and his sensitivity to the real atmosphere of any European place he describes—and he describes many—non-existent. It is all so one-sided, and much of it so flat. Yet I got to the end. It seemed to me to take awfully long—400 pages—to make its point. But that is the American in Sinclair Lewis. And he attitudinizes so.

John spent his summer holidays in California: Los Angeles, Carmel and San Francisco. He then went on to Davidson, North Carolina, to see his friend Bob Cumming.

TO JOHN MAUTNER   *c/o Hertz*
31 July 1960   *Los Angeles*

The oranges are just in front of me, did you know that they bloom and have fruit simultaneously? I wish I could say the same for all of us. I finished the tale of Salamander and Holunderbäume,* but was not as exhilarated as you had led me to expect. It is very charming—and has some fine *dichterische Passagen*, though I may not have understood all the parables. However, I did enjoy it, and thank you for bringing Hoffmann to my attention, as I had of course not read him before. I am now trying again *The Marquise of O*† which I started once before, but am determined to finish this time.

I hope to leave for Monterey in the next week if my car and my health permit. I have been having some glandular trouble all of a sudden, which having got better in my throat has started now in my groin. I had no idea one had so many glands. Nevertheless I went to the beach today, and indeed the days before, and sat in the sun, and swam in the sea, which is red, of all colours, because of a sudden visit of plankton, the stuff that whales feed upon.

I am beginning to feel more tolerant of this country, just at the moment where I am reaching the high point of irritation with it. There is after all nothing one can do about it. It is necessary to hope for the best—but yesterday for instance I discovered another absurdity. I met two friends of my cousins', a boy from Caltec [California Institute of Technology], and a boy from MIT [Massachusetts Institute of Technology]. They were quite intelligent and nice, but what they

* E. T. A. Hoffmann, *Der goldene Topf.*
† H. von Kleist.

had to report of their colleges! They both work at some frightfully important things, like space and atom-splitting, paid by the government of course, and are worked terrifically hard. One of them told me he saw no point in working that hard and had now stopped doing so. He tried to find time to read, and attended a humanities course on the 'Six Metaphysical Systems'—naturally he was surprised when I didn't seem to know what these six might be. I suggested that there were after all more than six, but having been taught a selection of that number, he has dismissed the rest. They seem to forget that idleness, as one vice-chancellor at Oxford put it, is an integral part of education, and that it is necessary for the languor of youth, to borrow a phrase from Waugh, to flourish, otherwise they will never learn anything satisfactorily above being the manipulators of electronic brains—and in that way of course the slave of the 'brains'.

Education at these colleges, and it is hard, really hard work there, seems to be more directed to beating the 'goddam Russians' than making human beings out of these potentially agreeable people. Both the US and Russia have convinced each other that human values are the least important, in spite of all their protests to the contrary. But what is so extraordinary to me is that there are hundreds of people, even influential ones, who think as I do, but they manage to change nothing. Do you think that when the political Midas of Hyannisport is in the White House things will change, and human values will once again be stressed? I doubt it. If he had vision he'd make Stevenson Secretary of Education, and start something new. *Die Welt war nicht für uns ausgedacht.**

---

* The world was not intended for us.

I have read on in Henry James's *Roderick Hudson*, which
charms me a great deal: a picture of a life which is in some ways
familiar, since intellectually we are so much the children—at
least I am—of the European 19th century, and which in its
leisurely way was highly satisfactory. It was also prim,
prudish, and morally the atmosphere was very close.
Nevertheless, I like to read about it, set in a Rome which sadly
no longer exists, the Rome with a Colosseum still covered
with weeds, a Janicolo full of gardens and backstreets, dirty
and yet riddled with palazzi in decay, and courtyards with
dripping fountains. That Rome has some remainders it is true,
but it has all been cleaned of course, and the tourists have
discovered the poor quarters and the fish restaurants. Liking
Rome as I do now, how one would have been captivated by it
then! The Campagna—the large area of meadows and fields
which stretch from Rome to the mountains, formerly made
up of marshes, and across which the Via Appia runs—was in
those days a high sea of yellow grass, and James describes
going for rides among the ruins of the aqueducts. Now we see
Pepsi signs and asphalt, the marshes have been drained, so the
malaria has gone—but aren't the twenty thousand houses and
tourists and cars and noise almost worse? Still, it remains
beautiful. James manages to bring back the flavour that has
escaped into the realms of historical imagination, and the
memories that other generations of travellers recall.

On the way up here I stopped for the night in a little place by
the sea and went early the next day, Saturday, to see the Hearst
museum, a great castle built on top of a high hill near the coast,

filled with the pillage of the after-war years, 1920–40. In some ways it reminds one, the gardens and lay-out, of Monte Carlo: everywhere concrete Herms support electric lamps. Pretty flowers and trees, however, cover the hillside—all artificially watered. The main building is a jumble of horrors—with some good moments. Moorish towers, an Indian teak roof and eaves, a Gothic doorway, and cement, make up the main façade. It is terrible as an idea, vulgar in the extreme, and quite successfully pulled off. Inside it is less good and the side views with the steel and concrete clearly visible (nothing was ever finished) are hideous. A dining hall worthy of an Oxford College has banners from the Palio (!), choir-stalls from a Spanish cathedral, a fire-place from a 15th-century château, and tables from a monastic refectory. It is a ghastly jumble of bric-à-brac. Occasionally of course a good piece creeps in: his agents could not cheat him all the time. In the guest houses there are some pretty rooms, and a few good pieces of furniture. Much of the antique stuff was never good anyway. *All* the pictures are bad, though I didn't see upstairs, because the public is not allowed there. Unfortunately some of the best and most awful rooms are there—displaying his vulture-like taste in all its grim glory—but one can only see them in post-cards. The reason why upstairs isn't shown is because the stairs are not considered safe, which seems to me to be a reason for repairing them quite simply, then we could see them. But everybody in America hates to spend public money on something which is an artistic curiosity—if it were a 'ball-park' now . . .

TO ROBERT CUMMING   *San Francisco*
20 August 1960

I have become very excited, internally, about the state of America, and what the business world and the Republican party between them have been doing. One can say at least that the battle is on in this country: the battle between those that think that there is still time before all human values and educational principles are discarded in favour of rank *keeping-up-with-the-Kremlin*, and those that believe that *keeping-up* is all that is necessary, and hope to make big profits from it on the way. I have become violently partisan, as you can see, in favour of the 'liberal' democrats against the disgusting laxity of the Eisenhower regime—the mere face of Nixon makes me irritable. In this highly excited state America would soon kill me: because both as a foreigner and as a private individual it is so difficult to get anything changed. In fact impossible. But there are still opportunities here. If I was an American I think politics would be the only activity I would be really anxious to pursue—there is so much to do, of a really *interesting and worth-while* kind in that field. That and—education—and finally race. From you I acquired a sort of sentimental affection for a romantic picture of the old South: but how it must be there now I daren't think—I have heard only bad things—though I would be interested to see you there, and see how people like your parents for instance fit into a society where most other people have such grotesque views.

I find that in some ways the Jews and the Negroes are the two racial types of America who are both most interesting and most vital in the society I have encountered. I dislike a great many rich New York Jews with no education on aesthetic, snobbish grounds—as I would dislike brash businessmen from Yorkshire or something. And I have had no contact with the Negroes of Harlem or the South—but those I have met, and those one encounters just walking down the street, have an air of vitality and 'bounce'—and sometimes are very charming to meet—that is infinitely more attractive than the dumpy Anglo-Saxons and the drearily correct New Englanders. I respect what Harvard has done for some Americans—*much* more than Yale and Princeton—but your Siftons and your Aldrichs are so complex, so careful, so childish in their search for 'truth', so false in their social relations, that one wonders how they can survive so much self-consciousness. I regard vitality as the only gauge of decadence—and they have in some ways so little of it—though I respect Sifton for his devotion to work.

Well there you have some mixed-up attitudes and reactions I have developed over the months here. I have of course hundreds more—and it is impossible to schematize them, or to make up my mind over America. I feel I *ought* not to dislike it, on the grounds first of all of principle: that it is absurd to dislike a vast country of so many people and places. And secondly because I have enjoyed myself so many times, and found sufficient to admire, and finally I would have failed in some way if I were yet another European intellectual who came to America and found he couldn't stand it. But while one is completely absorbed into American life, especially as an Englishman, because it is so amorphous anyone can join it, I am also alien to the intellectual climate, alien to the artistic heritage, and alien to most of the values. The interesting thing is many Americans feel that way too, but they are tied because, like Sheila Lafarge for instance, they feel themselves to belong here—to the semblance of a static society that one has in the East, and in Boston in particular. So they lead a sort of split existence—Americans in opposition one might say. And that is perhaps also why they are so correct, so careful, so serious sometimes, and occasionally so unadventurous in their ideas, because, while politically advanced, they are culturally extreme conservatives. You know: the blending of the best in the European and American traditions! In England I and some of my friends are in the same position—but in England and Europe generally the cultural heritage is clear, we know what we cling to, and its magnificence has become clearer to me here, where every drop that filters through is drunk by those who want a cultural life, with avid thirst. Once accustomed to the bumper bottles we have at home, I get irritated with the sips provided here. I certainly have learnt just to which continent I belong. Ultimately I suppose the vast majority of people prefer the familiar, and find their beauty in it.

TO HIS MOTHER   *c/o Hertz*
25 August 1960   *Los Angeles*

Ernst Koenigsberg, who read some short vignettes I had
written about some places in New York, said I appeared to be
always in two minds about everything here. And I am: it is
difficult to reconcile one's actual reactions with a desire to be
fair and judge the place according to its own lights. I know for
certain, what I knew for certain the day I set foot here, that I
am not destined by character to live here. I think anyone with a
taste for works of art and culture has a meagre time of it in this
country—not because there aren't opportunities to indulge
one's taste, but because these opportunities are so hard to
make frequent use of, without separating oneself from the rest
of society. Among the people we know in Europe a taste for
the arts is not so extraordinary, because we have the self-
confidence of our class. But in America no class has self-
confidence, except those who are very rich, or those who
don't care about the arts anyway. And as for writing here . . . I
have found it terribly distracting. The pressure of thinking
about America and of adjusting my ideas to the reality I find
and trying not to condemn it out of hand has robbed me
temporarily (I hope) of much of my imagination. The
problem is to protect one's values in a society that doesn't
share them. Most people don't at home, but there at least some
people know what I am talking about. All this has taken up so
much energy—never again do I want to use so much of it to
stick to my beliefs—I am so glad we didn't emigrate here!

There, I have gone on again: you see I can't get off it. It
becomes quite obsessive—this criticism of the US. But I feel
oppressed by it, involved with its size and its power, and feel
for those who see their lives here as one long rebellion. The
magazines have taken over even that, and every shout of
protest that is heard is immediately bought up and sold as
entertainment. We have the same in England—gradually we
are becoming as hidebound and complacent and regimented
and closed in as the Victorians. The God of Hygiene conquers

116

all, and every criticism of society is simply disposed of by calling it 'healthy'. I long for the squalor of Naples, for the Edgware Road, and French lavatories—and everything that needs to be attended to because it can't be dismissed.

11 September 1960

Davidson,
North Carolina

I called Mr and Mrs Silver★ about 2 p.m. on Saturday and they asked me round for dinner straightaway. First, however, I ran across Harold Joachim,★ who showed me some nice things, and we had a couple of drinks, and then I had two more drinks with the Fairbanks at their house. The heat was very great, and it was terribly humid, as bad as New York at its worst, and so I was in a somewhat strange state by the time I got to the Silvers' house. It is quite a way out of the main part of the town in a suburb dominated by one of those orientalesque temples which the pseudo-masonic societies erect all over America. Nothing about the house either inside or out is indicative of unusual taste or views—but then out of cupboards Mrs S. pulled drawings and out of shelves Mr S. pulled the earliest Virgils and earliest Dantes and earliest Ariostos. First however I had to argue—for two hours non-stop. Over dinner and brandy and chocolates I was asked to talk about America and defend every criticism I made. He is a very legalistic arguer and as a result of his work in the courts knows how to argue better than he knows the things he discusses.

The crux of the matter is of course that he turned out to be a Republican—something I thought would never happen in an educated household—and that they really think that Ike has given the 'psychology of the nation something to be proud of'. This is the first time I have met people of any artistic inclination who also think that all's well with the US—with certain exceptions of course. The muddle arose because I made

★ See p. 54.

criticisms he would have made under other circumstances—only as I am a foreigner, and especially an Englishman, he resented my criticism, although having asked me first of course to give it.

His Rembrandts (eighteen of them) are magnificent, especially the best six, which are truly astonishing. The self-portrait and the Flight into Egypt are my favourites. I then saw six Watteaus which he recently bought from Mrs Slatkin, two of which I think you once had, showing actors. They are early of course and good in their way but a little stiff, though I think Joachim, who had told him to buy them, was right to advise him to do so. That was all, apart from some fine books, because it had got too late to see any more. A pity we had to argue so much. Anyway I am very glad I was able to see them, and in spite of his 'rough' exterior as Joachim put it, I think he's a man with a good heart and respect for anyone who is willing to put up a fight. They were *au fond* very friendly to me and patient considering my very antagonistic viewpoint in relation to theirs.

I saw John Maxton* on Sunday. He does not like Chicago, understandably, but has a very pretty apartment full of nice things often bought from you. He spoke very nicely of you, and said one or two things which I thought were very apt and made me laugh. Like everyone else he thinks you are terrific highbrows—it took me years to find that out myself.

Chicago is more ghastly than one can imagine. In spite of a fine position on the lake it combines every known form of ugliness. Only the museum is interesting—and it does have some lovely pictures, particularly of course the Impressionists. The new Guido, which John has bought, is good, but it hangs in a gloomy room full of other seicento stuff, and really one can't take more than one of those things seriously at a time. The big Seurat is nearly as fine as ours in the Tate Gallery, and there are some lovely Cézannes and Van Goghs. Even the El Greco is good. I was glad I saw it again.

My stay in Davidson has been very nice, in spite of damp

* See p. 54.

weather and the heat. Yesterday we drove up into the mountains, which were covered with a lush vegetation of many varieties of trees (more in that one district than in the whole of Europe), and had a very windy walk 5500 feet up. The mountain is called Grandfather—and consists of a long narrow rocky ridge. At times I would stand on one rock and Bob [Cumming] on another, great swirling mists blowing round us, and occasionally revealing brilliantly lit valleys far beneath us and sudden distant vistas across the Vosges-like Blue-Ridge Mountains. I tried hard to sing Hoyo To (is that how one writes it?) as from one Walküre to another—it was all very Wagnerian . . .

I had one very interesting evening here, seeing Mrs Cumming in argument with one of the younger professors in the college [Davidson College]—a remarkable man who is trying to 'liberalize' the college, and has more or less dedicated himself to this task. Mrs C. is a liberal of course but believes after thirty years of slow progress here that progress *has* to be slow. The two of them revealed their characters to such an extent that the rest of us just sat spellbound and let them talk. Mrs C. was telling him he was impetuous and tactless, though well-meaning—hence misunderstood and misrepresented by his colleagues—and he told her rightly that she is the dupe of her own determination to think no evil of her colleagues. It was like an Ibsen drama—though not electrically charged, as he is an old friend. I enjoyed the way that these people in this small backwoods town regard themselves as on the frontier of a great social battle which they are really anxious to win: and it was interesting to see the different ways they thought it should be done. The younger professor is a very nice man indeed I think, and the Cummings tell me he has already achieved a very great deal for the students and for liberalization. Dr C. is of course principally a scholar and retreats from the situation as much as possible—though he has refused to become an elder of the church since it would be an endorsement of their segregationist ideas.

I don't have time or space to tell you about the really nice

Kansas farmer I met in the train from Springfield, who kept me from sleeping with his talk, but only because it was so interesting that a man so entirely from the backwoods could have such a perceptive view of a country, which he can only interpret through bad newspapers and his own observation. I haven't heard more damning views of America from anyone since I have been here, nor more of an appreciation of its opportunities. A really nice man with the most agreeable and articulate way of talking. 'You may be surprised,' he said, 'to hear the way I speak—I know I have a better vocabulary than most people here. My mother studied English in college and taught me to be articulate. It shows, doesn't it?' I had to agree. So much depends on the education—and the education the parents had. In spite of only reading *Readers' Digest* and Westerns (as he told me) he was more balanced, informed, fair and appreciative than many 'intellectuals' I have met.

Returning to New York John chafed under the boredom of his job on the Wall Street Journal. *He hoped to persuade his mother to join him before his return to Europe, as he wanted to visit several places with her and show her the museums. But he was disappointed in this. Meanwhile life in New York continued to fascinate and frustrate him.*

TO HIS PARENTS   *215, East 25th Street*
23 September 1960   *New York*

Ben [Sonnenberg] was thrilled by the museum at Bayonne [Musée Bonnat] to which I sent him. He said of Bonnat of course that he was a very bad painter but a fine collector. So I asked him what he thought people would say of the various collections at Gramercy Park: 'They'll say he had a bad figure but a good eye,' came the immediate reply.

Last Saturday evening Arcadi and I gave Mela de Croy and

Polly [Grant] dinner at his flat, and were then joined by Victor Emmanuel of Italy and his Italian companion here. They work in a brokerage house here to learn about American business—how are the mighty fallen! After dinner we all went to the Italian section of town to see the festival of San Gennaro, and were joined by still more friends of Mela's. Naturally the Crown Prince was stopped by a young Italian who said (in Italian): Are you Vittorio Emmanuele? Do you know the name Roberti?—'*il mio babbo era molto amico del Umberto?*' Victor of course had never heard the name, but was upset by the incident and didn't really enjoy the crowds. He was very frightened of having more of them on his hands. I don't think he should have been taken along if he is that worried by such things. It is the first time he has seen a lot of Italians—having left Italy at the age of eight and not being allowed back. The American Italians are unlike other Americans but they are also different from the Italians in Italy. As a very amusing bumptious girl-friend of Mela's who joined us said: 'This isn't the right place for him to meet his people.' This girl had the nice name of Elizabeth de la Perouse (et de l'Allemagne).

We are having a sort of Congress of Vienna *à la vingtième siècle* here at the moment—making New York difficult to negotiate because there are so many policemen everywhere. They gather in their hundreds outside embassies and hotels, and occasionally have battles (as they do in London with rent-sufferers) with warring factions of Castro's supporters and enemies, or Khrushchev's detractors. The most extraordinary leaflets crop up everywhere with strange demands written on them, in which Ghana and Congo, Castro and Kadar are all muddled up and grouped together as tools of Mr Khrushchev. People have strong hatreds but little idea of whom or what they hate. I saw some protestors from Latin America walk in procession with a complex combination of slogans: Down with Castro, Down with Battista, Down with colonial intervention and exploitation and Up with democracy. Well, after one has worked all that out, one really is treading a very fine line indeed.

I am interested to watch the 'campaign'* which has got forced a little into the background by the congregation of horrors at the UN. Nixon has shown what an utterly revolting little smoothy he is by never once mentioning an issue properly but just saying in very general terms that all is well, that we need high ideals, that we must be tough with Russia, that America is a great nation and greater today than ever, that Eisenhower has been a blessing and that Democrats aren't really quite nice. At least Kennedy has got something more to say than just that and is making something of the issues. I still don't like him, but compared to Nixon he is a sort of new Roosevelt, which is of course exactly what he is trying to show himself to be. The accent is the same and he has even more money, but he doesn't have the material that turns a man into a myth. The mere sight of Nixon, with his saccharine pandering to the most complacent elements in this vastly self-satisfied society, is enough to make me feel slightly sick: a real middle-class uneducated swindler with all the virtues of a seller of fountain-pens in Naples.

TO HIS MOTHER   215, *East 25th Street*
28 September 1960   *New York*

Your and Daddy's rivalry over the house is nearly as intense as that of the S'bergs over theirs. Mrs S. loudly called the drawing-room vulgar and in the worst possible taste the other evening when I was there, which left Mr S. muttering furiously in one corner. He wouldn't mind so much except that she said it to a Tory MP—Charles Fletcher-Cooke—who was staying there at the time. A very nice man by the way, and we had a delicious dinner, the four of us, on Saturday. Very mild and mellow, rather prissy in an English upper-class way, yet quite forceful, he was the epitome of politeness and tact. I attacked him of course—not very hard—on all sorts of

* For the US presidency.

subjects. I said just now to Mrs S. on the 'phone that I thought 'he had never dirtied his hands', she agreed but added quickly with a laugh, 'You have—(I mean we all have)—a great deal to learn from him. He was so unaggressive.' I liked her little covering remark in parenthesis, so I wouldn't take the point too hard. You'd like Hilda I think—she is very human, even though she is a hearty Jewish momma. (And of course what is wrong with that?)

About writing: I know Daddy thinks it is a speculation—of course it is—yet I suspect myself of having some talents in that direction, but time is the main thing I need in order to see if I can do something about them. Time has of course to be bought. In a sense you might be right in saying that if I were to spend say a couple of months at Perridge I could write peacefully there. But it isn't true, because once in England I shall have to see people and employers and be captured for good. A few more months of wandering are essential I think, if I am not to sink into a provincial round of restrictive work. Arcadi says that he finds his and my friends are already asleep in their English bed, and sad about it at that. I get the same impression from letters.

I want you to know, however, how very much I appreciate the fact you have given me so much money to come here and to see things—without it I would have never had such a fascinating time, nor seen so many things. It has enabled me to know America in a year in a way it may take some people several years. It has, as Mr S. said it would, added ten years in twelve months. Nor do I see any way in which one can pay these things back within the immediate future—though I hope I may have the opportunity for that one day. Once more thank you for letting me breathe some other climates.

As to art-dealing: I don't reject it because I am against it, only because it won't go with the things I have set out to do. In many ways it is a great temptation, because I have the knowledge to some degree, the taste, would enjoy the life, and would of course have the great advantage of Daddy's backing and prestige. However, I want to see if I can make my way into the world of politics and journalism, even if it is more difficult. Everyone thinks it crazy that I try: but that's because they can't see themselves doing it. I have twice as much energy as all my friends put together—as any of them will admit—and I think I can put it to successful use in that field.

Now I have made out my case—and you and Daddy can tell me what's wrong. I am sorry if you feel that in some way I have let you down by not working as a dealer: but you'll at least agree I have never 'led you on' to think I would be.

TO ANGUS AND JOANNA MCINTYRE   *215, East 25th Street*
7 October 1960   *New York*

How moral you are in your judgement of me, which is flattering, I suppose, with your comments on my sense of balance while I wine with the rich and dine with the powerful. But I do these things less and less, and it is really easier to keep a sense of balance while doing those delectable things, than when one has nothing but the humdrum with which to entertain oneself.

I am following the gyrations of the Labour Party with interest—having more or less decided that when I return to England it will be with them and not with the Tories that I'll throw in my lot. Didn't William [Miller] always predict that? Those of my generation who have headed for the Tory Party represent all that is worst in the English upper classes (and I have no feeling of attachment to them as a result of birth or education). More important, I find that the Labour Party is heading for at least ten years of crisis: in those years if it is to become the new party of ideas and change, or improvement and adaptation—the role of Gladstone's party in the 19th century—it will need all the help and support it can get from intelligent youth. Its basically Socialist aspects are going to disappear—its position as the party with the sense of what changes the times demand must be enhanced.

Here we are having to divide our attention between the clowns in UNO and the jugglers in the 'campaign'. Arthur Schlesinger, America's answer to Trevor-Roper, has written a pamphlet for Kennedy, comparing the two candidates: he makes a searing attack on Nixon, but his praise for K. is a little too vague. The truth is of course that Kennedy is a shot in the dark. Nobody knows if he is going to be any good or not—all we can tell is that Nixon is a horror.

Internally this year in America has aged me: I don't know whether you'd see it in my face, as it were, but I can see England and Europe, and me in them, in a perspective that I couldn't before. Over the next twenty or thirty years—which are *our years*, yours and mine—all the 'niceness' of the Tory radicals (Altrincham, Fletcher-Cooke, whom I met here the other day, etc.), all the goodwill of the Welfare State, all the gerrymandering pacifism of the Cousins Unions, won't do us any good. If Europe, and the culture which we are heirs to, are to survive it will require a very tough approach to every part of our lives. Changes when they are made must be thorough— help to our black Africans on a grand scale, and the bullying of our American friends—careful, complete and effective. There is no doubt in my mind that Europe is in every way the most superior of the civilizations that we still have: it will require nothing less than ruthlessness to save it.

I am re-reading *Vanity Fair*—I suppose it was at school that I read it first. It is a brilliant novel, and its faults are immaterial in relation to its intrinsic merit. Thackeray knew his characters and they are very English. That at least has not changed over the years. The scope is magnificent, and the sense of absurdity very funny: the preoccupation that most people have with the little things of life in the presence of the greatest events foreshadows *War and Peace*. Tolstoy must have read the book. His theme is really hypocrisy—what a great emotion he makes of it, worthy of Stendhal.

Allow me straight away to correct one impression: that I think that my friends' lives are humdrum because they work. Far from it—it has nothing to do with their work, but their attitudes. I too would lead a humdrum life if my attitude to my work was the same as theirs—more so in fact because my work is *so dull*. I am really tired of doing so *little* and would like to *work* hard, if it was interesting work. During the next few days I am going to do my best to see people at the UN, and to write to people in England and elsewhere about my trip to Africa, and work I could do there. However, please understand I have no aversion at all to work—and that my interest in writing does not conflict with my desire to have a career. What I dislike is the fact that I am *underemployed* and that the things I can offer, intelligence, energy and a much wider knowledge of people and places than most people older than myself, are not being made use of.

Friday
Well, I have just had to revise all I said about my friends—having this morning received a letter from Nicholas [Deakin], in which he told me that David Pryce-Jones, Alasdair Clayre and William Miller are all publishing novels in the very near future, that Bill Anderson and he are translating classics for Penguin, that Adrian Lyttelton is about to enter All Souls, etc. Meanwhile I languish in the *Wall Street Journal* as a clerk, unable to write, but—and of course there is a but—I have had my eyes opened here to many many things. I sense even in Nicholas's letter that his are not open in the same way, and perhaps the standard of one's own achievement has nothing to do with what anybody else does. Never compare yourself, Samuel Butler wrote, with anybody else. But there is an irresistible temptation to do so . . .

I have now had lunch and the foregoing burst of impatience has of course died down. After all Cecil Rhodes was a millionaire when he was 21—if one bothered to compare oneself with everyone's progress one's own would seem so small that it might even become discouraging. I find on the contrary that my friends' activities make me hopeful that I might yet do something myself. *Il faut cultiver notre jardin*, etc. Perhaps in Africa I shall end in H. Oppenheimer's office too. The call of the Rand has always been particularly powerful in regard to Hamburg Jews.

England sounds so familiar in the letters I receive—but sometimes I feel slightly oppressed by the thought of this familiarity. I have developed such a sort of self-conscious internationality that everything has an air of being provincial. But everyone assures me it is so 'nice to settle down'.

TO NICHOLAS DEAKIN   215, *East 25th Street*
4 November 1960   *New York*

At dinner with the S'bergs the other evening and Alistair Cooke, I listened not only to the last of the TV debates, but to endless discussions of who'd get what in the Kennedy administration. They ruled out the possibility of Nixon getting in, and said that of course if it did happen just the same group of dullards would be in power, with a few insignificant changes in personnel. Ben had lunch the other day with former Senator (Dem.) Benton of Connecticut who runs a well-known ad agency called Benton and Bowles, and the *Britannica*. Bowles was there, and Adlai, and David Bruce (ex-Ambassador to Germany) and old Harriman. Ben described the occasion as being like a meal with a group of old actresses, all of whom had had their greatest roles and all of whom were now seeing a chance of doing the Queen in *Hamlet* or whatever: 'You take it (Secretaryship of State) Adlai, you'd be much better than I.' 'Oh no,' comes the reply, 'you'd be much better Chester.' 'Oh I couldn't, why not *you* David,' etc., etc.

I feel rather sorry now to be leaving New York, as one does get used to the tempo and atmosphere of the city, though its ugliness and its inconveniences still irritate me. I'd like to stay in America too, to see what Kennedy will do in his first months in office. However, it will be fun to get back to Europe. Also, I am frightened that the day will come when I get used to America so much that I will be willing to spend the rest of my life here—and I think that would be quite wrong. Not because I disapprove of America, but because I want to live in Europe and feel I can contribute something to that continent which I cannot in this one.

On Sunday I went to Philadelphia and saw the museum there: It has some magnificent things, including a splendid crucifixion by Roger van der Weyden, which is one of the finest 15th-century pictures I know. Also a lovely Van Eyck. How meticulous these Flemish painters were, and yet they managed to incorporate on a small scale such a vast variety of observations and pictorial inventions. The Van der Weyden, however, is very big and monumental, with only three figures, almost life-size—Christ, the Virgin and Saint John— in an unusual composition. All the meticulousness has been expanded to make every fold, every angle and corner have a dramatic significance: the red cloths behind Christ and behind the Virgin, hanging from a plain grey wall, are moving very slightly. The painter has shown us all the folds which the cloth received while still lying in some coffer, so it bulges and waves sufficiently for us to know there is a slight breeze in this scene of tragedy.

Naturally Bernard Berenson had great hopes for a 'humanized mankind'—I am turning suddenly to your letter—he was very much the child of late 19th-century progressive humanism, the same movement that produced hopeful socialism, the Webbs, reform, etc. I am sorry to hear that you have no such hopes—or less. It makes you seem a little cynical, though I know you are not. I certainly don't have the same hopes as BB had and I definitely dislike his view on aesthetics, which I encountered in his awful book on Caravaggio, and when I glanced at *Aesthetics and History*, the title alone made me dislike him. He was more concerned with saying things in a clever-sounding way than in a way which had any solid meaning. If one compares his later views with his earlier historical insight—as in his book on *Lorenzo Lotto*, or that on *Italian painters of the Renaissance*—one can see how his intelligence, at least on paper, had turned from the contemplation of art, to the contemplation of the study of art, from the enjoyment to the self-conscious display of it, which is a pity. In his conversation of course he must have been brilliant, and I am very fond of his war diaries—*Rumour and Reflection*. I went to his house many times when I was in Florence in the spring of 1954, but he was away and so I never met him.

TO HIS FATHER   *215, East 25th Street*
25 November 1960   *New York*

Yesterday was Thanksgiving, which I spent at the S'bergs. I gave Ben a drawing I bought a long time ago, it may be 16th-century Florentine, about 1570 or so, with a certain touch of Salviati about it. I had it very nicely framed and it looks well. Ben was quite touched but thought at first I had got it from you. I was at pains to point out I had found it here. We ate a great deal, which is quite as it should be—including yams, or sweet potatoes as they call them here, of which I am really very fond, and pumpkin pie which is ghastly, but Mrs S. said the chef had succeeded in making it taste of nothing, so it had become quite bearable. I like the word yams because every form of Robinson Crusoe or Treasure Island always described them and this gives you a feeling of the adventurers.

Your very nice birthday letters arrived today, for which many thanks. I had a very good weekend in Washington, seeing all the fine pictures, and feeling slightly sorry for you that you weren't there to see them too. It [the National Gallery] is really a magnificent collection, especially when one considers that most of it was acquired between 1920 and 1940—no one, not even Mellon and Kress, could afford those pictures today. Really it is also a memorial to Duveen and BB, whose taste is also seen in the excellent selection of the Italian pictures. So many Bellinis, including of course the *Feast of the Gods* and the *Flight into Egypt*, and many other extraordinary things. The Lottos are especially handsome, and the portraits by Florentines and Venetians uniformly splendid. Fifteen or so Rembrandts and four Vermeers, three or four Velasquez, etc. make up the 17th-century part, and the very best Genovese portraits of Van Dyck. Rubens is only represented by good sketches, but that is the only serious omission. And then dozens of Impressionists and a magnificent Picasso, *Les Saltimbanques*, which is probably the best picture painted in this century. The Matisses are there in large quantities, but I don't like them, and the Braques are entertaining, but not really very exciting except for one lovely vase of flowers. The lighting is not always good, nor do I like the over-grand layout and the fountains, but there are plenty of seats, which is a relief in such a vast place. Two lovely Giorgiones are perhaps the greatest jewels in the collection, with the Bellinis and the Raphaels (5). But it would be impossible to isolate anything in particular.

Ben said it was a pity that I didn't go to Washington a month later—'My friends of my political persuasion will all be there then.' When Alistair [Cooke] asked him if he'd get anything himself, he said: 'Oh no—I'm not nearly *conservative* enough for these young radicals.'

Just before Christmas John met his parents in Paris and they travelled together to Madrid and other places in Spain. John then retired to Perridge House in Somerset to write a novel. He finished it at the end of 1961 and began looking for a job.

TO ARCADI NEBOLSINE   *c/o Marthe de La Rochefoucauld*
7 January 1961   *Paris*

I am overwhelmed by the familiarity of everything, even of France and Spain, which after all are not my home countries. However, I am gradually coming to my senses and am deciding on my future, trying not to feel like a man who has been to the moon, only to come home to find everybody exactly the same, nothing changed, and no one in the least surprised to see him again. I found my parents much the same as ever—*they*, you will be pleased to hear, found me neither handsomer nor much changed otherwise, quite cheerful and so on. But when I am with them I feel as if I was still fifteen years old in some ways, and behave and think childishly. They don't realize that quite, and think it is just me, and act accordingly. They are still trying to form me, but it is too late for them to try to do so. Of course they are fun to be with in many ways, and we had a very good time in Spain and here.

Madrid, and the Spain we saw generally, has got much better than in 1955, though the poverty in the villages is incredible as is the backwardness of everything. However, whatever has been arranged for the tourists is luxurious in the extreme, and the Palace Hotel was more comfortable than even the Palais Sonnenberg. The Prado is magnificent, in some ways the best museum in the world for old masters. The Titians are astonishing, the Rubens and Van Dycks among the best, and endless in quantity, and it is here that Velasquez emerges as the superior genius which he is. He manages to invest the objective realism of which he is the sole master—the Impressionists are much more self-conscious—with immense humanity, so that *Las Meninas* has given permanent life, as a novel might do, to a group of children and to himself, and even to a dog, which lies in front of the picture. Then of course there is the one and only modern painter there has ever been—Goya. Modern because his outlook is so like some 20th-century humanist's, and the only one because what he observes in people and paints is essential and never dates at all: moderns always do. I think you'd enjoy both the cartoons for the tapestries, and the ceiling in the glorietta of the *Assumption* on the edge of town, both of which are generally lighthearted and youthful, as well as the wild fancies and hallucinations of his last years, and the terrifying drawings of the people he observed. A friend of a friend took us to the flat of the Duchess of Xuesca to show us the magnificent portrait of her ancestor, the Duchess of Chinchòn. Goya shows her sitting in a chair looking very irritated, with a very slight touch of amusement too. She is absolutely alive, and is a mixture of Rachel [Rodd] and your sister in appearance with fuzzy red hair. Very pretty.

We also went to Córdoba, whose cathedral I find the most interesting piece of architecture in Spain. Outside it looks like nothing, but inside it is an amazing forest of columns, the remains of a great mosque built in four parts, with (unfortunately) a very tedious 1530 church stuck in the middle, built against Charles V's advice. The Mahommedans had a sanctum on one side with a rococo shell of a most realistic kind—made of one vast piece of white marble—as a dome, built in the 10th (!) century. The doors are surrounded by a frieze of mosaic made to Moslem design by Byzantines, of remarkable invention and finesse. You would like the endless pattern of the columns, which are usually Roman ones found in the district with old Roman capitals, or copies by Moors. The moors apparently had the same attitude to Roman remains as the Christians elsewhere.

All this reads like Baedeker—it is very difficult to be entertaining about Spain, because what is good is very good indeed and serious, and what is bad is sad or dull, which is worse. Back in Madrid I was unable to leave on Wednesday morning as there is a strike of Air France and I spent the day with a Spanish lady and an English friend of my family's visiting Alcalà, where the University building has a very grand façade, but crazy as so much Spanish art is. We went on to see a town set in a splendid countryside called Pastarna, which has a fine castle where the Princess of Eboli was shut up for twenty years to teach her a lesson for being beautiful and passionate, and tried to see some tapestries there, but they were inaccessible. Then on to a nearby village with a spectacular ruined castle above the Tagus with the greenish river sliding past below and in the distance a vast sunset with clouds every shade of baroque gold, against blue and black and red, so that it was quite possible to imagine a putto or two, and perhaps a strong brown and pink body from Tiepolo. A shepherd of about twenty showed us round, and when we asked him if people often came to see this fine place, he answered: 'Oh yes, often. A year and a half ago there were two cars here.' He was very proud of his twenty sheep, which, he told us, made him the richest man in the village. After that we felt there was no need to tip him.

TO HILDA AND BEN SONNENBERG   *31, Carlton Hill*
12 January 1961   *London NW8*

Everyone wants to know what I thought of the US, and what the new president is like—they really know nothing about either—and of course I can give them a lot of shocks by expressing wholehearted approval or not, sounding like an angry young man about the 'South'. Just as you predicted I have found out how much I liked and enjoyed America and was interested in it, after I got back here.

   I am not sure I feel quite like living in England yet, which will make you laugh, because of course you'll say I am trying to escape my family. That isn't quite it—it is more because there is a certain stimulation in foreign-ness which I like at the moment, and which gets one used to being independent.

How deeply indebted I feel to you for all your kindnesses—and your patience—over the last year and how tremendously I enjoyed your hospitality at all times. I think it is one of the best things about my stay in America that I had the opportunity of occasionally sharing in your family life—it gave a unity and solidity to the whole of my time over there. I am old enough to know that this is a very rare privilege and thank you for it again.

TO ARCADI NEBOLSINE   *Perridge House*
4 *February 1961*   *Pilton*
                                                           Somerset

As you can see from my address I am in the country now, and have been here for a week and a half. Although it's still winter I am charmed by it all, the house itself, the garden, the view, the trees and the neighbourhood. In the mornings hundreds of birds squeak rather well—even to my ear which is not in tune with bird-song generally—and owls are hooting in the dark at this moment. There are snowdrops everywhere, and even some primroses in the woods. In the glasshouses a gardener pots plants, and the under-gardener, a hefty lad from the army with a very handsome face, turns dark brown clods. The country round here is really country—not the suburban imitation provided by Long Island—with green valleys and ridges in which I walk, and one encounters neither houses nor people, let alone the endless traffic round Easthampton. Wells of course has a very fine cathedral, and Bath is an overwhelmingly grand city: I was very impressed by it, and ate very well in the Hole-in-the-Wall when I spent a day there earlier this week. I think Mr S. should get himself a house in the Circus and lend it to me for six months of the year, and you would come and stay, and write your Proustian memoir, which I know will begin very soon.

On Saturday we had lunch with the Hobhouses in their pretty house [Hadspen House], overlooking a park with a very grand avenue of trees. Imagine planting such an avenue, about forty yards wide, each tree carefully spaced so that it could grow to its maximum grandeur, the whole rising up a gentle slope for about half a mile, with only the Western sky at its climax, filled in the evenings with the gloriette provided by the sun— imagine planting it, and knowing that it will only be at its best for your children or grandchildren: how not to be jealous of the future when doing it? Over lunch in the Adam dining-room with white, pale green, dark green stucco-work and portraits of ancestors—Hobhouse the friend of Byron, Hobhouse the spendthrift, Hobhouse the Liberal MP, etc.— there were discussions on capital punishment, my mother and I and the younger generation against, the old couple for, on *religious* eye-for-an-eye grounds: it was all very English, full of anecdotage, remnants of the past, and even intimations of the future, in the shape of a small baby, the child of my friends of the younger generation. I am amazed already at the generation that has babies—it takes some getting used to, don't you think?

I had forgotten the heavy feeling of responsibility which hangs over England: Perhaps it is the socialists that have taught us this—but we seem to feel we owe the world something, that Africa, India, Asia, etc. are our concern. Americans have paid a lot towards all those but they are unconcerned with them, and I think that is why Eisenhower had so little success abroad. *Der Bube im weissen Häuschen* seems to me to be rectifying that with astonishing speed. He [Kennedy] has made a great impression—let's hope he keeps it up. His wife by the way is hanging Calmann drawings on her walls—my father had a couple of very nice letters from her. ('My address is The White House, 1600, Pennsylvania Avenue, etc. And if you have some good drawings in the future, though I know I am not an important client, I do hope you won't forget me.' Or words to that effect. *C'est charmant n'est-ce-pas?*)

TO RICHIE HERTZ   *Perridge House*
19 February 1961   *Pilton*

I have been reading Keats's letters: you must read them if you have not yet done so, though I am sure you have. They are magnificent—they make me realize that one is only a poor pedlar in words by the side of this department store of ideas and spontaneity. I wish it were possible in writing my book to achieve that much liveliness even at the risk of not writing the most stylish prose. Because his letters live—and though I have made a few brave attempts at letter-writing, and have a few passages in my book so far that will bear reading, his prose talks to me of all the living, while I can only talk most of the time of what is living in my head, but it doesn't seem to get an existence really independent of *me*. I don't know whether you follow this: but what I mean is that the best writing manages to reflect all forms of life, not just that of the author. There are good artists who have given the best of themselves, but there are better ones who have given the best of mankind. Compare in music Mozart and Brahms. Mozart is obviously of the second category—he is all of human experience in the fullness of its glory. Brahms is a great composer naturally, but it is always Brahms and never all of us. He was too self-conscious, I suppose, and one is constantly reminded of the 19th century, of the gloom of its rooms and the heaviness of the curtains and the seriousness of his purpose. Mozart's purpose may or may not have been serious—but he sings of man not just of Mozart. I hope this is not too silly.

This week an African musical is starting in London called *King Kong*, which I expect I'll see later; it had a great success in South Africa, where it played before mixed audiences, a great triumph. In any case, it being African, it's our duty to say it's splendid whether we like it or not: one has to give those people every kind of encouragement, especially as Macmillan, the old stick-in-the-mud, has made a disastrous bungle out of Rhodesia and we'll have another Congo there in no time. This will be the end of the period of people saying: 'Look at Britain—the peaceful development of Africa is the work of her genius.' Instead [they will say], 'Look at the Conservative government standing in terror before a few White settlers threatening a 1776.' In politics what England needs badly is a Democratic party as in power now in the US, with the courage to annoy a few people and the ability to dramatise its actions in the light of some ideological principles, which however badly put are sufficiently lively to make people say 'give them a chance'. Here we have an ideology of 'Let sleeping dogs lie', and if they growl and bark and even bite just pat them on the head kindly but show them the stick with the other hand.

TO ARCADI NEBOLSINE   *Perridge House*
10 March 1961   *Pilton*

[I made] a trip to London to see Benjamin Britten's new opera, *A Midsummer Night's Dream*, and *Fidelio*. The first was fairly good, but did not have the fullness I require of operatic music. I think it would be better in a smaller place than the Opera House, in which even grand opera is cut down to size. *Fidelio* was the best performance of it I have ever heard—really overwhelmingly moving.

The only mistake was a bad Pizarro, and one unavoidable thing in that the orchestra did not have enough strings, violins in particular. There simply isn't room for both an adequate wind section and strings, so they have of course to sacrifice the violins. Otherwise even you might have been impressed. Especially as they did not make the Met mistake of taking it

137

fast. It was a measured Beethoven performance, the last scene coming into its own as a sort of musical apotheosis of the characters and story, Klemperer getting remarkable clarity out of that jumble of voices and chorus, so that the melodic lines were each of them distinguishable. The set [by John Piper] was a bit wobbly which made Jeremy Lemmon and me giggle, but one was awe-inspired the rest of the time. As for Sena Jurinac, she shot up to *Ich bin sein Weib* with marvellous ease, and sang her big scene *Abscheulicher*, etc., with visible, but not audible, effort and, amazing to believe, with accuracy. Having jumped about on the octaves she finally leapt onto the last words *Die Liebe* and held them for all their required beats, unlike my record, where the Mödl having indicated that she could still get up there, switches off at once. John Vickers did an even better Florestan than the one he did for us in New York. Only Pizarro was bad—a great piece in ham singing and acting by Hans Hotter, a ghastly German monster, who wore boots and frogging on his tights that made him look like a circus trainer. At the end Klemperer appeared with his stick, 75 years old at least—my mother heard him first in about 1920 in Hamburg. His Beethoven is a heavy one, lacking some of the staccato that Furtwängler has on a record, but it was a moving, off-the-feet-sweeping occasion. I cried during the prisoners' scene, and again during the trio *Euch werde Lohn . . .* The mise-en-scène was terrific. *Un jour* you must come to London at this time of the year and hear opera—it is such a marvellous place to hear it, and they can do things well occasionally.

Last night I listened to Chopin's Barcarolle on the wireless —it was modestly well played—but a sympathetic piece of music. Then I played Schubert's Heine songs on a record— *Der Doppelgänger* and others. They are the quintessence, as my father said, of romantic music, but they have a solid core, I think. Poor Schubert, he was to die three months later. I think it would have been better to have died three days later—in the way of a swan song—and not to know, as he had to, that he was a genius. But of course he knew it already: all those

138

geniuses regretted dying young, I think. They did not have the confidence that Bach had of knowing that he had done all that was humanly possible to do.

Nobody is *in* my novel by the way. I find the hardest task really is to set the imagination free from one's experience: to write well is to imagine the people and the situations—at least in my case—and not to record what I know exactly, but to make a fruit salad of my knowledge. One has to use one's friends and knowledge as a *point d'appui* for writing—but only as that—and then *il faut sauter au delà du connu*. How we would have liked Keats, had we known him. But he would not have liked us. He was very *difficile* I think, and I am sure would have found us too sophisticated. He genuinely liked simplicity—he did not think it simply picturesque as we do.

TO ARCADI NEBOLSINE   *Perridge House*
21 March 1961   *Pilton*

My friend Bill Anderson read my novel—what's written of it—and liked it enthusiastically, which is encouraging, though he is always encouraging to me in a way, simply because he *understands* what I try to say, which some people of course don't. Anthony Blond, the publisher, thought it a bit long-winded and old-fashioned, but liked it. Thank God it's old-fashioned. There's nothing about social conditions in it except so far as it makes a part of the story—I don't provide a story to comment on social life, but on human beings. That's the difference between modern English stories and the old ones. People as part of the community have taken over from people as people. Tolstoy's characters could live anywhere and still be convincing, and even in social novels like *Vanity Fair*, the characters are the part we remember. Nowadays one remembers nothing but a vague idea of the story, perhaps one character and that's all.

I wish you'd write your book of the century soon. Then you

could afford to live over here and entertain brilliantly. However, I'll soon be a published writer—says he with more optimism than occasion for it—and we can set up a colony for brilliant people in—where? An island in the Aegean? The Tuscan Hills? Paris? No—not England I'm afraid. That's too near the knuckle. One has to make oneself sought after, then people will come. Like Frederick or Catherine. Which of us is which?

TO GRÄFIN CARMEN VON FINCKENSTEIN   *Perridge House*
(HIS AUNT)   *Pilton*
6 April 1961

I was in Ireland for the Easter weekend where I stayed with my friends the O'Neills. The family became Protestants in the 16th century when the eldest son of the chieftain was taken away by Elizabeth and sent to Eton to be turned into a loyal subject. His accounts for one of his terms there are kept framed in the library. We also went over to the Earl of Antrim's castle at Glenarm. After dinner there were charades. In one of the words we did there was the syllable 'pole'—and we acted the scene in the Antarctic when Captain Oates, who was dying, left Scott's tent so that the others might have enough to eat. Lord A. said afterwards: 'It surprised me that you performed that story—everybody knows of course that Oates did not leave the tent but *was eaten by the others*. In fact Scott says later in the journal that so-and-so died because he couldn't eat *Oates*. In the navy when a very good piece of meat is served it's referred to as Oates' toe.' He went on to describe how people used to eat each other during the war, etc. An Irish conversation . . .

America has gradually subsided into the past and I no longer feel as if I really had only left yesterday, though it begins to fill me with a certain nostalgia. I like the new government very much, so far at any rate, and would like to be there to see what they are doing. For the first time in recent American history a group of *educated* people are running the government, as well as the power-hungry businessmen who were there before, and whom the educated in America have learnt to dislike. It is difficult to imagine the difference in attitude between the new crowd and the old ones; instead of conservative millionaires with a love of golf, the new president's friends are young active professors and journalists with a belief that they can change the world. It may lead to disillusionment, but at least it is alive. Kennedy himself is as tough as is possible, but he works hard and has many ideas—I respect that. Finally he has respect for history and for people who aren't American, and that is attractive too.

TO ARCADI NEBOLSINE   *Perridge House*
26 June 1961   *Pilton*

I saw *The Misfits* the other day which is very Arthur Millerish and problematic and destructive of the American Dream, but has its moments, *and* is of course very well made. Imagine my surprise when I saw Clark Gable kissing a woman good-bye who was none other than Mrs Ronnie Tree. Then I remembered Frankie Fitzgerald saying that her mother had kissed him good-bye in the film (coz she thought it would be such fun to have a part in 'Arthur's marvellous new film') and he had dropped dead two days later. What can have been on her lips?

Sonnenberg was over here for a few days and we had lunch together a few times. He is a strange and impulsive man: we went round the antique dealers' fair and he bought £4000 worth of stuff in two hours. The lunch afterwards was excellent. Then I took him to the Soane Museum. He dashed through, terribly anxious that he could not get someone to build him a thing like that in New York—but I pointed out that the reason why it is so successful is because Soane himself designed it.

I listened to Bach's *St John Passion* on the radio the other night—the Evangelist was sung by a really baroque German tenor with a high voice full of sobs and decorations and vibratos and tone effects that made it immensely dramatic. What a marvellous work—you should turn your eyes to Bach at last, he is full of surprises.

I am tired of typing and have to think about writing my novel later today, though I don't feel like it. Goethe in his *Conversations with Eckermann* says that young writers should steer clear of writing very large works since it requires too great an effort of perseverance from them, and wearies their creative faculties to too great a degree. He says then that this advice is always disregarded by the young writers and they go ahead and tire themselves out by trying things too large for their powers, and have to find out everything for themselves instead of listening to those like himself who have paved the way. But that's the point—no one does pave the way. Everything is started from one's own scratch.

TO ROBERT CUMMING   *Perridge House*
30 June 1961   *Pilton*

My novel which is *now* the length of most modern English novels is just over *half* done. Perhaps it is too large, but I want to complete it, and I think I have the energy, as long as no one stands over me and says by such and such a day. I want one of my characters to be tremendously ambitious and ready to get on in the world. But how does he achieve it? I haven't achieved it myself so how do I know? Here I must confess I have to invent madly and it sometimes proves unconvincing, to me at least. After all one has been in love—dare I admit it?—and has known this and that experience and sensation. But the making of money is a mystery to me. I know some people have done it (and there are rich people in the book), and some people are doing it (and there are some of them)—but getting started? I

142

hope my character makes some by the end of the chapter.

I have felt a bit more enthusiastic about it all today than for quite some time. One is after all like the sea and the shore: some days one can pound away and there is water and spray far inland, and the rest of the time there is just lap-lap-lap.

I went to stay with Antony Grant at Whitsun and saw his father's magnificent Watteau: a nude Zephyr crowns a nude Flora with roses. I was enraptured by both of them in a heady classical frenzy of appreciation. Such a large picture too.*

The new President [Kennedy] whom I admired at first so much is getting bogged down by the size of the problems— but he may yet do something: he may turn from his present position of puzzled and dazzling do-gooder with badly placed shots in the dark, to a firmer position of getting a *few* things done. But the struggle most of the time is the one *inside* America and that's what so few people realize here. Half the time he has to be so dramatic in the hope of capturing the wayward American public, who don't think life can be improved. If he was prepared to let the rest of the world go hang he might be able to bring about that much desired transformation of the present lack of system into a quasi-welfare state (which is what must happen in the States gradually, as it is happening everywhere else)—but how can he settle peace abroad, *and* education, medicine, labour, social services, housing, the race problem and states rights at home as well? One almost begins to feel sorry for him—and wishes one could help. Isn't there an agency for which *you* could work after the army's over? The education department—but perhaps you've thought of that already.

Later on in my novel there is going to be a passage in which someone attacks America—there'll be no reply, really except for another character thinking: 'And yet, and yet, and yet . . .' The problems are infinite but fascinating, and distance from them doesn't make them less so. The problems are clear and the issues are blandly stated, but here they are much more confused and nobody knows quite what next: Africa, the

* It was later burnt out of spite by a gardener.

Common Market, the economy, the public schools—all the symptoms of getting older. But I haven't lost faith in Europe quite yet.

It is twenty to one and I am falling asleep. I wish I could see you for a long talk—and we could go for a walk in the moonlight. The heat has been very great for England—81 degrees—and it has barely rained at all in the last two months. The ground is much too dry and lots of flowers simply haven't appeared. But we have some good fruit. Do you remember our moonlit walk at Davidson—I did enjoy my visit there, in spite of losing at croquet—and our Wagnerian visit to the top of Grandfather Mountain?

TO BEN SONNENBERG   *Perridge House*
11 July 1961   *Pilton*

Thank you very much for your letter to Nicholas Nabokov.★ It was really very kind of you to send it to me immediately, and I understand from friends that other voices are being added to the chorus, so that the poor man must soon be thinking that he is going to have a visit from St Augustine or some other father of the church, rather than an unknown writer from the depths of Hardy's Wessex. I was also much taken aback by all the kind things you managed to say—if one were permitted to read nothing but letters of recommendation it would put priests and psychiatrists out of business altogether I should think.

All eyes and ears are turned to Paris where John Osborne's latest play† is being performed at the Palais de Chaillet. The critics have been very careful with it, not liking to say that it isn't to their taste because they think he needs encouragement —but also not liking to say that it really rises above the derivative. However, what they have missed is something

★ Secretary General of the Council for Cultural Freedom.
† *Luther.*

144

very new and startling: The German Wave. It is everywhere: even in my own work—both my plays and part of my novel are set in the German-speaking part of Europe. There are something like three plays about Germany running in London at the moment. People talk about nothing but Adenauer, and should we join his common market. The German 'decade of genius' in this century (1920s) is becoming more and more interesting: Brecht, Kurt Weil, Dadaism, Expressionism and so on and so on. The extraordinary duality of one's approach to Germany is of course finally brought home by the Eichmann trial. Has this movement touched New York yet? I am not sure I really like it.

TO ANTHONY GRIGG   *Perridge House*
12 *August 1961*   *Pilton*

I have thought about what you said about David's novel* last Sunday, and what you said about discipline in writing—and I think you are quite right, and that it is a virtue in his writing. But in order to make discipline really valuable you have to be clear about why you are using it: it is to intensify the quality of the work, not to cut it down to the bare bones, and there is *au fond* as much discipline required in expressing exuberance or the variety of life as there is in a distilled piece of social observation such as David's book. I myself think that social observation is the antithesis of art—it is harder to combine the two than people realize, while it is easy enough to observe *trends* in people or manners. David's people don't seem to me to be people but figurines playing in an artificial world. He has not merely selected the particular social field he wishes to observe, he has abstracted it into something dead and lifeless, hence unconvincing. This is discipline defeating its own ends.

To look at it in more general terms and to disregard David's work for a moment: I am sure in the long run it is better for a

* *Owls and Satyrs* by David Pryce-Jones.

writer, especially a young one, to put unnecessary demonstrations of feeling in his work, to overload it with characterization, to seem to be pumping his heroes with life, rather than the opposite. To err on the side of *life* in any artistic attempt is to show a proper respect for the things which in the main are the proper subject for art: the variety and largeness of the world, and the infinite number of experiences, pleasant and unpleasant, which it is possible to know. Discipline is needed to clarify and intensify this re-creation of experience, and in so far as David has used it he shows that he wants to write something *literary* and not simply journalistic, and though I have my doubts about how far he has succeeded in that, I think you are quite right in pointing out the attempt and praising it.

Well—I have no idea how my own efforts will seem to fulfil any of the aesthetic rules I lay down above, or how far those rules are interesting to you. I just wanted to say that I enjoyed our conversation and that it started lots of hares in my mind.

TO BEN SONNENBERG   *31, Carlton Hill*
23 October 1961   *London NW8*

Thank you for your letter, and the magnificent present of the book on Hearst,* which I have been reading with very much enjoyment. I must apologize for not answering sooner, but I wanted to let you know the outcome of my visit to the Congress for Cultural Liberties (I think that has a more genuine ring about it than the real title) and the negotiations dragged on rather longer than expected. And I'm afraid with a negative result.

In the meantime I am trying another tack which is to enter the European Economic Commission in Brussels which, while it will pay me practically nothing to start with, does have a much more interesting future in the long run, especially if Great Britain joins. It will mean living in Brussels, which is

* *Citizen Hearst* by W. A. Swanberg, 1961.

146

not unlike Jersey City in intellectual atmosphere, or maybe Newark, but like those places it is not far from the real centres. Perhaps you will see me yet as the Mongi Slim* of Europe!

Hearst's life makes a fascinating book—though it's a pity the author has so little sense of the romance of the thing. With all that wonderful material who could make a book dull? But the writing does not rise sufficiently to the level of the subject —and it seems to me that he has simply put down his notes. I don't think there was a more exciting era in American history than the period of Hearst's life: it was rough and even cruel at times, but in the modern America of Beverly Hills and Park Avenue glass-boxes the tremendous vitality and wildness of the earlier period has gone. It certainly touches the imagination—and the sentimentality of today as compared to the brain of yesterday. One need only compare Salinger with Nathanael West! You see the book has certainly been very stimulating for me to read. As for Hearst himself, I feel quite relieved he's not alive today. He would probably explode an atom bomb for his paper to have something to write about.

Paris in the autumn was splendid to look at and I wandered through the oldest part of the city, a sort of East End, made up of the dilapidated palaces of the nobility of the 16th and 17th centuries. They lived in great castles in the midst of the city. Now many of them are tenements or full of tumble-down shady offices and little factories of artisans. I would walk into a courtyard and would find my way to the staircase which would have, more often than not, marvellous old iron-work balustrades of a quality that is almost impossible to find nowadays. I tried rather wickedly to break off a fine iron sphinx (date 1700) at the bottom of one staircase but my conscience got the better of me. Perhaps one day someone will rescue the house and take pleasure in the sphinx. I also paid a visit to a palace which is still in working order—Alain de Rothschild's. His daughter Beatrice is a tremendous beauty

* In 1961 he was Tunisian Ambassador to the United Nations and President of the General Assembly. A leading figure in the fight for the independence of all African countries.

147

and very charming, and asked me to lunch and to a party one evening, which was made up entirely of members of the family. The atmosphere was thick, and rather splendid, but curiously lacking in gaiety I thought. Still the pictures weren't bad at all—and there were some wonderful objects. Fortunately the house has hardly been changed since 1880, so that it brought back the feeling of those palmy days. I slightly annoyed, or perhaps only startled, Baron Alain when I knew as much about his collection as he did—that is to say I contradicted him when he said that his two big Rembrandt portraits looked like Van Dyck. Fortunately they look exactly like Rembrandt.

TO JOHN MAUTNER   *31, Carlton Hill*
1 November 1961   *London NW8*

I am feeling terribly stale here in London. Nothing seems to be happening that I like, and I have no money, no place of my own. These periods pass, but it's a nuisance having to wait for news from prospective employers or publishers. It makes me feel horribly dependent on others. Sometimes I think it would be nice to disappear to a Greek island for the next twenty years, and then ambition raises its ugly head. What does ambition boil down to? That everyone should recognize the exceptional virtues one has. In some ways [ambition is] as necessary as sex. But you don't want to hear about my temporary blues (I'll be independently blue). I just opened a book on Heine in which the author quotes on the front page: 'Der Ernst tritt um so gewaltiger hervor, wenn der Spass ihn angekündigt.' Der Spass—wie gerne fände ich ihn wieder.* At the moment *Der Ernst* is beckoning to me with superficial tedious gestures.

* 'Seriousness has a more powerful effect if mirth precedes it.' Mirth—how much I would like it again.

You say your life has been only a few short stories. I can't imagine life being anything else. Perhaps when one is fifty some pattern emerges. Then one knows the tastes that are going to remain with one for always. But we are still, thank God, in a state of flux. I don't mind this slightly unformed being I still am. There is still a little to explore. If one was young and had energy *and* nothing to explore, and knew all the patterns, restlessness would be unbearable, don't you think? At the moment I'm not exploring, just living over patterns and acquaintances I know. I would welcome them more if they were things I turned to for comfort or relaxation or even inspiration, rather than distraction. Do you think when we are fifty it will be all like that? I suppose not, if we make sure that we find new interests or occupations—as my parents have done with their house.

Oxford is really full of sentimental attractions and associations and intrinsic beauties. Here I knew so-and-so, there stood Robert when photographed, there I entertained you for the first time, and here, brilliantly white, the part of Christ Church library that has been cleaned, gleams at me, full of revelations of architecture that I had not known before. The building is being tremendously improved by the clean and new stone: such delicate windows within the massive stone pilasters that flank them. And the smell of Oxford in the autumn: dank leaves and the gasworks, and the slightly cold air—it reminded me of my first term in Meadow Buildings and of my last autumn when I would plod somewhat sadly to Norham Road. '*Les premières fleurs qu'elles sont parfumées.*'

You ask me what I think of the world after my Miltonic retreat in Perridge. I'm pleased to see more faces than I did there. Often there were none. And as for the wide wide world it seems to me to be taking on the shape of a walnut: shrunk and disfigured and soon to be gnashed by some absurd self-made giant. And we will be part of the edible part. I'd like to

149

see you now and talk, and spend a few weeks near the Mediterranean. That is after all where I feel most at home.

I saw *The Lamb of God* by Van Eyck at Ghent, *quelle merveille*. I was amazed how absorbing I found it. At first it is just a large Flemish picture—then when at last you think you have seen as much as you can, you discover an hour and a half has gone by. So many details, so many colours, so many discoveries to be made by going up close, or moving further away. And the clouds! Little silver-golden and white wisps in a pure blue sky, drifting away into the blue; you *feel* the floating. I compared it mentally with the heroic work of Raphael in the Vatican—the *Disputà*—which is so much larger, so much less intimate, and obviously so much less Gothic. Of course I admire the Raphael, and love it, but it is a drama, whereas this has a richness and a contemplative quality that a big fresco can hardly have, although it is a big picture. In oil so many details are permitted—flowers and hands and hats and wings of many colours—that a fresco can't have because it isn't technically possible. And of course the colours themselves are unsurpassed.

I saw Bill Anderson today, who was as nice and pleasant as always. He is really a person of great humanity and expansiveness under his nervous exterior. I envy his sanguine approach to life and his good humour, and his lack of conventional ambition. He is not deceived by the appearance of glamour into thinking that it is really worth having. I am. In fact, I am not sure it is even a deception—while he does not even think about it at all. I mean things like politics and influence and fame and society glory! I read *Martin Chuzzlewit*. I can heartily recommend it. It has dull passages, especially in the first fifty pages, and it has *long* passages one can dispense with because they seem irrelevant and the end is terribly drawn out, but everywhere there is life and humour, and his terrifyingly misanthropic view of the world, like some medieval moralist. With few exceptions Dickens thought mankind was made up of ghastly people, and they only get worse, never (or only rarely) better. In all that he paints such a big canvas of his own contemporary life, at the end one has got to know people one did not know before. That is what I'd like to have people feel after reading my book. (If they ever do.)

TO SHEILA LAFARGE   *31, Carlton Hill*
1 January 1962   *London NW8*

It is just after lunch, and you are getting up in New York—I wonder whether you're looking out onto the pink and white panorama we have here: snow and sunshine, a very London sight. Thank you for your letter with its wonderful whiff of Third Avenue and 50th Street, of big new buildings with shining fronts, of the many rat-races. You have hinted at it all and make me feel very nostalgic. Here *Luther* and *Becket* are still running to packed houses and one can't get into the *Cherry Orchard*, which is the best thing in town, with Gielgud *and* Ashcroft. It has suddenly occurred to me that Osborne is our native Anouilh, and that for the next thirty years, year-in, year-out, there will be something new by him! *Imaginez cela!* I have been Christmassing in the country, which included a visit to a Hunt Ball at a house called Fonthill—built by Lutyens* not Beckford. It was atrocious and fascinating, so

* In fact built by Detmar Blow in 1900.

151

much so that in a way I enjoyed it. Four hundred people, some in red coats, danced round to a band that could not play in tune, though it was good at deb-deb rhythm, and we all wobbled together getting hotter and hotter. But the strange part was that on the walls was a very fine collection of portraits—the marvellously sardonic one by Goya of Carlos III of Spain in hunting costume (a version of the one in the Prado) stared at us in an amused contemplation of the spectacle of second-rate folly, and Louis Treize by Philippe de Champaigne looked down on our sweaty imitation of courtly life. And there were many others: Cosimo de' Medici by Bronzino, and the blind Johnson by Reynolds etc., etc.—faces which are justly famous because they are so much more alive than those of most of the living. Puddings of boys with sometimes quite pretty girls danced and with them their parents, addled mirrors of their own future.

I have been reading David Garnett's autobiography,* indulging in a wonderful world of reminiscences—'night time is my time for just reminiscing'—in which the characters are all larger than life because we knew them from books and plays and pictures and collective memories. No one I know lives in such a wonderfully self-sufficient world as Garnett, the Stracheys, the Stephens, the Keynes, and the rest did. And they had done it for generations before Bloomsbury. I feel envious of that, because it gave them a *tone*, an accent of their own, which they could fall back on and revel in, and use as a basis from which to write and paint and whatever else they did. And then their belief in friendship was wonderfully strong; I would not have wanted to share their particular accent but I would like to find their insistence on human relations as important in my friends as it was to them. Friendship in its way should be as passionate as love, but nobody seems to have the time or the willingness to make time for it now. We are much too ambitious in our generation—at least in Europe. In America, it is true, that ambition of the

* *The Golden Echo*, 1954; *The Flower of the Forest*, 1955; *The Familiar Faces*, 1962.

modern kind has been going on for so long that it has become possible to react against it, and I think that you and some of your friends have managed to avoid it in its worst sense. But here it is rampageous, so to say, and I see many of my best friends curiously attracted to the worst aspects of the success-psychology. The essence of a group like the one Garnett describes (almost too gently in almost too much of a sunset light) is that rivalry is only on a group level—rivalry in conversation, or games, or play-reading, or jokes—but never for the prizes of money and fame which are regarded as the natural deserts of all your friends, and you hope that they will all get them. Whatever the drawbacks—and there were enough for some people like D. H. Lawrence to feel stifled in the mere presence of anyone from Bloomsbury—I think it was a fine background for love and friendship, and for their conscious cultivation.

While travelling in Greece John's parents had made friends with a Dutchman, Jaap van der Lee, Director for overseas associated countries in the European Community in Brussels. Asked if there would be an opening for John, he kindly arranged for an interview. In January 1962 John was engaged as a trainee and sent to Luxembourg where he worked under Mr Derek Prag.

TO RICHIE HERTZ   *Brussels*
20–22 January 1962

I have been reading (skipping) Schlesinger's *Crisis of the Old Order*. It has many fascinating moments and I was amazed how clearly he was able to re-create the events at the Democratic convention of '32—making a sort of historical pattern out of them. FDR doesn't emerge as a really forceful man: rather as the figurehead for a group—or groups—of liberals, who managed to inspire them to act. It seems to me that it isn't always necessary for a statesman to be a great initiator—certainly FDR liked to wait for events before he did something about the situation, or so it seems to me—but he must have the magnetism that makes other people, who are possibly more intelligent or more precise, or more experienced, or more idealistic, *act*. It is an indefinable quality of giving people confidence, of stirring them to action, of persuading them that action will do them good, which is so well illustrated here (1932) in the contrast between the well-meaning nonsensical Hoover and the not nearly so well-meaning, but much more vital FDR. He was alive to the issues of the time and if he was much more power-hungry than Hoover, he had the sort of magic that makes men work.

I do think this leadership problem is important because people so often think that leadership means continuous action and initiation from the leader. It means much more the driving on of people with brains and energy, who without leadership would be too cowardly, too shy, too lazy, too sceptical to do anything. Kennedy wants to do too much himself, often is a little careless about the things he really ought to do, and has sometimes wobbled in the way people do who are accustomed to being led by others. Really good rulers are the ones who have got the best people to serve them. I'm not sure about Kennedy in that respect.

TO BEN AND HILDA SONNENBERG   *Brussels*
26 January 1962

Once more I am in the land of clouds, rain and no driving tests. My future with the European community has now been arranged, and I shall be working in the operetta-land of Luxembourg from about the beginning of February. (February always seems to be the month in which I start things—shades of the *Wall Street Journal*!) I have already

154

planned a musical comedy (I hope you'll arrange it for me with Abe Burrows) called 'Call me Sir'—but seriously it has come as a surprise to have to go there. I have no idea what one does in the evenings in Luxembourg—I'm afraid the range is not quite so large as in London or New York. Still, the idea is that it will give me a start in the European Community—and it certainly has been a great triumph because a lot of resistance was made to employing an Englishman at this time. I shall be a sort of apprentice—a *stagiaire* as they call it—and the first English one. Then when GB joins the community who knows . . .

TO ARCADI NEBOLSINE   *31, Carlton Hill*
1 February 1962   *London NW8*

Brussels has more appalling buildings in it than any city in the world and I am going to take my camera with me next time and make a series of photographs of two sorts of things: first hideous ensembles—streets or buildings—secondly fantastic details, of which there are more in the shape of art nouveau iron-work balconies, unspeakable stained-glass windows, monstrous turrets and domes, and lunatic porches and carved window-frames, than you can imagine. They had a law that no two houses were to look the same in the same block, so they gave free vent to their imaginations—but they forgot that they were living in 1900–1930 and the results are grotesque.

TO ROBERT CUMMING   *31, Carlton Hill*
5 March 1962   *London NW8*

About three and a half weeks ago David Winn gave a large dinner of about eighteen people which went very well. A gathering of the clan you might say: apart from the fact that nearly all my friends have now married—sometimes each other, sometimes not—there was nothing unfamiliar. A few new girls. I found a very merry one, whom I like a lot called Henrietta Guinness. You'd like her—full of bounce and life, *and* pretty. I can't bear dull girls. One of the sad things of last year—and indeed of America, though there it was different, and was the result of my having too many preoccupations—is that I haven't been in love at all. In the country there was no one, and in London I have been too distracted, too annoyed with life. But I miss being in love—even though my recollections of it are pretty painful.

I've been reading *Our Mutual Friend*—an excellent book if ever there was one. One has to get into it, but after that it's easy enough. Of course it's easier to write a novel like that after the age of 36 or so—in ten years' time—than at 26, because one has to have had the experience of human motives that Dickens manages to put in, such a fantastic variety of them. And they are all motives to do with money, or love, or sudden, unexpected (because always in bad characters) human sympathy. The variety is in the way they are expressed, but the motives are the essential human ones. In my novel I have tried to make of aesthetic experience an essential human motive—but I think it is an exceptional motive really, interesting perhaps, but belonging to decadent literature, one might say, as opposed to the broad appreciation of man that Dickens, or Tolstoy went in for. Is this the basis of their readability?

Now I am reading *La Côte de Guermantes*: much easier than I remembered Proust. I realize how much indirectly I was influenced by him—he reinforced all the circumlocutions of one's literary approach—but I also find him wittier, gayer, and more full of warmth and enthusiasm, almost baroque in expression, than I did before. I enjoy reading him, which I didn't really when I read *Swann*. And the traces of Dickens are easily found: the long elaborate sentences of description—so very like those of the English writer.

156

Luxembourg is rather less exciting than I imagine Stoke-on-Trent to be and has never heard of *camp*. It is filled with the Luxembourgeois, who are a kind of Luxus-bourgeois, as their name would suggest, and are as ugly as the Belgians and have the manners of the Germans. The country around is pretty, but it rains most of the time and is very cold. I went to Trier—now Trier is something. Strasbourg too is magnificent, such food! And of course a marvellous city. Unfortunately, I had to spend most of my time listening to the European Parliamentarians gassing away in the E. Parliament. They were not very interesting, though the ambience had what was to me, at least, the novel atmosphere of bourgeois diplomacy—a whole lot of rather tired-looking middle-aged men talking in corridors. It sounds, I know, like a bad court-room-scene film, but it was a little more real and dotty than that. Somebody told me that the parliamentarians 'are quite human really, and talk about beer and women, just like we do, when one gets talking to them'. 'Just like we do' was an odd expression. I can't remember talking about beer in my life—and women—well woman perhaps, but I do hate so these generalities of gender—genderalities one might call them (pardon).

After Strasbourg I went to Paris. I learnt to twist which I must say is a dance invented for me. I'm the Nureyev of twist. We went to a place called Regine's—it was filled with royalty and Françoise Sagan. It was a long and curious evening. The Rochefoucaulds organized it very nicely, but I was a bit tired by the end of the weekend of so many smart French people, who were very friendly, but a tremendous effort. Sometimes I feel I just don't *want* to be smart any more (good song that would make: think up another line ... ending in bore perhaps).

I didn't manage to see the Teylers Museum [in Haarlem], but the Frans Hals I saw thoroughly. He was an extraordinarily original painter, which is something one would not have expected of a man who could be so cheap. But who—certainly not Velasquez—painted in that impressionistic manner before the 19th century? As Pascal [Ruys-Raquez] said (we met in Amsterdam), it is surprising people liked his style in the 17th century—it is so much pastiche and short-hand and different from anybody else. Manet has of course lifted even more from Hals than from Velasquez—and Manet has so many similar faults. I was very impressed by the *Governors of the Poor-house* —a most sinister picture.

Saturday evening I went back into Amsterdam, and wandered on the canal in that peculiar part of the city given over almost entirely to prostitution. There were quite a lot of people on either side of the canal, loitering and looking around like me. I stopped on one of the bridges—the sky was pink and blue, and the houses reflected a sort of gold light. The trees were just touched by a little green, the lead towers of various churches floated over the top of the buildings. The women, still relaxing before working hours began, sat at their wide-open windows sniffing the air, and from a couple of bridges away, where an organ was playing, a series of melancholy, pretty old tunes floated like a cloud of tangible nostalgia over the whole thing. It was quite miraculous.

You must be getting ready for Provincetown, if you haven't gone there already. I am sure the house is as brilliantly white as always, and all the furniture gleaming indoors. A very blue sky here made me think of it—but my view is rather different: a cherry tree, a telegraph pole and the back of a football stadium. I hope no budding Washington will come along and attack the tree as it is the only nice thing in this slightly sad perspective. I have been living here for just over a month, and find the work very interesting. That at least is a comfort. I write pieces about the various activities of the European Community for our British and American bulletins, and this gives me the chance of learning a lot about it. I am most impressed (rare for me, you will admit) that they manage to do so much. I can't say I am terribly inspired by Hallstein, or our other European leaders as personalities, but they work very hard which is rare in bureaucracies, I'm told. And it really may be possible that at the end of ten years or so we will have a kind of United States of Europe, at least in principle. The effect will be, at least that is the hope, a great resurgence of Europe, but I think that will only happen if the Common Market stops being so commercially minded and starts thinking about education as well.

Luxembourg as a place to live in badly needs Pearl Mesta.* She must have worked tremendously hard here to lead the kind of social life she was supposed to lead, because the city and its inhabitants are a little dumber than some blondes are supposed to be, without the usual compensations. Even the movies are bad: they are all cut to fit into an hour and a half—which can have some ludicrous effects. They are also heavily censored by the all-powerful archbishop.

For Easter I drove up to Amsterdam. I was *most* taken by the city and was amused by the fact that here one can see the origin of New York architecture—the tall houses with thick cornices along the top, the stoops. The character of New York owes much more to Dutch town architecture than to British.

* First woman ambassador of the US to Luxembourg.

The Common Market is a fascinating business, but it is going through a big crisis at the moment, like everything else in the Western Alliance, largely because of the strange policies of General de Gaulle. Or perhaps they are not so strange, but they are nationalistic in origin, anti-democratic in intent, and supported by some reasonable political and economic arguments. Muddled like everything else about *mon général*. However, before getting onto the CM about which I could now address fifty farmers' meetings a week without any difficulty, let alone fatuous anti-marketeers in Beaverbrook pay, let me dispose of the main cause of my letter. You will be amused to hear that I have begun a flirtation (mentally) with the Liberal Party. The reason for this sudden change is of course the fact they are successful; that was always what one was looking for and now it has happened. *But*, and it is a big but, for an opportunist politician like me, are they likely to keep going? Another thing which has drawn me to them is that unlike the Labour Party they have seen the point of Europe. Although I left GB a Labourite the inability of Gaitskell to see Europe as the proper goal of the socialists has completely disenchanted me. Instead of recognizing our political opportunities in Europe, which are opportunities simply because problems *do still exist*, they have been frightened. They are also afraid of splitting the party. This hesitation and lack of vision have put me thoroughly off Gaitskell, and now there is something else to turn to.

Would it be worth my while, do you think, to try to offer myself as a possible Liberal candidate? Or do you think it most unlikely that they would ever consider me suitable in the first place, or that I would ever be successful in the second? I can hear low chuckles over the breakfast table: so he thinks he ought to be a Liberal candidate, does he, after all the rude remarks he made about the Liberals? But it is hard to know where else to turn now—and I would like to start working in politics as soon as I get back home. Working here in the Common Market has shown me how necessary it is that one does something *oneself* and doesn't leave it all to people whom one criticises (justifiably), but to whom one can offer no alternative. The trouble with the Labour Party is that it is so dull; no less dull than the Tories. If the Liberals could cough up a Kennedy then they would become a real alternative to the voters. (He'd have enough money to get the party going too.) Anyway I am looking forward to hearing your reply to all this—sarcastic or not as the case may be.

TO HIS MOTHER   *8, rue Michel-Lentz*
24 May 1962   *Luxembourg*

There has been an enormous amount of work to do—I have been writing all day today about the Belgian Coal Directorate: the problem is interesting, even if writing about it is troublesome. And the labour costs in the Common Market which I have successfully put off until now must be settled tomorrow. I learn a lot from all this—it is rather like studying history, but it is all happening *now*. It would be splendid in some ways to get a job in London as it would get me on a permanent basis, but of course it would limit the Continental side of my activities, just as I will be beginning to get used to life on the Continent. The fact that I worked in America has made an enormous amount of difference, and all the things I saw there through the Sonnenbergs and by myself. At the end of six months here the fact of being familiar with two continents should be of use in finding any kind of job I may want, especially as Derek [Prag] takes a lot of trouble in teaching me things and putting me right: I have had a lot of luck in having someone so interested and friendly as a boss, even if I don't always agree with all his opinions and his endless corrections of my work. I certainly find that my range of interests is much wider than most people's—and the nice

161

thing about the Prags is that they think that is an advantage and not a disadvantage, as some people have done—the *Wall Street Journal* for instance.

Did I write that the Sunday before last I went to Metz? A very grand but slightly cold cathedral with marvellous 16th-century glass. I was most impressed. It is very florid in colour and design, but amusing and original. A sort of Lorraine Mabuse, but more dramatic. The town is nothing—and the Germans added a lot of unnecessary gothic porches and sculpture to the outside of the cathedral, including the prophet Daniel with the face of Kaiser Wilhelm. The Nazis shaved off the moustache.

TO NICHOLAS AND ROSE DEAKIN *8, rue Michel-Lentz*
29/30 May 1962 *Luxembourg*

You ask a lot of questions about the Common Market and I could give you pages and pages of it—if you wanted them— fortunately (for you) I don't feel called upon to that extent. I do think GB will join in the end, but it may take longer than Heath, etc. hoped, and than the pro-British group here hoped. More detailed work is necessary if the so-called Commonwealth safeguards are to be at all workable. Also, De Gaulle (that idiot) has not made up his mind if he wants to be Louis XIV or live in the 20th century. He is universally mocked on the continent, and I suspect that most French politicians are heartily sick of him too. But one mustn't take French toughness in negotiations too seriously—because, for instance, in 1957 they prevaricated right up to the last minute just to see how far they could push their associates, and then they did after all sign the treaty, and since then, with much squeaking, have obeyed it. (But everybody has squeaked at some point.) The French believe as a matter of principle that negotiations don't mean finding a good basis for agreement:

they believe negotiations are a business of haggling advantages against advantages—and you can be as brutal as you like. Hence hints about the bomb, defence, political unity, etc., all to see if a) they can at least get the position among their Common Market colleagues they have hoped for all the time —i.e. exactly the position of Louis XIV; and b) they can force the British to swallow the worst terms of entry. Fortunately, the other members of the Community see negotiations in a slightly more modern and sensible light. After all CM negotiations are generally a form of inter-departmental planning. The ministries of transport getting together, or the ministries of agriculture, and they can't be treated like fights between great powers anxious to exchange Heligoland against Zanzibar or the like. De Gaulle is a good European in that he thinks that Europe needs to express its unity if it is really to be a political factor in the world. But he is a bad one because he still thinks France needs to fight like a wounded animal (as in 1940) to save herself. Finally he is under the illusion that Algeria has ceased to exist—like Louis XIV and the Pyrenees—and like his hero he might be in for a surprise. I think anyway that he is slightly gaga, and in Paris everyone I met—including supporters—seemed to agree.

What the Labour Party has to understand is that in the Community planning is not on a country-by-country basis but on a European, long-term basis, the aim being to give the consumers and workers in the *whole* Community the best deal, not just those in the Borringe or in South Wales or in the Ruhr. This needs imagination and information. Harold Wilson has shown himself to have much too much of the former (in the wrong direction of course) and too little of the latter. So he invents—and often fabricates like Beaverbrook. What Gaitskell should do is go and pay another visit to his mentors in the White House and get them to explain to him the difference between thinking about the interests of 58 million people and 180 million. He will find the latter is much more exciting, has many more challenges, and requires a little breadth of vision. In any case the most important contribution that GB can make to the Community when she joins is to insist on the world-wide importance and commitment of Europe and join battle with the 'Little Europeans' who believe that we needn't help India (and Asia generally) and Latin America, and should just see if we can't diddle them out of some trade. Progressive Europeans are looking to Britain to let in more air and more of a world-view into the Community and get rid of the slightly parochial type who follow De Gaulle and Adenauer. (Hallstein is not one of these funnily enough.) Like Mansholt they see agriculture, for instance, as a world problem, not just Europe and the US and the Commonwealth. But it seems that the Labour Party—if they accept Europe—will go on squabbling about the same little parochial problems of planning which all the Conservatives do here. By the way France and to some extent Germany are miles ahead of us, as far as economic planning goes anyway.

Oh well—all this is very dull for you—but it has got me very much in its grip I'm afraid. The exciting thing about the Common Market is that it does make one see economic problems in a new way—as American attitudes and situations do too—and realize that there is much more to argue about, and *do* in a society which is of the size Europe may one day be. The size of America which is sometimes so claustrophobic—because the problems seem so big you can't think about them anymore—is also stimulating because there really is the chance of doing something to help people live better. The resources of society are so great that the means are easily come by. This size is what the Community is trying to create. It gives reformers and planners more room for action and the likelihood of finding more supporters and helpers, as well as more obstacles.

I spend my time writing little articles on the Common Market and on the Coal and Steel Community for an English monthly bulletin we produce, and brochures on agricultural policy, or French industry, or ten years of coal and steel, etc., etc. Sometimes my articles appear more or less unacknowledged in *The Times*, reprinted verbatim, and sometimes, when I have no better source I take theirs and reprint them verbatim! The world of economic journalism is small and repetitive. But then I keep telling myself it is the first stage—I'm in this for politics not journalism. As spokesman [at the Coal and Steel Union] I'll get my first glimpse of politics at work (over reports on coal stocks in the Community no doubt). I still have a sort of aesthetic attachment to politics you see: a sort of gold hangings against black background feeling about it, and an almost American-style idealism. I must say the facts are gnawing away at all that!

After all this time of trying out love and sex I am beginning to want to have some permanent relationship. However irritating and limiting companionship may be, it's a kind of comfort, especially when there are no relationships worth speaking of to be had, as here. But I have seen no girl I even remotely admire—let alone feel that kind of *snap* inside one which makes someone else really important. The trouble is that I have become used to exercising my big appetite for *life*: I want art, romance, sex, work, leisure, time to write, time to travel, career—everything at once. And that's only really possible if there is plenty of money and responsibility—or else the sacrifice of at least half. Like you say in your letter (note my Americanism), I have got involved in the boring internality of myself! But that's also because I'm one of the more interesting people around—and I think that's a pity. I've never found this before really, and it's a bad disease. In order to cure it I leap into my little red car and rush off to see Metz, or Nancy, or Trier, or Mainz—sometimes alone—once with Arcadi, and

165

once with Philippe Jullian. I'm afraid I irritated them both—I was in such a hurry to get back for work, and there was so much driving, and I was tired. But at least I saw things—I enclose a card. Amorbach is a charming little town in the midst of hills and woods—it used to be a fairly deserted little resort: the day we were there hundreds of ugly people, mainly over fifty, in buses and cars, and horrible groups led by Führers (naturally enough) clambered all over the culture spot, like lice on a sore. Why should they all see and by seeing destroy these intimate things? A beautiful church is something that can't be covered by hundreds of thousands, but German education has taught these people that culture is something that is the reward of prosperity and everyone *must* try to get it.

Arcadi said that the masses taking in art was like Gargantua trying to fuck a goose. I'm getting very snobbish and nasty now, you can see. But art is something for the few—except in rare cases like St Peter's in Rome, where it is built for the many, or concert halls or theatres. But most art needs time and quiet to be enjoyed, not the hustle of Oxford Street. I'm afraid I'm less and less impressed with the Community's marvellous prosperity. It's built on the American assumption—the *Time* Magazine American assumption—that prosperity is the root of happiness. So it is if you don't try to put ghastly pretentious gloss on it. But the mood here is that wealth gives one the power to move, to see things, to take things in, to become the slave of guided tours and planned excitements. Sometimes I think all this prosperity really isn't worthwhile, nor all the tedious economic planning and boasting and boosting. You see I've become a terrible moralist. It must be the effect of this horrid hypocritical little town.

I was always telling you about the Frick in NY and we even went there together once but of course you were not impressed when the dame said inside the Boucher room 'Very Frenchy'—she meant very French and Company* of course, and up to a point she was right in *that* room I'm afraid. The Francesco Laurana Lady† is one of *the* sights of New York—I paid many regular pilgrimages. Frick is NY's answer to the Wallace Collection, but there is so much less that it makes a completer impression. The Rembrandt *Polish Rider* is of course a dream—and the Houdon *Diana*. You're mad about the Bellini [*St Francis*]: one of the most extraordinary pictures I know. The more you look the more you find. Try it again. Bellini gives a sculptural permanence to landscape as if he had ordered Time to do it for him. The Fragonards make one's mouth water: such a room would suit me. Now I sit in my blue flat and listen to radios blaring in those upstairs. Unfortunately all modern luxury flats, as in NY, are sound-carriers. But I play my gramophone when it gets bad—just now Haydn's *Creation* again. As I listen the stars are created and the Sun and the angels praise again and again in rhythmic fugues. It all seems so easy according to Haydn. Angels sang *et voilà*! I wish it were that easy for us to create our own littler worlds. My agent has refused to take my novel—so he is not exactly my agent any more. As I wrote before, Apollo asks us to have talent—I think mine may yet show. I'll try to work at 'Frederick' again—in the long run it is the most ambitious and exciting of my works—and the one with greatest possibilities. And I'll try another, shorter novel. But this time I'll try to put more passion into my writing. Today I was reading Dickens: *Bleak House*—the death of Jo. It is about a subject which ought not to touch us any more—vagabonds a hundred years ago—and written in a style that ought to be only sentimental. It

* New York furniture and art dealers.
† A bust of a member of the Neapolitan royal family.

should leave us weary, but it is exalting after all, because he really felt what he wrote, and the human situation is horribly alive. We are touched because we are alive as well—and it does not matter that the situation is out of date, that there *is* sentimentality, that it is laid on too thick—*j'étais bouleversé.*

TO WILLIAM ANDERSON   *61, Boulevard de la Pétrusse,*
13 November 1962   *Luxembourg*

I have just been re-reading your poems—which I like very much. It was very kind of you to let me have a copy of them. What I like particularly is that you write imaginatively—your poems are about *imagined* situations, *imagined* horizons, *imagined* worlds. You have *created* them, you have not merely written about your subjective reactions to certain moments in life. What I like also is that you have broken away from the contemporary flat idiom of stating in a shorthand version whatever the poem is about; instead you want the charm of intelligible language to engage the reader's attention as you build up your symbols or your images. Finally, they are *your* symbols—personal to you, and yet intended to associate the reader's mind with the whole range of humanity and history. 'All from tribes of the silent fog/Of history he rakes.' You have remembered, a lone singer (to use a metaphor borrowed from 'Westerns'), that the purpose of poetry is to relate the reader's thoughts to the continued processes of life, to the continued affections (mountains, friends, places) that people feel, to the continuity of gesture, and of the earth. Walter Pater said (in *The Renaissance*) that the Greeks portrayed the Gods performing the simplest gestures, such as the tying or untying of a shoelace, because these gestures are significant only in Gods—and are eternal to man. It used to be the object of culture to expose the endurance of life and the earth. It has become usual for poetry to speak of the insignificant *angst* of the individual writer. Symbols and legends, which are the large heroic portraits of our smaller individual dramas and aspirations, have been dropped from most people's imaginative equipment. The result is an enormous barren bourgeois introspection: arid and heartless. That you have completely avoided that was of course to be expected . . . but now I *know* you have!

I don't know if you really like Browning very much, but you do seem to have something in common with him. I like him enormously—or used to, as I haven't read him for years —but often find he is not a poet so much as a brilliantly evocative storyteller and versifier. Your intentions are very different from his, but your style is often similar. Am I wildly out?

I liked the poem on the poet, and the one for Robert and the one for Gillian particularly. I know what is meant by your poetry being old-fashioned—just as my novel is supposed to be 1910. It is a certain positive romanticism, and the desire to use one's cultural experience as a part of one's imaginative world—the use of themes, phraseology and imagery that are recognized parts of practised sensibility—that has changed so largely into sensationalism. Though I write so differently from you I do find an affinity with your writing that I find with practically none of the poets of our generation. Those I have read are at best brilliantly polished subjectivists—even Peter Levi's obscure aridity. Finally you are one of the few writers whose images and visual imagination are not dominated by the skilful camerawork of filmmakers. There are several things I would criticise as well . . . *Eh bien*—I expect the Goethe of Rosedale Road has had enough of Eckermann's comments for today.

I am reading a book by the French historian Halévy on his acquaintance with Degas when he was a boy.* The Halévys lived in Montmartre and the young Halévy took notes of what Degas said when he came to the house. George Moore, Sickert, Manet, and many others came there too. The artists of the time were in opposition to their society, to contemporary

* Daniel Halévy, *My Friend Degas*, tr. Mina Curtiss, 1964.

tastes and tendencies—aren't we too?—but what a fund of time and security they had with which to play and build up their ideas. Their friendships were treated with care; they had the time to make them grow and blossom and they had the chance to seek each others' friendship and help without having to compete as violently as we do now. They encouraged each other—and their motive was almost more to avoid profit than to gain it. Looking back on them it is incredible what a combination of charm and talent that large circle of artists and writers seems to possess. Their secret was that they were in no hurry for glory. It was their attachment to culture which mattered most. That is the first requisite for good art. On this moral note I lock myself back into my wintry Ardennes cage.

<table>
<tr><td>TO HIS PARENTS</td><td>61, Boulevard de la Pétrusse</td></tr>
<tr><td>20 January 1963</td><td>Luxembourg</td></tr>
</table>

One does much too much talking in this work—especially at the moment with colleagues of all kinds wanting to discuss the crisis in the negotiations.* I think they have taken a most interesting *tournon* in our favour in this sense at least: if the talks really do break down after the 28th January then it will be the fault of the French and everyone will rightly blame them. De Gaulle in all this has shown himself to be the European nationalist which one suspected him of being, with that basic anti-Americanism which comes from the knowledge that without America France would be nothing today. He can't forgive his wartime allies for having been more loyal to France than she was to herself. Here the *chef de cabinet* of Malvestiti (President of the High Authority), Almini, called me to his office on Saturday morning to say that as I was an Englishman (I explained 'of sorts') he wanted to tell me that he deeply regretted the state of affairs in Europe, the position that France had taken, and the dangerous effect on the negotiations. He

* On British entry into the EEC.

personally would regard it as a tragedy if Britain did not manage to join the Community and hoped I would understand that many people felt as he did. It was really very nice of him to say all that—a most friendly and agreeable man.

TO NICHOLAS DEAKIN   *61, Boulevard de la Pétrusse*
20 January 1963   *Luxembourg*

I was very sorry to hear of Gaitskell's death: I know how much you and Rose admire him, more perhaps than I did, and I know how much his death will mean to you. I think it will be a very great loss to England—especially at a moment when our political life so badly needs the few outstanding personalities it has. I never managed to make up my mind about him: he had so many admirable qualities, but sometimes I felt he lacked imagination. However, I think the best thing about him was his ability to keep some semblance of order in his party, many of whom lacked his great sense of public responsibility. Who'll be his successor? I hope it won't be Wilson—the lowness of whose character is only equalled by the crassness of his political ideas. For a leading socialist to write nationalistic articles in the *Sunday Express* clearly indicates that Wilson is directly comparable with the German socialists who accepted Hitler. In Britain he'd be the same kind of person. As for Brown, he is nothing outside his party. Perhaps something will now come of the movement to bring a fusion between the more progressive elements in the Labour Party and the Liberals. The Common Market may split the Tories in just as sharp a way as the Labour Party may split without Gaitskell to lead them.

It is the great tragedy of Gaitskell that he was basically a nationalist who neither wanted to understand the European issue, nor understood that the days of Britain's *island* story are ended. Still . . . there are many sides to the question and many criticisms possible. I am very critical of how the Community

171

is run, but not of its aims, nor of its achievements. There is so much Britain could bring to it, and it to Britain, that I hope with all this bickering that this main point won't be lost. In Britain itself there is a danger that it may be lost through the blindness of party feelings and old nationalistic suspicions. Perhaps if Gaitskell had been prime minister he would have felt this too. Probably better than the Tories. His position in the country may have forced his national point of view on him: but the Labour Party must change that if it is to survive into the future as a progressive party, and not an isolationist one, turning Britain into an equivalent of Spain in the late 17th century.

TO JOHN GRIGG   *16, Boulevard de la Pétrusse*
16 March 1963   *Luxembourg*

One must assume that an enemy's view is largely wrong, once one has recognized him as an enemy, otherwise one won't be able to resist him. I know of no one in the Community, apart from French foreign office people, who doesn't regard De Gaulle as an enemy of its autonomy, its political development, and its anti-nationalist ideals. He is giving encouragement to nationalism—a force which may or may not have value in newly emergent countries like Ghana or Israel, but which resulted in the death of millions of Europeans, including two-thirds of my family. When I go out to dinner here I eat with Germans and French and Italians and Belgians and Dutch (and, very rarely, Luxembourgers!)—we work together, and manage to communicate easily in all sorts of languages and dialects, and contribute a little to the development of European institutions. I think most people, even if they don't like to admit it, believe that. It is precisely this co-operation which De G. has consistently refused to believe in—he thinks it is unreal and impossible. He says it causes trouble and is complicated. It is both—but it is the only hope for Europe, and I can assure you, from a very close study of the Community and its mechanisms, De G.'s methods—never mind about his principles, whatever they may be—are opposed to the realisation of that hope.

TO ROBERT CUMMING   *61, Boulevard de la Pétrusse*
12 May 1963   *Luxembourg*

In London there were many friends, and lunches that lasted until four in the afternoon, and conversation, and absurdities, social and human, that make life worth living—at least in big cities. Here there is nothing, or almost nothing, and none of the absorbing human ties that can make small-town life exciting. Have I begun to lose my capacity for making those ties perhaps? It seems a horrible future if the great attachments are the ones made between 20 and 25, and later it is all chit-chat, and dinner parties and sex.

One of my greatest ties—though I saw her only rarely—died at the end of April, Elena Vivante. All generosity and humanity seemed to be concentrated in her. When I first met her in 1954 she opened my eyes to so many of the good things of life. She was not so unreservedly high-brow as my parents (or as they seemed to me), and she encouraged everyone in their dreams and hopes. For her, dreams were obviously the thing everyone is most attached to, and one should be encouraged to try to fulfil them. That was wonderful. And then living there, in that generous household, with the Sienese hills, and the lemons, and the warm earth, was in itself a sure way of giving nostalgia concrete form. This Christmas I was there again. She was ill, but from her bed she supervised everyone, and encouraged, and loved, and welcomed me. Within five minutes I felt as if I had never been away.

John was appointed British spokesman for the High Authority of the Coal and Steel Community. However, that did not satisfy him sufficiently to want to remain in Luxembourg. He left at the end of July 1963 and later took a holiday in Greece. On his return to England John found a flat at the top of a house in York Street, off Baker Street. On the strength of his experience in Luxembourg he was appointed editor of Opera Mundi—Europe, *a weekly news supplement started by* The Times, *in co-operation with* Le Monde, *with the aim of preparing the British industrial and commercial world for the United Kingdom's entry into the Common Market.*

TO FIONN MORGAN (NÉE O'NEILL)   *Monemvasia, Greece*
22 September 1963

I have been reading *Tom Jones* here, and gobbled it up, all of it, with greed. It is splendid—such life and variety and humanity and wit, all jumbled together, and surprisingly few dull moments. He does two things: he invents well and describes well. I think it is much more in that kind of direction that my talents lie—as you say in your letter—than in introspective Jamesian analysis. I am reading *The Ambassadors* just now, and it is very hard work after the romp with Fielding. For all his long-winded sensibility James doesn't really tell you that much more, nor that much more subtly either.

TO FIONN MORGAN   *28, York Street*
2 December 1963   *London W1*

Your letter was wonderfully gay, which is really the only worthwhile thing to be—but it is hard this year to feel that way: friends—Burgo [Partridge] in September among others —have died or disappeared for no real reason at all, and then

174

Kennedy, in whom I really believed in many ways. I feel like a character in Scott Fitzgerald—a feeling which I get anyway about twice a day—and things are slipping away. I have moved to the address above—which is a nice cosy little *garçonnière* (bachelor-flat to you) and which will make a nice home once it is in order. It has low rooms and pleasant 18th-century windows, and a bath the size of those at Christ Church, with huge brass taps, out of which the hot water comes steaming. There will be comfortable 19th-century chairs, and a certain amount of disorder, and I'll see if I can get a tiger skin to sit on. But I'm glad of Perridge,* where I am now, because it is funny how one needs a place to fall back on, which isn't a flat but *home*, in an enveloping sentimental way.

The news of the deaths of David [Winn] and Sara [D'Avigdor-Goldsmith] was too strange to believe when I heard it in Greece from Constantine Mano.† For me they were the essence of London life after you left. On each visit they were generous and friendly and full of plans for entertainments and fun. They were tremendously social people—in the best sense that they were the best company one could hope for. And they were intelligent at the same time, which is the rarest combination. Already one is getting used to their absence, but it has made London quite perceptibly duller.

I had lunch with your erstwhile step-father Lord Rothermere, whose minion, the editor of the *Sketch*, finally offered me a job as the author of a column euphemistically called 'The *Sketch* Thinks'. It would pay terribly well and I'd have some fun with it, but I'm not sure I'm really Tory enough, cynical enough, or enough of an ambitious young journalist to do it ... I am also considering a job under the auspices of *The Times*, running the English edition of a weekly news service about the Community. This would leave me a certain amount of time for my own life and writing, which the other would not, and be more up-my-street really. *The Times* interviewer was a gent—something one could not remotely

* His parents' house in Somerset.
† They were drowned while sailing.

call the editor of the *Sketch*—but just as much of a caricature. I am not sure I don't prefer the editor of the *Sketch* telling me over the lunch table at the Ivy that 'this country is being demoralized by people like the *New Statesman* crowd and the *Observer*. You know, Marghanita Laski.' (Why her?) I felt like ringing up the *New Statesman* afterwards and saying, 'Do you know there is actually somebody who thinks you have an influence!'

TO BEN SONNENBERG   *28, York Street*
25 December 1963   *London W1*

You'll be interested to hear that the boy armed with a letter from you, who worked as clerk at the *Wall Street Journal*, is going to edit a weekly news service on Europe for *The Times*. The thing is called *Opera Mundi, Europe* and will at first be a simple adaptation of a French bulletin of the same name. Later it may branch out into something of its own. It's all about Europe on the one hand, and something called 'inter-penetration' on the other: the main international developments in the setting up of subsidiaries and exchange of directorships etc. between companies in different countries of the Atlantic world. We hope to sell in the US too one day— but I'll talk to you about that, and ask your wisdom on it (if I may!), when the time comes. I finally turned down the *Daily Sketch* on the basis of the psalmist's philosophy: 'Better be a porter in the house of my Lord, than dwell in the tents of the ungodly!' It may sound pharisaical, but I suspect the psalmist knew what he was talking about. I have decided that for the time being at least I must be a professional 'European'—those books on art will have to wait until I have established the right to dictate my own terms to life!

TO ARCADI NEBOLSINE   *28, York Street*
9 March 1964   *London W1*

I actually quite like my work; for the first time I'm the boss,
and that brings a certain *soulagement* to the ego. It is a cheap
satisfaction—but my dear the effort of expensive ones! *The
Times* is an amiable institution in which to work—people are
very polite and British. In it I feel like a barracuda in a tank of
cod. My ambition has turned into a different direction: what I
hope for is to have financial independence—from tied jobs
that is—by the age of thirty-five. Then one might begin to
have the right of Cocteau talking to Diaghilev: '*Etonnez-moi.*'
But the energy that goes in London on the smallest most
transient items in life is depressing: it is the ability to rise above
them that represents the first stage of real independence. And I
wish one could leave sex to the weekends—but it has a nasty
way of being wanted on Wednesdays too.

TO ROBERT CUMMING   *28, York Street*
25 April 1964   *London W1*

Have you changed a lot in the three and a half years since we
last met? I have outwardly I suppose: by which I mean I can
deal with working life much better than I used to. I have
discarded my romantic belief that things would fall into my
lap. Inside the romance is still there—and I show it to those
who are willing to be interested. But it is money and career
that most people around think about: there are exceptions, like
Bill [Anderson], who goes struggling on, writing his poetry
that nobody will print, and who still hopes that something
will come of it. Are we simply not as talented as we thought
we were, or are we genuinely undiscovered because we are
unlike our contemporaries? I think we are too diffuse in our
interests—the single-mindedness of the tycoon or the great
artist is lacking—but perhaps it will come later. It is this hope

of arriving later, but carrying a better gift, that we have to sustain ourselves with.

To return to writing . . . I am sure that it requires all one's attention, or at least all mine if I am to do it at all. I can write fast if I do it, but it takes up all my energy. Other things take away my imagination, which has to put down roots and grow. And yet, with discipline—giving up sex, friends, parties etc.—one can combine it with other things. But how to give those up? And big cities are full of easy temptations—the cinema which keeps one cosy when tired.

I imagine you unchanged—full of wistful seeking after something. At Oxford, when I was rather anxious to tell you what to do, I used to be irritated by that; now I respect it, share it, but don't express it as you can, even in your letters.

TO FIONN MORGAN   *28, York Street*
8 August 1964   *London W1*

To be a great artist now, I think, is like trying to find places which have not been touched by the modern world: they really don't exist. But to be talented, to be sufficiently good to take advantage of modern society, with its enormous appetite for books, and pictures, and poems and music, that really should be possible. Just as it is possible, in Greece for instance, to find places where one can enjoy the remnants of the past, with just a few of the conveniences (cleanliness) and inconveniences (people, cars, noise) of modern life thrown in. The trouble is that genius must be rare, but in our super-comfortable world, talent is everywhere, and talent in a strange way makes it much harder for genius. Not that I either thought I ought or could be one, but there has always been a nagging hope in my mind that it would be worth putting up with a lot to produce one thing or two even that could last, that could be turned to at the end of life as a real product of one's own energy and mind. This may not need genius, but it needs

178

concentration and the good use of opportunity—and the opportunity, as Scott Fitzgerald points out, is always *now*.

His letters [*The Letters of F. Scott Fitzgerald*, ed. A. Turnbull, 1964] are sad and moving and well worth reading, at least a few at a time. So far I've read only those to his daughter. He wants so much for her: as one does with people one loves, he wants her to do what he failed to do, to make the most of everything in the way he would have done, so of course he is disappointed because she has to do it in her own way. He himself felt he had been robbed of opportunities by life—by his wife's madness, by his failure to write during that period, etc. And there is always jealousy of the opportunities of youth. But the daughter was no genius, no writer, just a nice young girl, and could not live up to all that. The disappointment one may yet feel with oneself for not living up to what one expected of oneself will perhaps be even sharper. Not that it is necessary, but in some way I expect nearly everyone feels it at some time, if they are not complacent fools.

This summer I'm going to Greece. I look forward to it enormously because I find the South the only place where I really relax. It seems to be made for people to live in, which is not really true of the North, which is more for people to work in. And who likes that?

TO DAVID AND CLARISSA PRYCE-JONES   *28, York Street*
21 December 1964   *London W1*

It was very touching to hear from you—such a rare pleasure to receive a good long letter which one can read and then read again. I was also impressed by the heading 'Program in Creative Writing', which made me feel I was receiving at last an offshoot of the new culture, to which I don't yet belong! (I am always troubled by that term 'creative writing': it has always meant to me some kind of very elaborate and generally unreadable prose or verse, as opposed to just plain writing—

179

of the 'uncreative' variety I suppose—which is readable and possibly interesting. However, this is just a thought; couldn't you persuade Iowa that it would be more in keeping with true 'creative' writing to drop the 'creative'?) I have just been watching the 'telly', which showed that venerable doyen of British scientific intelligentsia Julian Huxley telling us about the population explosion. In fact he was rather charming, and made one think that the explosion which produced him wasn't reprehensible. 'Life', he assured us in a very close close-up, which showed how old he was and how he would escape the doom he was announcing, 'is soon going to become unbearable.' But said with such a modest look as if he was genuinely hoping he was wrong.

Life in London progresses with that mixture of elation when one forms a new attachment and depression that the things for which one really cares don't materialize or drop out.

Make sure your children have everything as late as possible: luxury you will unavoidably give them soon, because you know how to use it well, and I don't think you should withhold that. But knowledge (Julian H.: 'I remember how Bertrand Russell told me, "It is so delightful to know facts" ') should be gained at some point around the age of thirty; a gentle breaking-in, when the youth meets Cyril Connolly for the first time, dines at Maxims, is bored by a museum (imagine that!) and sleeps *partie-carrée* with his mistress and two discarded boy-friends of hers. Keep all that forbidden, so that they never even feel tempted—and then let it be a satisfying deluge. Early disgust, and early self-satisfaction are the diseases whose first symptoms are already producing tiny lines in the faces of some of our friends.

The French tantalize me: I went to Paris for an engagement party for Michael of Greece and his Greek fiancée chez the parents of Marthe de la Rochefoucauld. *Grands salons*, seventy-five people, very few good-looking women, le Prince de Lippe-Detmold and the Princesses de Croy, Violet Trefusis and Mme Ralli, who could be heard: 'My dear when you were in London did you see the Prince?' 'Yes, he was at the

Duchess's.' 'And whom are you asking with the Duchess on Thursday?' 'The Prince.' Then Violet licked the caviar off the piece of bread she had taken from the platter, and replaced it. 'I think,' I suggested sharply, 'that would be better on here,' and put the ravished morsel on an ashtray. It was very lively and almost enjoyable, but somewhere, like the late Consuelo Vanderbilt in Petersburg before 1914, I 'could sense the emptiness of it all'. But *now* we know she was wrong—so perhaps the emptiness was imagined. The real trouble was that the party was so little different from a London one; the grand people were grander, and the people I didn't know, I knew even less, so to speak, but the conversation was almost exactly the same. Very occasionally I leave a party or a dinner with that extraordinary feeling of elation which people can give even more than wine: suddenly one is *sure* that the wit and intelligence and the significance of what one has to say—and is saying— are apparent to everyone; a kind of brilliant Bacchanalian *entrain* that makes me laugh and think of things to say long after I am alone. Fortunately this is rare. But I look for it all the same. I say fortunately because I might be a little mad if this happened often.

Why do you call Goethe mad, by the way? (*You* must be mad!) Goethe is everything—and he knew all about us long before we were born. In the conversations with Eckermann he says quite emphatically that we have come too late. The meal has been very largely eaten by his generation—and for some time to come this will still remain true. The last of the heroes were practically gone by 1830: what a frightening change there is from Goethe to Tolstoy, from Beethoven and Schubert to Brahms, from Delacroix to Manet. Better or worse is not the comparison I'm making—but extrovert and subtle, voluptuaries but prudent, aristocratic and almost sentimentally human, in the first instance, and with that hint of realism and gloom that has now completely overtaken art and ideas in the second. Oh, this is a generalization all right, but I feel a hankering after the carefree, for unhampered sentiment, overwhelming tunes, and the mysteries of the private life—a sort of year-end irritation with the passing of time perhaps. But never mind, you wanted gossip, and this is listening in on certain secret thoughts and hesitations which creep in at letter-time. (But read Goethe's 'An den Mond'—the essence of romantic poetry—almost perfect in thought and diction. Schubert set it to music exquisitely.)

Will you visit the West Coast? If so you must visit my cousin who is *charming* and intelligent and difficult, but you'll conquer that. Also *your* delightful cousin by marriage, Biene Goldschmidt-Rothschild, whose walls are hung with pictures *by* Goethe, and who thinks of life *damals*★ while humming-birds play round her fountain. Ah, California . . .

TO ARCADI NEBOLSINE   *28, York Street*
13 March 1965   *London W1*

When you telephoned I was, as I told you, in a state of having discovered a new attachment—one which now has already been dissipated, or rather, which exists on a much less intense level. It was a momentary belief that I had found someone who was not only beautiful, charming, tender and intelligent, but who wanted to be those things for me. As it turned out, however, she wanted to be those things for just as long as it needed to raise my hopes. Since then she has been friendly, but that is all, and my feelings have given way to slight disappointment.

Art, music, literature continue: but it is astonishing how archaistic we are. Can there ever have been an age when people thought so strongly that the art of the past was better than that of the present—since the early Middle Ages I mean—and have been so right? The old Europe to which we belong is over and we recognize that—you by teaching the past to a society that will only know of it from teachers and people who have given their memories that third dimension that comes from history

★ Long ago.

and art, I by turning to the economic force which is the expression of the new society and which I study as if it were some new historical twist in the story told by the writers and artists of the past I love. But of course it isn't—because this society does not merely reflect the *ordinary life of people*, it glorifies it into the be-all-and-end-all of society. The more I look at what is happening in Europe, the more clearly I recognize that there has been a break with the past: at first I felt that what was happening was a kind of continuation of the Europe that we were brought up to know; instead it is a force which will systematically destroy it.

Sorry to sound so gloomy—I am not in fact so. I can't understand with all this going on how I am still cheerful, but I suppose it is because for a while there is still a hang-over from the old life which deceives one into feeling relaxed. Solitude, privacy, leisure, the opportunity to enjoy the best of life in quiet—gradually they are slipping away. That is why you must come to Greece now, while we still can, and drink the last drops of the honeyed cup that is soon to be completely empty.

TO BEN SONNENBERG   *28, York Street*
14 March 1965   *London W1*

I had in particular a very interesting visit to Brussels and Luxembourg where I renewed my acquaintance with my former colleagues in the institutions of the European Community. I was amused to note that coming as an outsider I was provided with privileges that I never enjoyed when I was a civil servant myself. The head of my department in the High Authority in Luxembourg, whom I had seen at the most for about ten minutes at a time once or twice over the eighteen months I spent there, took me out to lunch which lasted two and a half hours while we discussed every subject under the sun, quite apart from our discussions of Europe. My former boss not only gave me his views of what was happening in the world of politics, he also gave me a full account of his dissatisfaction with Luxembourg—a dissatisfaction he never allowed me to utter without pouncing on me when I lived there! The President of the Common Market Commission received me for more than an hour, and we had what the papers call a 'full exchange of views'. And so it went on.

President Hallstein by the way impressed me enormously by his frankness and his willingness to discuss things without any of that official restraint which the 'Eurocrats' usually manage to spread over their talk. He was professorial—talked to me as if I were a student—and I don't doubt that that is how he talks with the President of the United States too. He is a strange mixture of theologian—only the theology is Europe and the bible the Treaty of Rome—diplomat—only he represents a state that is not yet, but will be—and professor—he teaches a subject he has created himself. He reminded me a good deal of some of my mother's professorial acquaintances at the Warburg Institute here in London, and so we were able to get on to the right footing straightaway, since I found the matter so enormously familiar. I must say I thank my central European origin for that; it has prepared the way for certain encounters which leave some of my English friends a little breathless. Nothing could be more foreign to the English manner than the German professorial style, and I think this goes some way to explain Britain's difficulties in entering the Common Market.

TO BEN SONNENBERG   28, *York Street*
12 May 1965   *London W1*

I have made up my mind that what *The Times* has to offer me is not much, unless some dramatic change takes place in the next few months. My aim is to start a small concern of my own. In the field of publishing over here—I don't know about the

States—more and more work is being divided between small flexible firms with ideas, and large dull firms with sales and money. Initially at least I would like to run a small flexible firm, with people who do well because they are involved in the success of the thing. The great boredom of working in a large organization is that even at the top one is 'hired help' (as you once described the President of Cheeseborough Pond), and on the way there at the mercy of absurd intrigues between the personnel. If the chairman is a dud a sort of dullness can descend down to the office boys even, and that is what I fear might happen here. In addition I don't see myself as a reporter . . . Well, I think the answer is to find one's own act and perform that.

TO ROBERT CUMMING   *28, York Street*
3 July 1965   *London W1*

Now here at Perridge I miss you. You would like the great masses of flowers that my parents have planted, the overflowing quantities of fruit and vegetables—raspberries, strawberries (wild and cultivated), beans, artichokes, peas, and everywhere roses. My parents have put in 1000 at least since they came here; they clamber in trees, up walls, stand in rows, mount banks, descend old tree trunks, and hang in festoons. We play croquet furiously, the victor invariably crowing while the vanquished displays his wrath in bouts of bad temper. It is a cruel game in which the sad truth about life's little hopes is enacted by wooden balls in front of iron hoops. Bang, bang—and the enemy for reasons that are not rationally explicable puts an end to the carefully planned manoeuvre; the revenge, also carefully planned but inexpertly executed, never quite gives the satisfaction hoped from it. It is all very instructive and moral and frustrating.

   It is the hardest thing to keep up the different sides of life. I wish I knew how it is possible to combine all the things I would like to do. I still have the feeling that I would like to change the world in some way—a political feeling I suppose, not a religious one anyway— and to write some good things, and travel, be amused, have friends, and enjoy the many 'pleasures of the flesh'. But what a problem to have time and energy for more than one thing at a time.

Apart from John's own misgivings Opera Mundi—Europe *did not find the anticipated readership in Great Britain. John left* The Times *and joined the staff of the Institute for Strategic Studies, an international organization under the directorship of Alastair Buchan. John made new friends at the Institute, including François Duchêne and Graf Coudenhove-Kalergi. Unfortunately he had to work with someone whom he found uncongenial. This caused some friction and he left the Institute in 1966. His article on 'European Cooperation in Defence Technology: The Political Aspect' was published as No. 1 in the Institute's series called:* Defence, Technology and the Western Alliance *1967.*

He was asked by the publisher Anthony Blond to edit A Handbook of Western Europe, *published 1967, and he also edited as an introduction to it 'The Common Market, The Treaty of Rome Explained', Booklet No. 5 in the series:* The Great Society, Anthony Blond *1967.*

While working at the Institute John went on a research visit to the United States.

TO HIS MOTHER   *c/o Sonnenberg*
31 October 1965   *New York*

We [Ben Sonnenberg and J.C.] had a very welcoming reception in Northampton, Mass. from a most interesting and likeable artist, Leonard Baskin. We argued a good deal over 19th-century art, which I find duller and duller. Next day we

186

saw the Sterling Clarke collection at Williamstown, a pretty college town in the midst of New England woods. There, in a white marble mausoleum, are some magnificent drawings, a marvellous Rembrandt, Fragonard, Piero, Maître de Flemalle (type), etc., and forty Renoirs. The Renoirs were absurdly silly: what a dreary painter he is en masse—no taste, little skill, much sentimentality, like Turkish delight, only more expensive. There are many other good things, in fact in all other respects it is a delicious collection. I could do without the Bouguereaux, but I dare say Sterling Clarke really enjoyed them more than anything. A Degas self-portrait was exquisite, but then the Degas in America are better than anything we have of his in Europe. He is so much better than any of the others that one sees here in such quantities that you cannot believe it. Rooms and rooms and rooms of Impressionists: and after all there were only about ten of them who were really any good. Unfortunately they had nothing to do but to paint, and so they did much too much . . .

On Tuesday I took a walk up Madison Avenue from 57th to 83rd streets—about a mile and a quarter—with Ben, which was very revealing of his New York personality and position. He was like the Ancient Mariner and stopped nearly one in three: art dealers, businessmen, Kennedy's sister Jean, Truman Capote, fashionable women, etc., etc. At the end of our walk we visited Lucien Goldschmidt, who had one or two nice things, and sent Daddy his regards. He is a nice man, reproachfully nice almost.

Washington was rushed but very interesting. I saw a large number of officials, including George Ball who is more or less a member of the Cabinet and is in charge of relations with Europe. Everyone was very talkative and frank. I was surprised how much time they had in which to talk, how friendly they were, and how easily approached. The European Community Office was very helpful to me—gave me an office, a place to stay, a telephone and announced my arrival to various people whom they thought I should see. I made notes on all my talks with officials which I'll show you when I get back—

certainly interesting as a picture of what people think, and the atmosphere in which they work. They had all heard of *Opera Mundi-Europe*, which astonished me, especially as the State Department does not receive it, but it proves that that was not quite useless . . . I saw a copy of it in Washington—already full of stylistic errors, but who cares?

TO ROBERT CUMMING   *28, York Street*
15 December 1965   *London W1*

Today is your 30th birthday—many happy returns. It is a dismal feeling in a way—the forgiveness to which one has been accustomed as a child is now at last withdrawn and one feels a kind of nakedness, that is discouraging and troubling. I dare say that one will survive—I am told also that no birthday will seem so sad again!

Are there any books you would like? I am also going to send you a page from Philippe Jullian's sketch-book of Charleston, from which he has given me two pages, one of which I'll have mounted for you. Then you can frame it and remember our trip. What a pity we are only able to take photographs and not sketch. In a way they give a much warmer feeling of the place than my photos can. In fact our art is becoming mechanical and I suppose decadent in the sense that it is less and less inventive and more and more the perfecting of what is already known. But once one has accepted that—and it is disillusioning to have to accept it but now at 30 I'm beginning to accept some disillusionment—the best one can do is to get to work like an ancient Egyptian perfecting the well-worn tracks. (But of course I don't really believe that.)

My new work is among people who are openly one-sided— at least, in their approach to their work they prefer to appear more as technicians than as thinkers, and this is of course the biggest mistake one can make in life, since it condemns one to the narrowest interpretation of one's activity and not the

188

largest. The result is that they often seem to me to be too concerned with the trivia of military affairs in the studies which they conduct, and not with the political and economic uses to which the facts they discover could be put. In a really *scientific* institute—not a semi-speculative 'think shop' like mine—this kind of narrowness is alarming. I think for instance of a distant relative of mine* who has worked for Nazis and Communists alike, gathering all sorts of prizes, and making all sorts of vital discoveries, but never bothering about what they were to be used for. That kind of extreme is more often to be found among scientists I suppose, not the little academic beetles who populate the Institute for Strategic Studies, who can't do much to change the world anyway!

I must not be unkind after only a fortnight but so far no one has been able to impress me with the clarity and intelligence of their thinking as some people in the Community have done in the past or as some of the officials I saw in Washington (especially Henry Rowen at the Bureau of the Budget—*voilà un homme*), or as a few of the 'Europeans' in Britain have. These people have no political passion—and that oddly enough is essential to get an interesting view of the political world. It need not be a narrow passion—in fact strict Communist or strict right-wing views are deadly—but there must be a desire to see something happen, to contribute to a particular end, if a person is to develop a sense of what is happening in the political world, and to get a feeling for the pattern of events. Without this passion their views are grey and they seem to have little insight.

What does this matter to you? I'm sorry—riding on a hobby-horse that may bore you. If it has, I give you leave to skip the passage the next time you read my letter. I think of you eating racoon pie and persimmon fool and pecan pudding or whatever—cakes baked in wesson oil!

* Professor Gustav Hertz, a physicist and recipient of a Nobel prize.

Just a note to wish you a happy new year—and to tell you that I have sent you a book by Chaudhuri called *The Continent of Circe*, which gives a searing, or rather acid picture of India, and Hinduism, but accompanied by a very lively English style, and a real respect for what the author thinks is real Hinduism. I find the whole thing entertaining, specious, and often brilliant—a mixture as a stimulating book usually is—none of that grey and balanced tone the work of scholars has nowadays.

Christmas here has been very pleasant—I have a Dutch friend staying, and my parents are here—and we sit comfortably in the library (as it now has rather grandly become) with a wood fire blazing, nursing our righteous indigestion. My new work is becoming more interesting—the people in the Institute not more so, however: I'm afraid I will never be a great admirer of my colleagues as I always expect them to be full of ideas, love of the arts, and immediately understanding of the shorthand I like to use in conversation with my friends. All this is of course out of the question as one chooses one's friends but not one's colleagues.

What I like about your life is that you have done what you wanted to do, and did not, like me, obey too carefully the rule that one must do what is expected of one, which our *bon bourgeois* backgrounds have inculcated. I have to admit that I did not entirely dislike my twenties (!) and did not entirely waste them on stuff I did not really want to do, but I do sometimes get the feeling that it is only recently that I have discovered that it is for oneself that one must live life, not according to precepts which suit other people. (I don't mean one should be terribly selfish, but just that in choosing the work one does, it should help to further one's own aims, not the ones people expect one to further.) And you have explored the world well, and have written the things you wanted, which is good. Albeit with that tremendous conscience of yours which makes you worry all the time!

TO BEN SONNENBERG *Perridge House*
24 July 1966 *Somerset*

Perridge is as pretty as when you left it. Your visit, by the way, was much appreciated: I enormously enjoyed our dinner in Bath, and was very glad that you saw this place at last. It will not, I hope, be your last visit.

As I told you I am very interested in becoming a publisher, and have been looking around—not very actively yet I admit —for a new job in that field. After working as a journalist and a 'European' in America and Europe, and having got together what I hope will be quite a good book on Western Europe, I feel this business is one which I would enjoy and could possibly do quite well. I would also want something in which I could stay for good, I think. I like working with authors and getting them to work on ideas and problems of which they had not necessarily thought. Publishing is also a business, which journalism in the end is not; one always feels with journalism, as with Institutes and Foundations, that they are for life's waiters rather than for the diners themselves.

As you know, I am also very interested in art history. Something which would be very useful would be a book on the subject-matter of Western art—especially the Christian and mythological themes which kept cropping up over the ages, and which have been traditionally depicted in more or less the same sort of way, but which are often unintelligible to a young person who sees them for the first time. The result is that much pre-20th-century art is almost suspect even for a number of educated people.

Most publishers still seem to find it difficult to make an art-historical book both serious *and* attractive—though Phaidon has succeeded sometimes. It can be done, but it needs a great deal of attention and enthusiasm. It might be a good idea to republish some of the old masterpieces of Wickhoff, etc., in illustrated editions, or Bode's *Botticelli*, or Justi's *Velasquez*.

I must apologize for this very self-centred letter, but as usual I am taking advantage of the encouragement you gave me to pour out my hopes and fears. You are always so generous with your patience and interest.

TO ROBERT CUMMING   *28, York Street*
12 September 1966   *London W1*

I paid a short pilgrimage to Solaia [near Siena] for dinner—one must never go back to places where one was happy or sad or discovered something which changed the world in some way; the secret of the place was Elena [Vivante], and in her absence her ghost floats like a great inhibition over the children, and over the servants and over the food. We ate in a desperate attempt to return to the past, but Paolo, Arturo and Charis were pale shadows. The few guests were made of cotton wool and after dinner we rushed back to Siena, with 'never again' firmly branded in my mind. It was and is a wonderful place, but Elena was a great nymph in my private Arcadia, and with her gone, it is too painful to be there. Much more than I realized at that time, she gave me eight perfect weeks in 1954, which coloured my view of the South, of Italy, of the perfect life of happiness, for good; of all the things I would like to live through again it is that summer—but I won't.

I still travel to discover myself, I suppose—and the discoveries are getting painful. Intellectually I was brought up for an intensely romantic world in which entirely beautiful and brilliant people make love under Byronic moons in an atmosphere of pagan freedom. Inject into that a Puritan fear, carefully nursed through my English education, of the physical world and especially of love, and the whole vision is made irksome and painful, as well as being absurdly fantastic.

I miss you and especially some corrective cold-douche in this welter of taking myself seriously.

TO ROBERT CUMMING   *28, York Street*
13 December 1966   *London W1*

My life centres round four books which I am writing simultaneously: the first is a handbook on Western Europe which has been worrying my weekends for nearly two years —but which has been my main job since I got back from Greece. It is now nearly finished but the publisher wants an extract to be published separately as a 'pre-run'; then there is my study for the Institute for Strategic whats-it which should come out in February; and then a novel which is three-quarters done—it is quite short—but which I find the most amusing part; finally, my play about Frederick is coming on French television next year.★ So you see there are a lot of business things going on; ideas, work, secret hopes, all coming together for a change, and not totally in conflict.

I interpret your silence to mean that you've fallen in love—I have not since I last saw you, and I miss it; perhaps it is not going to play the same role in my life which it did between 18 and 25 again.

We are not in an age when letter-writing is satisfactory as a way of communication. We are too bothered both by ourselves and by minor affairs to make them interesting; a leisurely conversation between two cultivated people by post

★ It was not performed because De Gaulle, on his return to power, dismissed the staff at French TV who had accepted it.

is impossible because our business lives are so important. Cultivated people—even supposing we are such—now means people who fit in culture between earning their bread and butter. And yet, foolishly perhaps, we were brought up, both of us, and encouraged at places like Oxford, to believe that culture was essential to life and that leisure would be available in which to enjoy it.

I should like a long talk with you, after a visit to some great cathedral, in the shadow of a tall cypress and the hills vanishing in the distance and near at hand a peach grove. Talk with one's friends, and I mean people to whom one has opened personal sides that aren't shown to the world, is really the most enduring of pleasures, especially when intermingled with art or books or travel. There is a charm in friendship which I think too many people miss. I used to want to know the most famous and the greatest—and I don't deny a certain satisfaction in touching the hems of their garments from time to time—but it is journalistic satisfaction, like reading an amusing article in a paper, forgotten, or at least without significance, the moment it is over. Slowly one gets nearer the few things which one knows are worth doing—I mean worthwhile for oneself, because they may not be for others— and the meaning of being adult is I think to realize what these things are and to get them done, even if it means patience and surmounting a lot of barriers. I think, looking over an old letter from you, that you have always seen these barriers loom too large; forget some of your obligations, and concentrate more on your wishes. And if you have to feed yourself too, see if you can compromise the two in some way so that there is an overlap somewhere. I think I am feeling my way towards all this—but perhaps I'm being too hopeful. I'll let you know how it works out; let me know how it is working out for you. You deserve the best.

On Tuesday John Craxton comes to dinner—his show at the Whitechapel is pleasant, sentimental, ever-so-slightly slick. Actually he is more talented than I thought, especially when he is in his most pastoral mood—then he is like a modern Bassano. But then he tries experiments—and they are sometimes amusing, more often too slick and successful, not experimental enough. Anyway *I* liked his pictures after seeing them all together,—the critics have said idiotic things, both as praise and damnation. They get paid for saying them too, which is so absurd.

Oxford looked marvellous—in the street a glimmer of Oscar Wilde as a young man; Maria [von Katte] tells me it is his grandson and next time she will invite him to meet me as she knows him. Very odd. Here I saw a brilliant revival of Otway's *The Soldier's Fortune*—I hope it is still on when you come back. It was written in 1680, and is more up-to-date than any play written in 1967—pansies, pimps, blimps, perverts, silly girls, pretty girls, cuckolds, the lot. They knew it all— but with so much humour and *no* psychological explanation. What a relief!

An article I wrote in a moment of enthusiasm has been accepted by James Chace for *Interplay*★ and another commissioned, my play† passes from one expert in Paris to the next as they try to decide whether it is literary enough, historical enough, TV material, pro-De Gaulle, or something

★ An American magazine. The article was entitled 'Communiqués From London', April 1967.
† *Prince Frederick.*

else—anyway I'm assured that by the end of '67 it will have appeared, nine years after I first wrote it, on return from our trip to Sicily.

So you see I'm playing a waiting game—nothing in the world so demoralizing. Anyway, in a month's time I suppose I will have a job, of some kind, and will feel less sorry for myself. But I feel that I'm 31 and neither Prime Minister, nor Walter Pater, nor Aldous Huxley. What's gone wrong? Everything is done by working at it slowly, I keep repeating to myself—but how slowly it seems.

I have been reading five of Disraeli's novels in succession—they are immensely entertaining, readable, lively, and far too long, so one has to skip some passages especially about religion. You'd enjoy *Endymion* and *Lothair*, which he wrote at the end of his life, especially if you want a complete contrast with what you are doing! Of course he is completely extrovert—anyone who has the bad luck to have doubts about themselves ought either to get over them or to put up with the consequences: ruin, disaster, suicide, misery. Someone commits suicide, 'as most people do,' says Dizzy, 'through want of imagination.' I would not commit suicide I don't think, but sometimes I am 'plagued by doubts', which means that one is paralysed from all action. Then I rouse myself and say 'I'll survive', but I still manage to get very little done.

I wish your letters were not so short—I have no idea of what you are becoming or what you are thinking. I am as you see the same as ever, if a little depressed for the moment. But that will change again, I hope, soon. I would like a small recognition from the world that it thinks my doings worthwhile. But this kind of hope is absurd, I suppose, because it reveals such a limited horizon on my part. Still there is this craving I cannot get rid of, to be able to turn round and point at things I have done—works written, works stimulated by me, works achieved at least partly through my effort—and not journalism which fades into total uselessness in less than twenty-four hours after it has appeared in public.

196

*John was now looking for a job in publishing, and in the summer of
1967 he joined the publishing house of Paul Elek, where he stayed for
two years. He also pursued his interest in politics because he felt it was
not enough just to criticise politicians but that one had 'to dirty one's
hands'. He applied to the Liberal Party and was later accepted as a
candidate for Hampstead.*

TO ROBERT CUMMING   *28, York Street*
4 June 1967   *London W1*

You will be relieved to hear that I have taken a job in a
publishing house, that I have got out of the doldrums that I
was in when I last wrote and that life is rather more cheerful.

My novel about the 'Foundation World' has not met with
success, in that I found no buyer and will probably have to
re-write it, which I may do. My literary career is therefore still
in the backwaters, although I am having a little amusement
with the Liberal Party, who seem to be anxious to further my
political one—you may yet see me as a Liberal candidate,
which would alarm me more if I could believe that there was
any reality in it. When I attend political discussions I always
feel an atmosphere of total unreality—just as in academic
seminars at the London School of Economics or at my
Institute for Strategic Studies. The discussion of politics is like
ants talking about clouds: we are so small in relation to those
vast amorphous issues, and we seem to have no influence on
them: and yet we are assured that we do. Looking at Vietnam,
for instance, I feel that this assurance is absurd. But the
discussions go on and I can't deny they have a certain dream-
like fascination.

Have you written any more poems? It is so tremendously
difficult to express what one feels without keeping any of it
back, when one's whole life is organised to keep feelings under
control, and not express what might be painful. To be a poet in
this kind of world is very hard indeed, I think, or even a

197

novelist or playwright. And artists now have so few feelings that they have to resort to pastiche, or hysterical abstract pictures. I thought the other day of doing a Dutch flower picture—but all in plastic flowers, with the little plastic tomatoes they have in Hamburger bars containing ketchup, and plastic lemons and a bottle of 'pure' lemon juice in the background: this would rival Rauschenberg perhaps. The boredom of all that official dada-ism is extraordinary.

My life here is entertaining but not moving, I laugh a bit and very occasionally make a new attachment—but it is all social and very little from the heart. I still have school-boy visions of a world of heart-rending attachments, but they do not increase in number with the years. Politics is a good complement to this unreality—one must make do with it I suppose.

TO ARCADI NEBOLSINE   *28, York Street*
22 July 1967   *London W1*

Thank you for your postcard—of course we will be serious, *very* serious—I am never anything else as you well know. And of course we will exchange ideas—if we have any. And we will take the business of life at the level it requires—a tragic cast of face, a mournful tone, a respectful lack of humour before the splendours of Rome. And if you are the kind of moralist that J. A. Symonds was then, my dear, I will be especially pleased because the morality he preached and practised was very similar to my own. The only thing in your card which I resent is your phrase 'silly Oscar'. He has left us with two or three perfect plays and for that we are to be eternally grateful—you see how serious I usually am—whatever his shortcomings personally.

I was in Rome a few weeks ago at a conference where I represented the Liberal Party (a new thing in my life about which I will tell you, not *too* seriously), and was amazed that of my colleagues, some of whom were moderately distinguished in their way, practically none had the vaguest idea of what the Gesù was (and is), who St Ignatius was, or why his tomb was there. The conference took place just opposite in the Palazzo Altieri, with magnificent rooms by Giulio Romano—that too was a closed book. It is the age of specialists who know all there is to be known about concrete or machinery or transport but are children when faced by anything else. But real children have curiosity—these middle-aged experts are childish only in their inexperience.

Friends continue—that is a relief, perhaps one that is harder to find in America than here. In Paris Marthe and Jean Dominique and Philippe, in London the old gang, and some new ones; for instance a very nice poet and writer, François Duchêne—and our neighbours here in the country, including David Cornwall (John Le Carré). And then there are curious new groups and types among whom one finds oneself through work or by some other accident. The opera is a great source of excitement always, and the nearness of the Continent, to which one can always turn whenever one is bored here! Finally, this house in the country gets pleasanter and prettier, the garden a kind of nostalgic backwater, and life is lived as it ought to be; arguments are over flowers or croquet or nothing more divisive than that. So in spite of difficulties and upheavals I can't say I mind life, or that I find it impossible— quite. There is too much to whet my curiosity, and enough small triumphs to keep one's competitiveness alive.

TO ROBERT CUMMING   28, York Street
19 November 1967   London W1

I have seen your parents twice—they had dinner with me and a very pleasant girl from my office at my club (yes, my club, a sort of college in the middle of London with better food and rules and pictures, and large comfortable rooms, called the Garrick) and I had lunch with them at a restaurant near the

199

British Museum. After our lunch your father and I had a long chat on a sofa in the middle of the King's Library in the British Museum. I had asked him if he would be interested in contributing to a series of books on 'Discovery' which we are planning, and he explained to me how and under what circumstances he might be. We talked for almost two hours and he was remarkably warm and alive and perceptive about the series—about everything we discussed. He is strangely like you but with a determination which I know you have too, but are careful to hide behind a façade of indecision. (But I have never believed in your indecisions.) I enjoyed this talk very much—your father has such a perfect *style* that I am left feeling a little vulgar and mundane; it makes one realize what a stable, almost innocent world America used to be in a way—full of a republican decency that is now on trial, but which has its strengths. All in all it was very good to see them.

I have been to the Frankfurt Book Fair. At the end I had a long (and equally exhausting) day in the Staedel museum—but it was a relief. They have a magnificent collection of pictures (Van Eyck to Picasso), including the strangely moving portrait of Goethe in the Roman Campagna by Tischbein: wisdom, flamboyance, romantic self-consciousness and immense power all conveyed by a thoroughly second-rate master—which shows what a subject can do to a painter.

After that I went to France for a week chez my friend Marthe de La Rochefoucauld in her house in the Auvergne. French aristocracy in the country—very good food, old-fashioned conversations, interspersed with a good deal of giggling on our part, fine houses and the strong scent of a way of life that was once almost perfect—like a bowl of slightly too old dried rose-petals—the immense identification of family with a *place*, which we are gradually losing in the west everywhere and which, oddly enough, is essential for civilised existence.

Your letters aren't depressed or depressing. You have always underrated yourself, you always manage to do everything you do very well, even though you complain all the time how badly you are doing it. And that goes for your friendship with me too. You always seem to imply I ought to reserve my affection for someone worthier; that's asking too much— once one likes, one does not really ask any more if it's worthwhile or not. Of course one does invest people and things with a certain quality, which is more in one's own mind than in the thing itself, but that is the power of some people— and some works of art—to suggest qualities to one, to provide associations, to make life come alive as it were.

Christmas has been calm and overeaten, but enjoyable with my Dutch friend Aart van Deth here and a pleasant evening at Hadspen with Paul and Penny Hobhouse—a very quiet family party, with backgammon afterwards between myself and the small son David, and the older generation chatting around the fire—everything Christmas even in a large house in the country should be. In spite of everything England and English life still have a lot to recommend them. You are so Centrally European in your romantic vision of the world—brilliant conversation, brilliant clothes and beauties, exotic loves—and so New Yorkish in your practical vision of ruthless parties and cut and jab. Things here are in decline in some ways, but the quality of life is, oddly enough, none the worse for that, in fact it is a little improved by it. France is not all that different but there are all sorts of pretensions because they are all so political and reflect their silly government.

The smartest society here is rather boring I admit—first because I don't know it very well, and my contact with it tends therefore to be spasmodic and a little out of touch, secondly because the rich here still don't know what to do with their money—money and really imaginative brains rarely go hand in hand—thirdly because society is not cut out for being smart now, rather for small groups with brains and culture in common and an ability to cultivate their friendships. The rich run after pop and TV stars, after tailors and hairdressers (literally)—people who are always more amusing to look at than to talk to. So one has to cultivate one's own little garden of acquaintances, and there sure enough are a number of exotic blooms—not least *mon cher* yourself, who is sadly missed over here, but who will I hope be descending like Apollo (or possibly Silenus) out of a cloud in 1968 . . .

TO BEN SONNENBERG   *28, York Street*
6 March 1968   *London W1*

It was very good to see you here even if only for tea—but short as our meeting was I still have ringing in my ears the magnificent political speech to which you treated me. I had no idea that oratory fitted into your rhetorical repertoire: what a pity you have never been persuaded to enter the political lists yourself. Since we spoke I have been formally adopted by the Liberals of Hampstead as their prospective Parliamentary candidate, and there has been a rapid succession of meetings, discussion groups, 'wine-and-cheese' parties with ward-workers, etc., etc. Surprisingly even *I* am beginning to find that the sound of my own voice wearies me after a while— although in the last week it has been a relief to find a platform to sound off from, when thinking about the Government's extraordinary behaviour to the Kenyan Asians. Calmly and you might say brazenly, our mother of Parliaments has decided to keep out 60,000 people from this country who have valid British passports, simply because they are brown. It's a comfort that the Liberals were leaders in the fight against the bill, but it did not make much difference. The effect of the bill will probably be, however, to make the middle-class idealists who form the basic group of the Labour Party's workers in England much more reluctant to help their party back to office in the future. This could be helpful to the Liberals ... but better still in the long run it may make a link-up between the rump of the Labour Party and the Liberals possible in the mid-70s. That's what we hope for anyway.

In the meanwhile work continues to fascinate me—I really think I have found both a profession and a firm I'll be able to tolerate for more than nine months...

TO ROBERT CUMMING   *28, York Street*
10 May 1968   *London W1*

Your parents have come and gone from Perridge—we had a most enjoyable weekend. Croquet balls went clicking back and forth amid cries of dismay or pleasure—my father badly letting down yours in a foursome in which the two of them played against my mother and me. Most of the time the weather was good which was a great advantage because it meant that they could see the garden and in spite of a very wet trip to Wells we had sun on the ruins of Glastonbury. I enjoyed their curiosity and interest in everything they see—something which they share with my parents and with you and me. They have read and seen so much and have absorbed and remembered it all, so that listening to them is to be taken through an enormous variety of interesting and enjoyable experiences. I always feel a little like a naughty boy when they are there because they have much higher principles than mine —but they have a great deal of tolerance and warmth to bridge that gap!

At this distance America seems like a pot on the boil with

evil things swimming about in the mixture, but at the same time you still have in America that 19th-century enlightened hope that the 'liberals', the humane, the people who think that things can be improved are slowly winning. Every victory in the 19th century was a victory for those who wanted to make things more tolerant and more decent in their societies (in Europe)—in spite of temporary set-backs. But this has changed in Europe in the 20th century where the liberals have simply been squashed when they have not been wiped out: of course they have managed to survive, but at what cost! In America I have the impression there is still the conviction that the society is *capable* of improvement—and slowly perhaps it is moving forward. Here instead we have a kind of political and cultural immobilism in which we are always trying to ensure the preservation of the virtues and great inheritance of the past.

TO ROBERT CUMMING   *Perridge House*
2 June 1968   *Pilton*

Your parents like mine think that it would be a very good idea if you got married (and of course I should too). The two mothers were wholly in agreement. They want grand-children—and they want to see that sense of responsibility develop which apparently comes only with marriage. But I think I belong to a generation that does not—or should not—get married, and if I have children, let them be illegitimate—I'd look after them if need be. Our parents have had such successful marriages, in the sense that they continue to put up with each other, that they automatically suppose that their children will do the same. But I might be horrid to live with. It is curious how the convention of marriage is getting stronger. There used to be nothing wrong with a bachelor in his thirties—now automatically one is supposed to pursue appall-ing vices (homosexuality is the very least people suspect—that isn't a vice any more, it's a religion), to be impotent, to be arrested in one's development or I don't know what, if one isn't married. The fact that one just likes one's own company is quietly overlooked.

You cannot imagine how pretty it is here now (I am at Perridge as you may have guessed): how fat and succulent the strawberries are, how everything is pushing and growing so you can practically hear the plant life at work. Wild orchids have spread in one part of the garden—and the thousands of things my parents have encouraged over the years are beginning to make themselves felt at last: huge viburnums and hydrangeas, lilacs, a tulip tree and a paulownia, magnolias (not so large as in South Carolina), honeysuckle and acanthus. You would enjoy it—just the profusion by itself is a tribute to what a little ingenuity and patience can make out of the soil.

TO JIM RIDGEWAY   *28, York Street*
13 June 1968   *London W1*

I'm surprised in a way that you're still with the *New Republic*, but your natural dissatisfaction with things keeps you restless —perhaps you have accepted that now and have decided to become an official progressive instead. (It happened to me some time ago, I didn't even notice then.)

Paris is bubbling quietly—I'm not alarmed by the students since they have no real programme and talk in the language of forty years ago. For them the *only* revolution is the traditional revolution, and that is Marxist (what a bore and how irrelevant to those swinging boys and girls with their English clothes, American food, daddy's car and mummy's weekend cottage, pot and homosexuality). And the government's reaction isn't all that surprising, since we always knew that they were fascistic underneath. Alarming is the extraordinary panic on the part of the fifty-year-old intellectual bums and journalists, academics and 'leaders' to jump on the bandwagon: we want to be even younger than the young, even more hip. Middle-aged pansies talk of Mao, and journalists spurn consumer values, failed artists sprout new pretensions and youngish socialists, vaguely aware of their hopeless future, eagerly hurl bricks by the side of their gorgeous juniors. And Stephen Spender is writing it all up for the *New York Review of Books* (youth, youth, lovely youth . . .).

TO PROFESSOR SIR ISAIAH BERLIN *28, York Street*
29 July 1968 *London W1*

I am writing to you merely to say how very much I enjoyed, was impressed, and was moved by your introduction to Alexander Herzen's autobiography.* I had been attracted to the book as soon as I read the reviews of the new edition, having heard of it all my life, without ever reading it. Now I am feasting on it—delighted that there are four large volumes—delighted too that the promise of excitement which you give in the first pages is borne out by the book itself.

You capture not only the predicament of Herzen and his generation and his class in the Europe or Russia of the 1850s but really also the whole contemporary problem of being a *European*. There is a moment in Goethe's conversations with Eckermann, where G. says that he feels sorry for those who come after him, because so much of what they *will* feel has already been expressed by himself; this is precisely what I feel Herzen does too—and a quality in him which you have brilliantly described.

Having worked for only five or six years in and around the European Community, with its vision of integration and technical bliss, I already feel a sensation that once achieved, that kind of Europe will destroy or forget all the values, all the ideals of privacy, leisure and human contact, which our

* *My Past and Thoughts. The Memoirs of Alexander Herzen*, 1968.

206

inherited culture stands for, and which has after all survived tremendous attempts to destroy it. And yet I still believe that Europe must in the end be brought into some form of unity, however alien the society that results will be for me. It is an enormous comfort to see Herzen, with all his energy, his vision, his much larger culture, having so much the same conflict between his ideals and his personal preferences, and in a sense resolving them by the mere exercise of consistent courage.

You introduce one to this vindication of being an individual with an infectious enthusiasm and sympathy. I hope you won't mind my taking up your time in saying how much I appreciated that and what a relief it was to feel that you *wanted* to write about Herzen in the warm way you have, at a time when the gasworks of sociology are covering every memory and every aspiration with a thick layer of dust.

TO ROBERT CUMMING   *28, York Street*
27 August 1968   *London W1*

I have been reading the memoirs of Alexander Herzen—still am, four fat juicy volumes of fascinating, astonishing humanity—ideas, events, comments, people, brilliantly presented: a whole world comes alive and a strangely modern one, set in 19th-century Russia and then among the romantic exiles in the West, Marx, Bakunin, etc. The more I read in it the more he fascinates me, though I find him as a person less totally likeable in the second volume than in the first. He hates the Tsarist regime, but didn't much like any other, and ultimately I suspect he wouldn't even have much liked the socialist paradise of which he occasionally dreamed. On his friends and on friendship he is most revealing: how I wish one could open one's house like that—with people in and out in a casual way, talk, food, affection, argument mixing—but he was accustomed to a world in which there were always servants, however revolutionary one might be, and a few with money who were willing to spend it. I would like to do that—but friends today are busy and things have to be arranged. It is only when they come to stay that one can sit down and talk to them—and then the weekend is over and they are gone for the next few weeks or even months. In our time we are losing increasingly the art of human relations— the pleasure of coexistence. There are *arrières pensées* and there is the wristwatch warning us of the next appointment, the next job, the next chore. I think we—you and I—have managed a friendship in spite of distance and jobs and our own disagreements—but it is a pity that it has to be across such a distance, because one needs the few friends, in the full sense of the word, that one has all the time.

I am very dominated by what people expect of me—such as earning a living and making a career—to such an extent that I often believe I need those things. I need a different world, where Russia doesn't march into Czechoslovakia, where there is no Vietnam, where people including oneself are content with what they are, where sophistication has not reached the masses nor spoilt the 'happy few', where my great-uncle Hertz's radio waves are unknown, where genius resides in small corners, Goethe in Weimar, Voltaire in Fernay, Stendhal at Civitavecchia, Mozart in Salzburg . . . It is a vain dream, all right, but it is also an ideal. How is one to lead this huge empty mass of over-fed rich people in the West, with their idiotic racial preoccupations, their philistinism, their selfishness and banality, their touching ordinariness, into some kind of comprehension of life—of a life worth living? I have an Indian friend in London who says that in his village in Orissa, where they have no shoes or electricity, they understand this better than we do. But it is too late to have no shoes and electricity. We need them because we know them. You'll say I'm being sentimental. In fact I am being realistic. 'Art and the summer lightning of individual happiness' are all that life has to offer— does that lightning (Herzen's word) touch you from time to time?

I must congratulate you, but especially the Institute for Strategic Studies, because as I said many weeks ago, I never thought they'd have the imagination to offer the directorship to *you*. But they have and (as you must realize yourself) they are jolly lucky to get you. Naturally *I* think you are the most dastardly turncoat, but that you may say is just a combination of sour-grapes and romantic illusions. The trouble is that Samuel Butler-like I cannot reconcile myself to the idea that success so often means that one acquires the things which one used most to hate—and while no doubt I will reconcile myself to the paradox if success touches *me* with its butterfly wings, I am still perturbed when it happens to those I most esteem and admire. *Eh bien!* that's nice and pompously put but I would not dare say it if I didn't wish you genuinely the greatest success in the Institute, and that you will leave on it very firmly the stamp of your ideals and character. I hope it will give you the opportunity to spread your views among people who ought to listen to them, and could act on them—this is not said sarcastically: you are one of the few in the world of civil servants and journalists with an eye on the human issues involved in politics, and you ought to be heard.

You'd be amazed at the Garrick Club these days—we've got them all now: Auden, Spender, Betjeman, C. Day Lewis, Lehmann, A. J. Ayer . . . we're waiting for Duchêne to join us. But isn't it funny how the old radicals are coming home to roost, how wonderfully concerned they look about the issues of our time over the hock, or the champagne? John Le Carré in his new book, *A Small Town in Germany*, says the enemy is apathy—his story as always is excellent, but his philosophical observations are balls. I don't think people are apathetic, they just have no good vehicles for expressing themselves. In the age of super-communication, all discussions at a public level —and so often at a private level too—have turned into *dialogue de sourds*. And when at last someone is heard, like Enoch

Powell, it is because he reflects the reactions, the dim hopes, the base aspirations, the niggardly flatulence of the scum of humanity. Even Nixon is better than that. But *we*, who pretend we are not scum, or hope that we can preserve and extend the better things of our society, have no better means of speaking out than he has—in fact we are bad at it, worse at it, even. We are level-headed or even well-informed, but we are not passionate. Perhaps you found in America that the *goodies* are better at communicating than they are over here—perhaps they still have the knack of making an ignorant person believe the better side of an argument, at least sometimes. Here the ignorant merely feel lost, while the informed (whom you will meet in their droves at ISS, and good luck to you) are confused by their information and have no hopes, no ideals, no vision— they have just a few possessions and a style of life, which they desperately hope they can preserve for the rest of *their* lives at least. A revolution in the *attitude* of the informed is needed— more than currency reform, more than participation, more than the Common Market, more than technological union. You know that as well as I do—in fact I partly learnt it from you. The test is, can you do anything about it?

Too much reading of Herzen, and a life of Goethe, have produced a sort of wistfulness for the individuality of their lives—but I have realized that our lives have grown out of theirs, our ideas are just a development of theirs. The strange thing is that the idealism which they represent is today regarded as a sort of aesthetic reaction—not quite conservative, but definitely out of keeping with 'the way things are going'. They were then visionaries—even dangerous. Who the hell is *dangerous* now? Some people, some governments, are crushing, some politicians like Powell stir up hideous gases, but what periodical is worth prosecuting, what vision threatens to change our society and needs to be suppressed? Our dearly beloved well-informed overlook, however, that the things that make life tolerable for them—dinner in Soho, freedom to make love when they like (or with whom), a garden at Henley, a visit to Greece, a football match,

210

Duchesses—and which are the alpha and omega of their social and political philosophy are actually endangered, not by outside forces but by their own inertia. All these things, so dear to Herzen and Goethe too, are fast disappearing. No one knows how to protect them from the flood—let alone increase their number.

So I'm gloomy . . . not really, just aware that our nice easy fairly friendly society, in which I can comfortably publish books, and drive down to Perridge, and visit Italy, etc., sits on a curious vacuum—a world in which most improvements actually make life worse, in which we are always hankering after the *abuses* of yesterday.

TO ANSON KIDDA NÉE JORDAN   28, York Street
18 December 1968   London W1

Mr Sonnenberg was here on top form full of cracks ('Women journalists would be wonderful to make love to, if you could only go to bed with their by-lines and leave *them* behind'), dispensing dinners at Claridges with total relaxation but a bit nervy in museums as he doesn't like collections where nothing is for sale . . . Do go to see him and the palazzo—it has a mustiness that is rather splendid and endearing—and he admires your grandpa [Learned Hand] reverentially.

Van Gogh has been shown at the disgusting Hayward Gallery—that nightmare of concrete and tinware across the river near the Festival Hall. The pictures are all in little wooden frames that make them look like stamps on the wall. Only one is surrounded with a frame as VG himself made it—immediately it comes alive. It's strange that frames help—but they do, and I can't see why modernity requires that pictures should be unframed. Some of them are marvellous, some merely dull. But one remembers him, he goes on being an artist that I can love—nothing chocolate-boxy about him as there so often is in Renoir. Cecil Beaton in the afternoon—

glamorous photographs of people over the years—but there is something coldly pansy about photography, which freezes the cockles of my heart, *pour ainsi dire*.

TO HILDA AND BEN SONNENBERG   *Perridge House*
14 May 1969   *Somerset*

You have been, over the past five weeks, so very hospitable and kind to me and gave me such an enjoyable stay (in spite of illness and all that) that I feel almost embarrassed by my debt of good living. Your house remains the most comfortable and the most welcoming in two hemispheres. I felt this time more than ever how much its style is an expression of yourselves— both in its elegance and in its sense of humour. And then it is such an oasis in the dingy atmosphere of the city—an atmosphere which I hugely enjoy, but from which one wants to escape. You shut it all out in Gramercy Park, or at least you keep only the best of it and reject all the dirt and discomfort. I must say that I have never yet enjoyed a visit to America so much—and I'm afraid you spoilt me so much that it took quite a time to get used to the simplicity of this house! As for my illness—I apologize for it, and thank you for being so very patient about it. I don't think one could have shingles so comfortably anywhere—it was almost worth having to stay a little longer.

One especially good thing about your house is that in the nine years I have known it, it has not changed—so that even though I've changed quite a lot in that time, it is like a home-coming. Having dinner with you last week was just like dinner in 1960; it makes one believe that some good things in life are permanent, that they don't just live on in memory. It was good too to see Alistair [Cooke]—it reminded me of our dinners in 1960, when after a day as, what Hilda called 'the talking dog' at the *Wall Street Journal*, I would come to Gramercy Park to find comfort, a good story and some sharp minds at play! And then you see I have been very carefully brought up, so that I believe that no entertainment is worthwhile if it is not also instructive—and the classrooms at Gramercy Park are really the most delightful as well as the most effective one can find.

So you see you have overwhelmed me again—I just hope that later in life I shall be able to return the favour by overwhelming someone else. These things cannot after all be repaid, they can only be passed on, each generation to the next; it is just outstanding luck to find friends of such good nature in an older generation than one's own.

TO HIS FATHER   *28, York Street*
16 August 1969   *London W1*

Many happy returns of the day—it is very hard to think of you being 70, as that is more than twice my age, and as I grow older you seem to remain very much the same. Fortunately the passage of the years has left almost imperceptible marks, so that one does not think of you getting older, nearly as much as of oneself doing so. It must be strange too for you to think that when you were my age you had no idea that your whole life so to speak was before you, in that you had to start from scratch in a foreign country. But how good to sit at 70 in the garden at Perridge (when you are allowed to *sit*) and to think that you have managed so satisfactorily to survive all that, and that surrounded by your trees and flowers have found so different —and so much more wonderful—a setting from anything which you could possibly have imagined thirty or forty years ago. How good too that you have found that you could not only be a banker and an art dealer but finally also a gardener, to start on the most exacting and the most absorbing career as your third choice. What next? You have chosen such diverse careers that I'm sure you'll find another before long, and that

213

at 100 you will have perfected your fourth or even fifth expertise.

Most surprising in a way is your ability to survive family life—and to have given your children, or at least me, the impression all through what has after all been a perfectly ghastly period of history, that all was really quite all right, that certain values, certain aspirations, were not merely legitimate, but quite within our grasp, that Pangloss-like we would survive, and survive with the good things of life stable and available. You share an incurable optimism with Mummy, which should see you comfortably through to 100. Unlike most optimists you have been justified by the event—perhaps even you are surprised by that. Perhaps the secret of your success is that you have always matched your optimism with generosity and that too explains why the impression of stability was always so strong. In the end it is generosity which I associate with you most, and from which I have learnt most.

In November 1969 John went to India with his parents, a country which made a deep impression on him, aesthetically and emotionally. He had joined Phaidon Press before this journey. He stood as Liberal candidate for the Borough of Camden in April 1970 in the GLC elections. Then each elector had three votes in a joint contest. John's poll was 4·7% of the total. In the General Election on 18 June 1970 John polled 3550 votes which was 7·8% of a low turnout of the electorate of Hampstead and thereby lost his deposit. Geoffrey Finsberg (Conservative) won the seat from the sitting MP, Ben Whitaker (Labour). It was a bad year for Liberals throughout the country, and the worst results were inevitably in close marginals which Hampstead had by then become. In 1966 many Liberal supporters had voted for Ben Whitaker, because he claimed to have a Liberal outlook although he had joined the Labour party; and many Liberals again voted for him in 1970 in an unsuccessful attempt to keep the Conservatives out.

His travels took him to Greece, but also to Italy, New York and

Frankfurt in connection with his work. He left Phaidon Press in 1975 when it was bought by the Dutch publishers Elsevir, and moved to No. 7 Cleveland Square, where he established his own publishing firm and office above his private flat in 1976. His letters were now rare, as his time was fully occupied. In January 1980 he moved his firm to new premises in Great Russell Street where he enjoyed the fact that he could look at the façade of the British Museum from his office window.

TO HIS AUNT GRÄFIN CARMEN VON   *Clark's Hotel*
FINCKENSTEIN   *Benares*
9 January 1970   *India*

It must be amazing to you to see yet another decade of this strange century—certainly it is to me: I can hardly believe that the 60s, which started as it seems only yesterday, should have already come to an end. During them I discovered an enormous amount—first about myself, later about the world. The first voyage of discovery is after all inside oneself—but gradually that becomes too familiar a territory and one turns outside. Here in India a journey does both, because one simply has to reassess life.

TO ROBERT CUMMING   *Perridge House*
1 March 1970   *Somerset*

If you want to know, as you seem to do, I do often feel bitterly about my limitations. I started life at 18, say, believing that human relations was all that mattered, that being in love was the best thing possible, that sex was a tremendously exciting business full of passion, longing, fulfilment, etc., that my attachments to people would be the thing both they and I would care most about. I felt like this both instinctively and consciously. My feeling was to enjoy other people's affection and to give it to them, and my thoughts quite consciously went in the same direction. Lots of illusions accompanied these feelings and ideas but they were absolutely genuine. Everything discouraged me—or nearly everything. I believed, as I said, that love was everything, without enjoying it properly however, with the wrong objects and without getting it returned in anything like the strength I demanded. And there was a relentless pressure to make me work, to conform to what other people (not only my family) expected of me, to be normal, that is: with middlingly strong feelings, mild desires, and sensible short-term aims.

It's easier to rely on myself for most things—but it still jars when I think about it. I'd like to lavish, pour out love over someone and have it poured back and I'd like to live in a circle of people who adore me and whom I adore, and who are within constant and easy striking distance. I'd like to live in a world in which everyone has their place and I had my own (glittering) position, I'd like there to be no form of social glamour and human passion which was not within my reach. But obviously all that is unrealistic and I'm having to adapt in a strange way to what I've actually found. People like me more if I'm slightly distant, and I like them more, with a few exceptions, if *they* are. I'm not perfectly frank, not even with you—and you aren't with me. And so it goes on. Human relations may be the most important thing in life, but it's best perhaps not to expect too much from them. Acceptance of all this boring side of life has made it easier for me—more livable. The trick is to create a private life within the framework which has forced itself onto one's life—and I'm trying to do it. So are you.

I could be happier, I could be more intelligent, I could be free-er of problems, I could depend less on my parents or on my creature comforts or on my work, etc., etc. But isn't the real point at this stage to try to make something of one's own within our limitations—and what does it matter if we don't

216

marry, don't have children, don't work in banks, don't write textbooks, don't teach, don't make £1 million, don't do dozens of other things people still expect of us, provided we do some of the things we want to do and maintain an adequate relationship with the world?

What a frightful letter. It started as a tease but ended as a sermon, or rather a mini-confession. But you want me to tell you about myself and so I tell you over and over again, and I rely on your warmth and tact and discretion to put up with it. I haven't told you all this because I want you to take me as an example. I want to explain simply why I've come to accept the limitations on my life. Some people never accept theirs and this often makes them do *better* than I am doing—to make more things that are recognizably theirs but are enjoyed by others. And that is the most exciting thing left to us, given the type of life we are forced to lead: to make something of one's own, which can excite others, make them share in one's own hopes and dreams and feelings, even if only momentarily.

TO SIR JOHN BUCHANAN RIDDELL   *28, York Street*
30 March 1970   *London W1*

I have seen a few of our friends—an evening with Serena [Rothschild], Griselda [Grimond] and Si [Baring] to watch Paul Scofield as Uncle Vanya. I awfully wanted to join in the conversation on the stage from time to time to say 'shut up', and I suppose that is a measure of the success of the production. The trouble with Chekhov is that one does want to say that so often. Who cares about the misery of provincial Russian life in 1900? Watching them doesn't make one's own burden any easier to bear.

I was amused by your description of visiting the seminar on the wickedness of capitalism—it corresponds to the hippies we saw at various points in the Indian sub-continent. Puffing away at their pot, receiving delightful capitalist cheques from

217

home (Wyoming, Oslo, Düsseldorf, Wigan), nude on the beach at Goa (and very pretty at that), long-haired and well-covered in Nepal (not at all pretty there), begging in the streets of Bombay, enjoying poverty as an adventure in a land where poverty is very much not a thing to be enjoyed, they made me feel quite illiberal and disgusted. The Indians regard them as idiots to be tolerated part of the time, to be thrown out at others, but certainly not as serious converts to the Asiatic way of life (or love) as which they pose. One in particular struck me; he wore a long grey-white garment draped round him, on his head a mass of knotted once blond hair, but now so filthy that it had turned a greasy yellow, on top a bun (in imitation of an Indian 'rishi' or holy man), in his hands he clutched some sacred (to him) object. It was with difficulty that he got onto the plane to Nepal as he was well over six foot tall, and his hair and bun made him about six-foot-ten—altogether too big for the Fokker Friendship. At the other end some poor Nepalese made a sort of obeisance to him as if he were a genuine rishi—so California's exports are beginning to make their mark even in the religious field. But do rishis fly I ask myself? On carpets yes, but in the tools of Western capitalism?

It really reveals the incredible childishness of the Americans that they can think of no better way of breaking with tradition than these pathetic imitations of the East or bohemia, capitalist gypsies without romance. But I gather you are enjoying the greatest suburb of the world. I love my American friends— but I'm feeling rather anti American 'culture' at the moment. I'm sick of their tastelessness and lack of ideas, their thirst for other people's culture, for reach-me-down ready-to-wear intellectual garments. Oh, and their knowledge: they have far too many facts.

Just before my belated attack of mumps I was a Liberal candidate in the Greater London Council elections—it was an unmitigated disaster as I knew it would be—and it makes one wonder why one puts in the effort. Politics could be fun—or even useful, if one had plenty of money and time to put into it. The necessity of speaking always in clichés is incredibly depressing, however; the idea that politics is the art of making good ideas work is forgotten in the welter of effort it requires to make the system work at all. Our society is so large and ideas get so diffused in it that all discussion turns on the immediate question and not the long-term. The world is an unhappy place—if one takes into account all the information one continually receives about it. And the interaction of all this information is to confuse issues and people, and make local action dependent on things like Vietnam which have absolutely nothing to do with it. So many of the 'great issues' are irrelevant to our current needs or local issues: but it is easier to attitudinise on the first and harder to have the necessary information on the second, so people align along the great issues and don't work hard enough to make their own world habitable at least. The concern with faraway issues is amazing: everyone wishes apparently to indulge in the fantasy of being a great revolutionary hero, liberating South Americans, Vietnamese, South Africans or what have you. But a bit of cultivating one's own garden would do the world no harm.

The biggest burden really is the feeling that one must make a mark—that one must be known, must have caused a small ripple—must have captured an immortal moment and given it to others. That's the effect of an education which says that we are a little higher than the ants if we create works of art, an effect one cannot throw off—once imbibed it is a distorting elixir which keeps one on the move like that wasp which the Goddess Hera used to pursue the unfortunate maiden who had caused her jealousy.

I go back to London in a couple of days. Wednesday I give a dinner-party in my club—I still feel the urge to entertain, I don't know why. I suppose I enjoy it while it goes on, and I always hope there will be a sort of magic generated which will give us pleasure. Sometimes it works. Basically I like very conventional pleasures—and rather conventional people, in a way. At least I like their ideas to be unusual, but their manners not. It's hard to find such a combination! Nowadays we wear our ideas on our sleeves, and if our ideas are to be lively our sleeves must be filthy. So I fall back on the good old British upper-middle class, with its tolerance and sense of humour, and complacent acceptance of the world. Friends are after all one's own in a sense—once you have them, it is best to try to keep them, and have one's adventures in the mind. But I'm still curious about all those millions of people I don't know.

TO MR DAVID STEEL   *43, Cleveland Square*
LEADER OF THE LIBERAL PARTY   *London W2*
29 June 1970

I was amazed to read in *The Scotsman* on Friday (26 June) that you had said that, 'Liberalism is better served by saving Labour MP Ben Whitaker from his 474-vote defeat. He had an excellent record in the House of Commons of stout independence on many liberal issues.'

Leaving aside for the moment your assessment of Ben Whitaker, I must say it was extremely painful for me to read this panegyric which was so remarkable for its failure to commend the many Liberals who have fought London constituencies in very adverse circumstances.

The theory on which this election was fought was, that the more Liberal votes there were in the country, the stronger would be the position of the Liberal MPs actually in the House: on this basis, all my supporters and I worked tremendously hard to get as many votes as possible. I certainly

220

feel it very deeply that you should say *now* that the whole thing was a mistake. (If you felt indeed that it *was* a mistake to fight Hampstead, I wonder why you did not bother to inform me before the election: it was well known for two years beforehand that I was the PPC.)

TO BEN SONNENBERG   43, *Cleveland Square*
10 September 1970   *London W2*

The election was a disaster for the Liberals as you know. I enjoyed some of it but was disappointed by the results. If ever I go into politics again it will be where I have a chance of winning—and for a party which has a chance of forming a government. Actually the two go hand in hand. The British don't really like parties that aren't likely to govern, and however much they like *you* (and my constituents said very often they did like me) they won't vote for you on a personal basis as a rule. And if that's the way they want it, there's very little one can do about it.

TO SARAH AND JOHN BUCHANAN   43, *Cleveland Square*
RIDDELL   *London W2*
7 December 1970
At a launching party at the Bodleian Sir Isaiah Berlin turned up and gave me his views on Hannah Arendt: he said that the first sentence of her most famous book contains two propositions which are manifestly wrong. 'She says the difference between Greek and Jewish civilization is that the Greeks despised work while the Jews admired it. She forgets that the Greeks admired Hercules, who spent his life carrying out labours of an extremely tedious kind, cleaning stables and the like, while the Jews were chased from paradise and believed work was a curse.' I have shortened it, but it was masterfully done.

How does one acquire a position in which one is universally admired (or at least sought after), has enough money, interesting and successful work, *and* a large amount of free time in which to indulge the passion for human relations and romantic dreams of beauty and poetry? You, Sybil of Connecticut, must have found out the answer in your endless researches in English literature. I hope you aren't becoming fierce—when I was in the US in November I got the impression you were getting fierce. You squashed that poor nervous girl-friend of Bob's—and there was something fierce too about your jeans . . .

I regret there are so many people in the world—it would be easier if one's thoughts were not shared with quite so many others with similar education, ideals and problems. It is shocking how banal one is. And yet everywhere one goes one gets the impression that there are actually only 10,000 people since the paths that cross ours are all interconnected. Who are all those faceless nameless broad masses of the intelligentsia? And apart from making up the sheep in the fashionable intellectual movements of the moment, I wonder what all their studying does for them? My sister would say my attitude was snobbish. But I would so like to hear of some group of people who have arisen out of the morass of university products, and who have something to say I couldn't have thought of myself, or would like to have thought of myself. I'm afraid I'm not in sympathy with the world you have chosen—I don't know whether you are yourself: the universities are the dreariest symbol of a barren age. But for you it is a way, I do see, to forge your private world, in which you can live for your own ideas without being disturbed. I suppose that's as much as one can ask for in life, certainly it is very much what my mother asked for, and did not, to her dismay, get.

To hell with all this philosophy—I'm sorry I haven't

cracked any jokes, but jaundice leaves one rather barren of all that. The garden is looking enchanting with daffodils and violets and primroses in masses, but the skies are very grey and it is cold. So I feel a bit grey and cold too. In the end I feel a stranger in England, just a little anyway, and not quite at home anywhere else. That's the effect of being an immigrant, and it makes me understand American life very well, with its lack of family connections and influence—at least for most Americans although not for you or Sheila [Lafarge].

TO ROBERT CUMMING   *Perridge House*
11 April 1971   *Somerset*

I often wonder why the art of the 19th century in every sense is so much more attractive to me than that of the 20th, even though I think I would have hated much of the 19th-century life, just as much as I dislike so much of life today. I was very amused the other day when I was visited in my sick-room by the editor-in-chief of Praegers, a pleasant plump balding shortish man of about 44 from rural Georgia, but Jewish and very nice if a bit plodding. He is married to a go-ahead Jewish wife from New Jersey, they live in the 90's on the West Side by Riverside Drive, have two or three charming children and are concerned about everything that forward-moving middle-class people should be concerned about. He told me that some book or other I had recommended him to take from my former employer was 'terrific': the reason—'it really undermines a whole lot of accepted middle-class ideas'. It is amazing the extent to which nice middle-class people *want* to be undermined. It gives them the satisfactory feeling, if they are undermined once a week, that they have had an intellectual motion. They are on the move, as it were, which is the main thing, and in the meantime they live exactly as they did before. The desire to regard oneself as absurd is about the most accepted middle-class idea of all. And here am I wanting to

223

indulge in fantasies, and not think about social problems at all. I think the only real view which would undermine the current middle-class outlook is that the traditional values governing human relationships are right. That will really cause a furore.

TO THE EDITOR,   *43, Cleveland Square*
The Times   *London W2*
10 July 1971

Sir, When the Labour Party holds its special conference to consider the case for supporting or opposing British entry into the Common Market, it is to be hoped that it will invite one or two leading socialists and trade unionists from the Six to address the conference, so that it can hear about the European Community from socialists who have experience of its workings and effects.

In particular it might be a good idea if British socialists were able to hear a member of the German government either at the conference itself or at a meeting held within its orbit, since the German socialist party is now in power. A trade unionist from the Six should also perhaps be given the opportunity to explain the generally favourable attitude of the socialist unions to the Community.

It would surely be helpful for Labour supporters to know what the conference has taken note of, what socialists from the Six think, before it attempts to define a view on the negotiations on behalf of the Labour movement as a whole. [Printed 16 July 1971.]

43, Cleveland Square
                                                London W2

If I taught in a university like you I would find it awfully hard not to be very influenced by the students—not to fall half-in-love with them and their appetite for and their willingness to believe in every big idea that comes along. I share this appetite to some extent but one's enthusiasms are mitigated by scepticism and one's prejudices are so strong that it is hard to have the adaptability of the very young—and hard not to be overwhelmed by it.

I can't by the way understand why you are so concerned to have 'a view of your own' as you put it. We take over lock, stock and barrel other people's vision in all sorts of areas, and there is nothing we can do about it—just as evolution has given us the shape we have and the brains we have. Getting your own vision means adapting this inherited stock to your own purposes. What does it matter if your parents have influenced you? What does it matter if you understand or don't understand the workings of ordinary American lives? You will never understand them—and if you do what will they care? Perhaps it will help you with your writing, that is true, and I hope it does, but writing is the work of the imagination as much as the observation of the finer points of contemporary life.

TO RICHARD NIEMICE   *43, Cleveland Square*
23 September 1971   *London W2*

If you can get to India do go. I was there for two months in the winter a year ago, and enjoyed myself hugely. It just is *visually* more beautiful than anywhere in the West—not because of the cities, which are mostly awful, but because of the people who look, walk and dress marvellously. The temples I thought magnificent or at the least extraordinary, but the colours of saris, dresses, silks, jewels, sculptures, mountains, were continuously exciting—all the lost excitement of the medieval world which modern manufactures have destroyed. The people were generally charming, if occasionally crooked, and one has to raise one's eyes from the sadness of the city streets. But that's true in New York and London too.

I enjoyed an evening in Naples—giant palaces built in the 17th century for Neapolitan nobility, now turned into slums with washing hanging from ornate baroque windows. Then on the second floor perhaps one aristocratic apartment left, with windows open, and velvet on the walls of the rooms inside and a uniformed servant looking out. In the square tall columns with Virgins and saints perched on the top, grass growing in between the stones, angels and cherubs in stone and plaster dancing all the way up and down, and little boys playing football below. In the central area a huge number of prostitutes of both sexes offering a room in an official brothel, where 'you pays your money and you takes your choice'.

TO ROBERT CUMMING   43, Cleveland Square
7 November 1971   London W2

Life here proceeds rather too rapidly, with a swarm of small pieces of work pouring in, small events, contacts, visits, talks, and rapid readings that make time fly by, but product hard to identify. It would be good to have a reminder of your existence—to know that the process of assessing the world is continuing in Thompson Street, and there is one mind at least which is still wrestling with the question 'why?' while the rest of us assume there need be no answer.

Sometimes we look at our slides of India and it is astonishing how much we saw, what variety there was there, what extraordinary richness of beauty. One forgets it all so easily and photographs strangely are a help. I could perhaps become someone who would simply revel in all these pleasures of the past and do nothing else—pleasures of the eye, I suppose. It is therefore quite a good thing that I am made by my work to follow up so many things, and be alert all the time. But I would like to live among the dreams of others, and otherwise dream myself. We are at the tail-end of the Aryan civilisations perhaps, and they have no more to offer? Just the past to remember? Of course one cannot believe that: it is simplistic decadent philosophy, which rationalises one's laziness and lack of inventive power. Invention has become hard though, terribly hard. You find it too—I wonder what it is that has dried it up in us, in you and me, in dozens of others. I don't say we have none: I just think we find it difficult to produce anything which comes anywhere near the high standard which we associate with the creators of the past. And that high standard is off-putting precisely, perhaps, because we understand it so well. All this is an old observation—to you most of mine are, but it hits me every time I think about how oddly my life has developed—from the endless productivity of my early twenties, however bad, to the frenetic work but lack of creative product now. Will it start up again? I think it would if I had a stable life—a long-standing love affair, a home around which I built my life, a tie that let me relax the quest for human events, a tie which really bound me. But it has not grown, such a tie, and so I must try without.

TO ROBERT CUMMING   *43, Cleveland Square*
31 January 1972   *London W2*

Your deciding to get married calls for a letter—a handwritten one, as a special honour! Many good wishes, congratulations, and acclamations (if that's correct) to you both. Though I mean this letter for you, *please* give Deborah all my love and good wishes. With your usual alarming sensitivity you noticed a hesitation in my voice [on the telephone]—you thought you detected disapproval: there was none. There was surprise (I had thought you'd never make up your mind) and I must admit there was a little jealousy—first that you could decide at all (I don't think I *ever* will), and secondly because marriage does mean that even in one's relations with one's closest friend there must also inevitably be someone else present. But that was a passing feeling and wasn't important— and it certainly wasn't disapproval. I think you are very lucky to have found someone you want to live with—and who is so charming and intelligent and good, *and* who wants to live with *you*! My only disappointment is that I can't persuade you to come and live in Britain! I often miss you—married or unmarried I'd like to see you and talk to you often.

You sometimes say I always tell you 'you are wrong', but in most of the really important things in life I think you are right, and your instinct is *always* right. I love in you, your absolute sense of loyalty and goodness and instinct for truth and if I argue with your point of view, it is because you so often show a sense of insecurity, which seems to run counter to your instinctive sureness of values. You became the closest acquaintance I have ever had (in the sense of *knowing* you and vice versa) fifteen years ago, and everything good I found in you seemed wonderful and remarkable then—and I think still is. You will bring an extraordinary warmth and affection and gentleness to your marriage and I hope Deborah will help to give you a sense of direction and a confidence which has oddly eluded you. I think *she* can—I certainly never could, and perhaps I am a little jealous of that! (But that too is not important.) Whatever you do I shall always wish you the best, and hope that you will at last find what you want. So good luck and let me hear from you soon.

TO BEN SONNENBERG   *43, Cleveland Square*
25 February 1972   *London W2*

I have been enjoying myself in the last few weeks planning an edition of the Bible—this has involved negotiations with Oxford University Press which as you can imagine is rather like negotiating with God. They have a substitute and composite group—called 'The Principals'—who are responsible for the *New English Bible* which we propose to publish with illustrations. You cannot imagine how reverently we have to approach them. If I bring it off it will be a small triumph—and rather a pleasure to be publishing what consists largely of one's own family history!

TO ROBERT CUMMING   *43, Cleveland Square*
27 March 1972   *London W2*

In these last three months I have been rather mad—less so now than in January—but the illness lingers on. I suppose my whole love-affair was part of what Bill Anderson calls 'the adolescence of early middle-age'. From 30 to 36 or perhaps 28 to 37 I felt a great confidence about my ability to cope with life, with my career, my family, my love-life: I was alone, but I could make it. Suddenly I was offered the apple of passion (what a title for a romantic love-novel), and a few luscious bites into that and I was made aware of a whole new range of uncertainties. What happened to those nineteen years between when I was 19 and now?

I returned to find the office in complete chaos unfortunately—
our accountant had made a mess of the accounts, which was
very worrying (like cars, I only know *when* things are wrong
with accounts, not *what*) and our production was similarly
topsy-turvy, so that needed straightening out—which has
finally been achieved, more or less, but the mess prevented me
from doing essential things such as writing to you.

I had some light relief by giving a big dinner to celebrate the
third anniversary of my 40th birthday (I've decided that there
is no need to alter the basic age I've reached—I'm going to be
40 for a long long time) and then we had Derry Moore's
wedding in Paris, of which I had first heard when we met in
Los Angeles. We all (his friends) went over there, and after a
long service during which we stood for fifty minutes, there
was a dinner for 350 in the magnificent embassy, and a ball
afterwards. The building was put up for the sister of
Napoleon, Pauline Bonaparte, and has a splendid staircase and
huge reception-rooms. We all sat at tables for ten,
unfortunately my table had pretty dull people—my friends
being scattered elsewhere. A rich Greek lady beside me and I
discussed ninety-two Greek islands one by one, after that there
seemed little to talk about. At least the food was delicious. But
once the dancing had begun, the fun began, and we twirled
away until 4 a.m., with a band that played real dance music,
with waltzes and tangos and the things of one's childhood,
which is infinitely more fun than disco. Biene [Goldschmidt-
Rothschild] would have been amused: the Rothschilds were
there in full force, and lots of very elegant Greek ladies.
Anyway I tell you all this because it's funny to think of such
things still going on—a glimpse of the past, and very nice too.
In Paris the next day I visited a delicious flat, on the ground-
floor at the back of a big 18th-century courtyard, and looking
out over a vast garden behind, right in the middle of the city:
the essential Faubourg St Germain worshipped, rightly, by

Proust. If I could have a place like that I'd certainly be content to live in Paris. It has so many cheerful cafés and restaurants where everything is good, and one could be happy as a kind of perpetual visitor: to be deeply *involved* in French life would be more difficult.

TO HILDA AND BEN SONNENBERG   *7, Cleveland Square*
14 February 1978   *London W2*

I used to enjoy writing letters so much—now for some reason I find that they don't express the things I want to say, but come out much too formally, as if I was always writing business notes, which of course I am. So please forgive this silence—it was in no way lack of appreciation of Gramercy Park and its lord and lady. You were really *very* nice to your perennial visitor over Thanksgiving, and I always find when I come to New York that it is really your warmth and good will that make my visits there worthwhile.

London has not been so overwhelmed with snow and ice as America, and we have had a very hard-working winter, but not a particularly bitter one. My real problem was my business: January is the month when I have the largest printing bills—I had somehow to find £170,000, which is more money than I have ever had in my life, and I did find it. It was nerve-racking, but curiously now that I have done it, I feel, as one is told that women feel after having children, that I would be quite prepared to do it all over again. Given the fact that the business plans to go on for some years, I suppose I *will* have to do it again, but I hope it won't be quite such a struggle to get the cash together as it was this time. With these, you might say, mundane preoccupations my life is now principally concerned, which startles me sometimes: after all one was brought up with the idea that what mattered were books, music, and learning. Instead it appears that the business of survival is more pressing than these, which are the decorations of life. In any case I suppose I'm not sufficiently monastic to wish to concentrate wholly on 'higher things'.

We had a very good visit from Alistair and Jane Cooke, who came to dinner here and were quite dazzling. The first as we all know is the king of guests if the table is small and the atmosphere relaxed: table-talk takes on a much better meaning on these occasions than the reports we have of O. Wendell Holmes or Coleridge. He is the autocrat of the dinner table and we are glad to be his slaves. Jane was quite another matter—time was not on my side by letting me be only a boy when I first knew her. We had lunch too and she captivated me as she always does.

TO HILDA SONNENBERG   7, *Cleveland Square*
9 September 1978   *London W2*

I was (and am) so very sad to hear from Helen that Ben had died on Wednesday. He has always seemed so completely indestructible—100 years old as he always claimed to be. There seemed no possibility of his not being always among us, ready to goad one into action, to keep one endlessly amused and instructed by his immense sense of humour and extraordinary wisdom—and above all to make one feel boundlessly grateful for his generosity, which itself seemed to know no bounds.

You and he have since the last days of 1959, when I first came to Gramercy Park, been a second family to me—as dear to me and as much part of me as my own. So it is very hard for me to believe, as it must be even more for you, that Ben isn't suddenly going to be *there*—his astonishing personality so much stronger than anybody else's. But the 'personality' was in many ways a public thing: the great privilege he extended to me was to know him privately—to have known well someone of such great gifts of intelligence and humanity was at all times so exciting and stimulating and, above all, touching, that I shall miss him always, and find life much harder without him.

One aspect of his life that I feel particularly privileged to have known something of is his relationship with you—I hope you won't mind my saying this. You were so much a part of him—so much a source of his strength and power, because you understood him as no one else did and unswervingly believed in him. Together you showed me how two people, with such different temperaments and different interests, could give each other so much love and respect and tolerance and laughter. Among the most treasured memories I have of the last eighteen years of our friendship are our dinners and evenings together at Gramercy Park, they were always such fun.

Ben inspired a great deal of love and gratitude among his friends—for whom he was always willing to do so much— and his memory will remain alive in us always. His influence on me, in some parts of my life, I am indeed only becoming aware of now, as it emerges in a subterranean way long after the event. This is just as he said it would be. So I hope it will be a comfort to you, as for his friends, that Ben will go on living in our thoughts and memories and understanding for the rest of our lives, so that we will go on loving him as we did before.

TO ROBERT CUMMING   *7, Cleveland Square*
24 December 1978   *London W2*

The last time I spoke to you I had just arrived in New York and was staying, probably for the last time, with Hilda Sonnenberg: the house seemed very empty without Ben, his vast collections in no way making up for his absence. Diminutive, he was nevertheless larger than life: a curious mixture of energy and imagination and will-power. Increasingly I believe that the people who succeed in life are those whose fantasy of what they wish to be or achieve supersedes all other considerations—be it millionaire or writer or nurse or politician or painter; the dream must be there, so strongly that affection or the lingering pleasures of contemplation are secondary. And then of course there has to be energy. And Ben possessed that in superhuman abundance so that he electrified any atmosphere he entered.

My New York trip was largely taken up with business—my big book on the Metropolitan Museum has stirred up such a hornet's nest of jealousy and animosity that I have no idea just now if it really will ever be published. I think it will, but the lawyers have now got into the act so that it may take for ever.* I then went on to California for a few crazy days in Los Angeles, which is as horrible as I remember it, but yet in some weird filmy way fun: it reminds you somehow of every movie you have ever seen, it is so American, such a dream world, but yet a dream gone wrong, conceived by a crowd, not one energetic individual, so that it is diffused and vulgarized and hugely impersonal. A friend [Brendan Gill] and I are planning a book on the houses of L.A.†—they are curious, such a conglomeration of styles, and so pathetic, or so cosmetic, that it's quite painful to contemplate. But it is a part of the American dream, and some have 'architectural merit', but I no longer know what that means, since there are now enthusiasts for every style of architecture that ever was and the classical lines of good building on which one was brought up are regarded as dull by the side of ghastly Victorian fantasies. In the end everybody will like everything and there will be nothing left to prefer. The Los Angelinos have already reached that stage, having nothing really good to compare anything with, they like the mediocre and the indifferent in the way we might like the Parthenon. But the book will be serious (or at least semi-serious), and (here is of course the key, and I apologize for it) it ought to *sell*.

Commercial publishing is my working life now, and it gives me an enjoyable existence, up to a point. If it hasn't made

---

* The book, *The Metropolitan Museum of Art*, dedicated to John's memory by the author, Howard Hibbard, was published in 1980.
† Published in 1980 as *The Dream Come True*.

me quite a bit of money after five or six years, I will think again—but at least I am working for myself, which is infinitely more fun than working for other people. It is very tiring, and occasionally worrying, as I now employ five people, and am, in some way, responsible for their existence. But then one must be careful not to let such considerations get one down, as it impedes work. Keep one's eyes on the dream: to make enough money to be able to have an amusing life, and occasionally produce a book that's really worthwhile. As for my own writing, I dream of that too sometimes, and perhaps I now have something to say as well as the facility. But the problem is to combine it with the rest of the things I like doing: working, entertaining my friends, travel, etc.

From L.A. I went on to San Francisco where I met Alistair Cooke for the day. I was amused by his latest role of elderly celebrity, basking in the adulation of the crowds, who literally came up from all sides to greet him. 'Funny,' said one man, 'you look just like Alistair Cooke . . .' S.F. is a delightful place, quite dotty in appearance, a miniature Manhattan, with several little hills with buildings of all sizes cheerfully scattered about on them, and the vast bay on all sides, blue and dotted with sails: the bridges very grand, and the sleazy quarters very gay—if you see what I mean.

TO HELEN TUCKER (NÉE SONNENBERG)   *Perridge House*
Saturday, 22 December 1979   *Somerset*

I was so sad when you rang to tell me of Hilda's death that it has taken me a couple of days to gather my thoughts together sufficiently to write. Life will never be the same without your parents—not only for you and Ben, but also for me. I looked through Stevie's pictures of Gramercy Park after you called me and thought of all those times past, of conversations in Hilda's room, of dinners, just with the two of them in the Den over so many years, of Hilda's teasing Ben in the library, of her constant devotion and her capacity to submerge herself for his sake, however hard she may sometimes have found it. To me she was an outstandingly loving friend, who so often made me laugh—'he's my best audience'—and who was, like Ben, invariably generous and kind.

Most extraordinary of all was Hilda's refusal to become anything other than herself, to be anything even Ben might have wanted her to be. I loved that strength and her total disapproval of affectation, stuffiness or pretentious airs. Her approval was specially worth having because it was not extended to *anyone*. Looking back I'm particularly glad to have been with you and her at the Cape last summer. I enclose a picture I took of her at the time (which you won't like, though *I* do, because you never like my pictures)—also one of you which *I* like too. She's looking a bit pensive. But sometimes she was that too—and her thoughts could be devastating.

How right you were to say in your note with the album of Gramercy Park that we had both grown up there. For me it will always be a memory of great intensity and warmth. I really was looked after there and cherished as if in my own home and taught so much that was fun, interesting and valuable. It was doubly remarkable in that both Ben and Hilda were from the start such good friends and that with both in quite different ways I could share so much.

May I say also how much your immense strength and courage over the last year meant to her? You have been so devoted and good and I do admire what you managed to do. It was tremendous.

From the last entry in John's diary
Perridge House, 13 April 1980

A marvellous Easter and week following has brought me down here twice—the fields green, the garden full of flowers

236

and bird song. The air almost warm—just as April should be. ('Oh to be in April . . .' as Mutti started to quote the other day.)

So New York slipped by—with a mass of visits and meetings, and encounters, etc., as it always does, but I find the stimulation much less than I used to, and I miss the musings with Ben in Gramercy Park: he and Hilda provided a background and a home really for me which has gone, and makes NY just another place. When my parents have gone, Perridge will have to be kept, just for that. Places give one security, almost as much as people.

. . . 19th-century novels are still fascinating to me in that they provide my main reading for pleasure. *Wives and Daughters* by Mrs Gaskell was a bit soppy though well told. Now *Shirley* by C Brontë. I find it dull in parts—a sort of curate's egg in reverse. But all the contemporary preoccupations are there: the lack of sympathy felt for the North by a Tory government; the need to adapt to modern machinery and methods that put people out of work. The help needed by the poor. The paradox of new wealth being created by methods that make people poor, and by people who themselves want to help the poor with money. They need to help them with training in new methods of work too and that seems to be so slow and behindhand in English history and so hard to do. There are far too many arbitrary situations, loose ends, and literary conversations in the novel. And the women are much more interesting than the men. But it's got something: I keep turning the pages.

This really explains my attitude to work. It too has enough interest to make me want to go to it every day—but not enough to make me passionate about it just now. So many problems with 'cash-flow' are really quite harassing and make for an uncomfortable and unproductive life. One spends too much energy circumventing those problems and not enough on the books themselves and on improving them and selling them. I *hope* sincerely that all that will get much better later this year, otherwise work will begin to depress me. For all our efforts the cash problem is hard to cope with—we should either be better capitalized or have made *much* larger profits. I hope I can keep it all afloat till September. Then things will improve.

So many other things to tell of: internal and external, but lunch calls and my time allotted to this book is over. It's fun to write in it with this pen I got in Wells, which for once seems suited to *me*.

A bientôt.

Towards the end of April 1980 John went to Italy to see his printers and Hugh Honour and John Fleming, the authors of his World History of Art *(1982, Mitchell Prize 1983, published in seven countries). On his way back he went to see his parents, who were staying at Tourtours near Draguignon in the South of France. He left them on the morning of 26 April and drove off in his Bentley. He was murdered that same day by a hitch-hiker near Bollène.*

Index of Recipients

Index of Names

The abbreviation JC represents John Calmann

Adenauer, Konrad, 84
Aldobrandini, Prince, 103
Aldrich, Nelson, 69
Almini, *chef de cabinet* of Malvestiti, 170
Altrincham, 2nd Lord, 125
Anderson, William, encourages JC as novelist, 139; foreword by, 1–7; JC's opinion of, 95, 150–51, 177; literary works, 7; at Oxford, 50, 51n; quoted, 229; translates classics, 126
Antinous, 103
Antrim, 13th Earl of, 140
Arnold, Matthew, 107
Attlee, Clement, 101
Auden, W. H., 209
Austen, Jane, 107
Ayer, A. J., 209

Bach, Johann Sebastian, 139, 142
Bacon, Francis, 82
Baldwin, James, 106
Ball, George, 187
Baring, Si, 217
Barocci, Federigo, 21
Barry, Sir Charles, 33
Baskin, Leonard, 186
Beaton, Sir Cecil, 211–12
Beaverbrook, Lord, 163
Bedford, 13th Duke of, 62
Bellini, Giovanni, 167
Benton, Chester, 127
Berenson, Bernard, art collection, 19; art collector, 85; JC assesses, 128–9; and National Gallery, 130; Sprigge's book on, 90–92 *passim*
Berkeley, Lady, 22
Berlin, Sir Isaiah, 221
Bernini, Giovanni Lorenzo, 70
Berry, Adrian, 33
Betancourt, Rómulo, 81

Betjeman, Sir John, 209
Betjeman, Mrs (*later* Lady), 28
Bevin, Aneurin, 101
Blond, Anthony, 139, 186
Blow, Detmar, 15 1n.
Bosis, Lauro de, 23n.
Botticelli, Sandro, 23
Bowles, Governor, of Connecticut, 66
Brahms, Johannes, 136
Braque, Georges, 130
Britten, Sir Benjamin, 137
Brontë, Charlotte, 237
Brown, George, *later* Lord George-Brown, 171
Browning, Robert, 169
Bruce, David, 127
Brueghel, Pieter, 36
Buchan, Alastair, 186
Buffet, Bernard, 82
Bullock, Alan, *later* Lord Bullock, 34
Burnshaw, Mr, 61
Burrows, Abe, 155
Buttery, *picture restorer*, 29–30

Calmann, Gerta, 82, 120, 237; abroad with JC, 17, 39, 131, 214; background and history, 3–5 *passim*, 75; character, 78; Cummings and, 203, 204; house in Somerset, 74; JC's last visit, 238; and Klemperer, 138; Perridge, 78, 97, 205; unfulfilled aspirations, 222; and van der Lee, 153
Calmann, Hans, 89, 187; abroad with JC, 39, 102–3, 131, 214; art dealer, 75, 93, 123; attitude to JC's writing, 123, 124; background and history, 3–5 *passim*; character, 78; Cummings and, 203, 204; Jacqueline Kennedy writes to, 135–6; JC's last visit, 238; Perridge, 78, 122, 205; and van der Lee, 153

Calmann, Iris, 4, 24, 25, 222
Calmann, Marianne, 4
Calmann, Susan, 4
Caravaggio, Michel Angelo Merisi da, 15
Carritt, David, 17, 28, 54, 82
Castro, Fidel, 81, 121
Cecil, Robin, 64
Chace, James, 195
Chaudhuri, Nirad Chandra, 190
Chavasse, Christopher Maude, 29
Chinchòn, Duchess of, 132
Chopin, Frédéric, 138
Christus, Petrus, 13
Cima, Giovanni Battista, 19
Clarke, Stirling, 187
Clayre, Alasdair, 52 and n., 94–5, 126
Connolly, Cyril, 66
Cooke, Alistair, 59; as dinner guest, 232; as elderly celebrity, 235; at JC's birthday party, 61; JC meets at dinner, 127, 212; and Sonnenberg, 130
Cooke, Jane, 59, 61, 72, 232
Cornwall, David (pseud. John Le Carré, q.v.), 199
Coudenhove-Kalergi, Graf, 186
Courbet, Gustave, 32, 81
Crane, Mrs Murray, 76
Craxton, John, 195
Croy, Mela de, 120
Croy, Princesses de, 180
Cumming, Betty, 34, 35, 37, 119, 199
Cumming, Deborah, 227, 228
Cumming family, 37, 203, 204
Cumming, Robert, and Ginsberg, 47; in Haute Savoie, 39; history, 34–5; JC and friends of, 58, 95; JC in North Carolina with, 110, 119; JC on, 35
Cumming, William, 34, 119, 199–200

Dali, Salvador, 67
Dali, Mrs Salvador, 67
David, Jacques-Louis, 70–71
D'Avigdor-Goldsmith, Sara, 175
Dawnay, Andrew, 33
Deakin, Nicholas, 44n., 50, 126
Degas, Edgar, 169, 187
De Gaulle, Charles, and Common Market, 160, 162, 164, 172–3; European nationalist, 170; and JC's television play, 193n.; London visit, 90

Delacroix, Eugène, 71
Deth, Aart van, 201
Dickens, Charles, 24, 151, 156, 167–8
Disraeli, Benjamin, 10–11, 196
Dominic, Father, 28
Dos Passos, John, 105
Duchêne, François, 11, 186, 199
Dürer, Albrecht, 36
Duveen, 1st Lord, 130

Eboli, Anne de Mendoza, Princess of, 133
Eisenhower, Dwight David, 41, 114, 117, 122, 135
Eliot, T. S., 107
Elizabeth II, Queen, 33
Eristavi, Princess, 65
Eve, Zara, 19
Eyck, Jan van, 128, 150.

Fairbanks, Douglas, 33, 34
Faulkner, William, 45
Fielding, Henry, 174
Finikenstein, Carmen, Gräfin von, 2, 4, 29n.
Finsberg, Geoffrey, 214
Fitzgerald, Frances, 94 and n., 96, 141
Fitzgerald, F. Scott, 179
Fleming, John, 238
Fletcher-Cooke, Charles, 122, 125
Forsdyke, Lady, 25
Forster, E. M., 32, 106, 109
Fossi, Maria, 21
Fragonard, Jean Honoré, 167
Freud, Lucien, 82

Gable, Clark, 141
Gage, Nicky, 26
Gaitskell, Hugh, 100, 160, 163, 171, 172
Garbo, Greta, 69
Gardner, Isabella Stewart, 85, 91
Garnett, David, 152, 153
Gascoigne, Bamber, 48n., 62 and n.
Gascoigne, Veronica, 48n., 91
Gaskell, Mrs Elizabeth, 237
Giacometti, Alberto, 66, 74
Gibbon, Edward, 24
Gill, Brendan, 234
Giorgione, 18, 36, 130
Giotto, 21
Goethe, Johann Wolfgang von, advice to young writers, 142; Eliot's opinion